Lecture Notes of the Institute for Computer Sciences, Social and Telecommunications Engineering

101

Anthony L. Brooks (Ed.)

Arts and Technology

Second International Conference, ArtsIT 2011
Esbjerg, Denmark, December 10-11, 2011
Revised Selected Papers

 Springer

Volume Editor

Anthony L. Brooks
Aalborg University
Esbjerg, Denmark
E-mail: tb@create.aau.dk

ISSN 1867-8211   e-ISSN 1867-822X
ISBN 978-3-642-33328-6   e-ISBN 978-3-642-33329-3
DOI 10.1007/978-3-642-33329-3
Springer Heidelberg Dordrecht London New York

Library of Congress Control Number: 2012946356

CR Subject Classification (1998): J.5, H.5.1-3, H.4, H.5.5, I.4.9

Typesetting: Camera-ready by author, data conversion by Scientific Publishing Services, Chennai, India

Printed on acid-free paper

Springer is part of Springer Science+Business Media (www.springer.com)

Preface

The Second International ICST Conference on Arts and Technology (ArtsIT 2011) was held at Aalborg University Esbjerg in Denmark, December 7–8, 2011. It was jointly organized with support from CREATE-NET; The European Alliance for Innovation; and Aalborg University Esbjerg (Denmark). Papers were varied covering a wide range of topics.

The conference included an opening keynote by A.L. Brooks, Aalborg University, with five thematic sessions consisting of 22 high-quality scientific papers. The sessions were titled: (1) Interaction and Art [i]; (2) Music and Performance; (3) Interactive Methods; (4) Interaction and Art [ii], and (5) Digital Technology. A poster session was convened on the second day presenting the research of PhD students and other delegate contributions.

Matteo Fuoli from the European Alliance of Innovation (EAI) presented the supporting organizations, i.e., The European Alliance of Innovation (EAI); The Institute for Computer Sciences, Social Informatics and Telecommunications (ICST); and CREATE-NET.

The event was supported by the opening of the Centre for Design, Learning and Innovation, which was presented by Eva Petersson Brooks, the center founder and leader. Esbjerg Deputy Mayor Jakob Lose cut the ribbon opening the center that is sponsored by industry giants such as IBM, Lego, and others. Opening speeches were made by Annette Lorentsen (Head of Institute for Learning and Philosophy, Aalborg University), Michael Mullins (Head of Institute for Architecture, Design and Media Technology, Aalborg University), and Anders Schmidt Kristensen (Head of Campus Esbjerg, Aalborg University). This was followed by keynote presentations by Lieselotte van Leeuwen, University of Sunderland, UK, and Bengt Tjellander, Halmstad University, Sweden.

A welcome reception on December 7 at a downtown main attraction provided traditional Danish food for the delegates to have a "taste of Denmark." The gala dinner on December 8 was at the same location bordering the main square where the annual ice rink is built for all to enjoy. A gala Danish Christmas menu was enjoyed by the delegates followed by live music performed by a top band.

I would like to thank the Organizing Committee members, Special Session Chairs, the Technical Program Committee members, and all the authors and reviewers who contributed immensely toward the success of this event.

Also, on behalf of the Organizing Committee and the Steering Committee of ArtsIT 2011, I would like to thank the ICST for sponsoring this event, alongside EAI, CREATE-NET, and Aalborg University Esbjerg.

April 2012   A.L. Brooks

Organization

Steering Committee

Imrich Chlamtac   President of Create-NET

General Chair

Anthony Lewis Brooks   School of ICT, Aalborg University, Denmark

Program Chair

Eva Petersson Brooks   Centre for Design, Learning and Innovation, Aalborg University, Denmark

Program Co-chairs

Kristoffer Jensen   School of ICT, Aalborg University, Denmark
Tatiana Chemi   Department of Learning and Philosophy (HUM), Aalborg University, Denmark

Publication Co-chairs

Andrea Valente   School of ICT, Aalborg University, Denmark
Emanuela Marchetti   HUM, Aalborg University, Denmark

Conference Manager

Elena Jane Fezzardi   The European Alliance for Innovation

Web Chair

Matteo Fuoli   The European Alliance for Innovation

Reviewers

Alexander Refsum Jensenius   University of Oslo, Norway
Anders-Petter Andersson   Kristianstad University, Sweden
Andrea Valente   Aalborg University Esbjerg, Denmark

Anthony Brooks	Aalborg University, Denmark
Anton Nijholt	University of Twente, The Netherlands
Antonio Camurri	University of Genoa, Italy
Barnabas Simon Wetton	Kolding Design School, Denmark
Christos Bouras	RACTI and University of Patras, Greece
Cynthia M. Grund	University of Southern Denmark
David Hebert	Grieg Academy, UK
David Lindholm	Aalborg University Esbjerg, Denmark
David Obdrzalek	Charles University in Prague, Czech Republic
Dirk Heylen	University of Twente, The Netherlands
Elizabeth Stokes	Middlesex University, UK
Emanuela Marchetti	Aalborg University Esbjerg, Denmark
Eva Petersson Brooks	Aalborg University, Denmark
Florian Mueller	RMIT University, Australia
H. Jaap vanden Herik	Tilburg University, The Netherlands
Jack Ox	College of Fine Arts, UNM, Australia
Javier Jaen	Universidad Politécnica de Valencia, Spain
Jean Detheux	Independant painter/filmmaker, Canada
Jean Penny	Universiti Pendidikan Sultan Idris, Malaysia
Jens Hjortkjær	University of Copenhagen, Denmark
Kjetil Sandvik	University of Copenhagen, Denmark
Kristoffer Jensen	Aalborg University Esbjerg, Denmark
Lucia Pannese	Innovation Network, Politecnico di Milano, Italy
Luis Girao	Planetary Collegium, UK
Marc Cavazza	Teesside University, UK
Margaret Weigel	Harvard University, USA
Mark Palmer	UWE, UK
Mitsuko Aramaki	CNRS-LMA, Marseille, France
Msrco Roccetti	University of Bologna, Italy
Oscar Garcia	La Salle - DTM, USA
Paul Sharkey	University of Reading, UK
Philippe Codognet	JFLI - CNRS/UPMC/University of Tokyo, Japan
Philippe Palanque	ICS-IRIT, Université Paul Sabatier - Toulouse III, France
Pirkko Raudaskoski	Aalborg University, Denmark
Richard Kronland-Martinet	CNRS - LMA, Marseille, France
Rubén San-Segundo	Speech Technology Group, Spain
Ryohei Nakatsu	Kwansei Gakuin University, Japan
Seungyon-Seny Lee	SangMyung University, Seoul, Korea
Sofia Tsekeridou	Athens Information Technology, Greece
Sølvi Ystad	LMA-CNRS, Marseille, France
Søren R. Frimodt-Møller	University of Southern Denmark

Table of Contents

Session 3: Interactive Methods

Session 4: Interaction and Art

Session 5: Digital Technology

Poster Session

Designing Interaction Though Sound and Movement with Children on the Autistic Spectrum

Wendy Keay-Bright

Reader in Inclusive Design
Centre for Applied Research in Interactive Arts and Design (CARIAD)
University of Wales Institute, Cardiff
South Wales, UK
CF5 2YB
wkbright@cardiffmet.ac.uk

Abstract. This paper documents the making of ReacTickles MAGIC, a series of exploratory technology applications that use multi touch and sensor inputs on consumer devices. The ReacTickles concept is based on cause and effect activities that are highly responsive to individual interest. Especially targeted have been individuals on the autism spectrum who experience the most profound impairments in social communication, and have limited opportunities for self expression and meaningful interaction with others. The paper will review the basic design principles that emerged from early research with this target population and describe how these have been embodied in ReacTickles MAGIC. With reference to the impact of participatory design methods, the paper will discuss the early formative evaluation, from which we draw certain conclusions for future concepts.

Keywords: autism, cause and effect, communication, playfulness, motion sensor, multi-touch, interaction.

1 Introduction

The original ReacTickles applications were designed as cause and effect activities in which shapes and colours responded playfully to interaction with a mouse, keyboard, microphone and interactive whiteboard. Throughout the development of the software autistic children aged 4-7 years, and their teachers, were involved in envisioning, exploring and implementing prototypes. Over a period of two years, as the design became more refined, teachers made many compelling videos that captured the engagement of children as they explored ReacTickles in the classroom. Data from videos, interviews and extensive field notes led to the conclusion that the key to unlocking communicative potential through this technology was to make the interface as uncluttered as possible. This meant stripping out any extraneous detail that might presume level of cognitive ability, and avoiding any references to real world objects or to characters that impose meaning. What became clear from these studies was that the simpler the interface the more relaxed, expressive, imaginative and dynamic the actions of children.

A.L. Brooks (Ed.): ArtsIT 2011, LNICST 101, pp. 1–9, 2012.

In recent years multi-player inputs have become readily available to the consumer market through game consoles and multi touch tablet computers. The affordability of consumer hardware provided an ideal opportunity to extend the ReacTickles concept of user-led, responsive interaction with abstract forms beyond the desktop, which is being exploited in a new project, ReacTickles MAGIC.

In the same way that ReacTickles put children and teachers at the heart of development, inspiring and informing the design throughout, this extension into gestural interaction and multi touch has come about through an opportunity to design at a school that provides specialist education for some of the most severely autistic children in the district. This paper will describe the background, rationale, design principles and methods that have led to the creation of ReacTickles MAGIC.

The next section begins with a brief overview of the communicative impairments that constitute a diagnosis of autism. This is intended to provide the reader with a context for understanding the complexities of designing for this group, and the challenges faced when designing user-led technology applications within a special school setting.

1.1   Background to Autism: Social Communication and Repetitive Behaviours

Autistic Spectrum Conditions (ASC) affect approximately 1% of the child population, [1]. ASC is diagnosed when impairments in social interaction and communication as well as restricted, repetitive patterns of activities and interests are present. One of the key goals in the education of children with ASC is to help them acquire competence in social communication [2]. Social communicative competence plays a major role in our ability to form those relationships that allow us to interact happily and effectively in the communities in which we live. Positive long-term outcomes for individuals with ASC are strongly correlated with competence in social communication.

When social communication is misdirected or misunderstood a negative feedback loop is created that hinders social development profoundly. This can become all the more problematic when children engage in off-putting behaviours, such as repetitive self-stimulatory acts, or making inappropriate comments. Deficits in social skills have the capacity to lead to a harmful developmental trajectory, causing social anxiety, depression and isolation [3] [4].

Autistic children demonstrate core neuro- and developmental challenges that impact on their ability to predict the intentions of others [5]. Repetitive activities that enable them to predict and control an environment, and in which others can join in, are vital in gaining self-awareness, and, ultimately, the desire for social communication [6]. Difficulty predicting the intentions of others impacts on the ability to attend to the most relevant information, process that information and problem solve within social settings. When situations arise as a result of an unpredicted change to routine, heightened anxiety and social withdrawal often results.

Whilst many interventions are designed to support young people in the development of social communication, there have been few studies that aim to directly target this need for predictability in a positive manner that combats the negative effects of poor self esteem. In response to this, the work reported in this paper aims to assist people with

ASC in overcoming poor feelings of self-worth by enabling them to predict sequence, predict how to engage, predict how to regulate their emotions, predict that others can be a positive source of emotional support and to predict why they are engaged in a task. Individuals who display a greater capacity to self-monitor their emotional state are more able to maintain social engagement, to problem solve, to cope with unpredictable forces and to communicate effectively [5].

2   Design Principles for a Positive Emotional Experience

ReacTickles has been commercially available since 2007. Research conducted following it's release has confirmed that certain features of the software have proved enabling for young people, demonstrating positive impact on concentration and flow, [7], expressive communication and creativity [8] and self awareness [9]. These features, described below, have been embodied in the design of ReacTickles MAGIC, a new series of applications that include multi-touch, motion sensor and sound inputs, which are amplified through a projector. The scale of the projected output makes interaction highly observable and palpable as an experience unfolding in the here and now. The look and feel of ReacTickles MAGIC remains consistent with the original ReacTickles; it is based on the use of shapes and high contrast colours that can enable children to focus their attention, and for this focus to be observed and shared with others. The cause and effect style interaction has been designed to mirror such phenomena as elasticity, gravity and inertia, meaning that as soon as the child disturbs the shapes, they respond by moving around the projected area in perceptibly magical ways, drawing the focus of attention away from the original location of the shape. The behaviours attached to the shapes, whereby they appear to be pulled, pushed, stretched, dragged or tickled are consistent in that they always settle and return to their start position. This playfulness and predictability has remained the most defining feature of the software. This is embodied in the following design principles:

1) *Meaning is discovered through action*: avoid unnecessary detail that presumes the user interest or level of cognitive ability, let the person add complexity in how they animate the interface through their interaction.

2) *Simplicity yields novel user-centred experiences*: depending on the mood of the user the interface can be surprising, joyous, relaxing, funny, energetic, cheeky and enduring. A design that does not overwhelm the user leads to experiences that are open to interpretation and purpose, thus avoiding the negative feedback loop that arises from perceived errors and confusion.

3) *Provide a rich playground for sensory exploration*: colour, light, texture and sound can specifically condition the experience and afford both an aesthetic and metaphoric surface for imagination. The main function of the interface is to trigger curiosity and to reward interaction with positive emotional experiences, for many people this will be the key to unlocking potential. This means designing elements that are naturally stimulating but that do not overburden the player with complex features that require an unnecessary level of cognitive processing and compliance.

4) *Trigger curiosity through repetition and flow*: the interface affords natural kinetics, rhythms that are created through a visual and aural syncopation between input and output. For example pressure may increase size; movement may change speed, scale, opacity, colour; sound may condition any of these, but the repetition of interaction can create rhythms and patterns that increase interest through the opportunity to personally choreograph the experience.

3   ReacTickles MAGIC

ReacTickles MAGIC has been developed at a special school for pupils on the autism spectrum. A small team of developers and the researcher established a base room at the school, which was a large unused space with little natural light. The room was set up with a laptop computer with in-built microphone, a projector and a Kinect motion capture sensor. Kinect is a consumer device sold with the Microsoft game console, xBox. No other technology was required.

The design of MAGIC was based on the simplest shape, a circle. A menu provides eight different MAGIC applications, each with three levels of difficulty. When the input devices pick up movement and sounds the circle will respond. Changing the levels of difficulty can increase amount of colour or make a new shapes, or impact on acceleration of the shape. Movement can cause the shape to cluster, spin, and trace the child's body position. When the child perceives the circle on a projected surface - in the MAGIC room this is the wall, or on the iPad it is the screen - the visual sense distinguishes it as different from the background space. The circle becomes more meaningful when it responds to input, moving as the child moves or makes a sound.

Fig. 1. ReacTickles MAGIC interface on the iPAD

3.1   Physical Directness

ReacTickles MAGIC combines a number of sensory inputs which are behaviourally and perceptually coupled with visual outputs [10]. Each input action is mapped to an instant graphical representation, affording physical directness through cause and effect. This notion of physical directness is of interest to interaction designers as it impacts on the level of cognitive processing required by the user to navigate an interface. Beaudouin-Lafon [11] describes three aspects of physical directness. Firstly, the *degree of indirectness* refers to the temporal and spatial distance between input and output, or cause and effect; secondly, the *degree of integration* refers to the degree of freedom between the input tool and the level of interaction afforded, and, lastly, the *degree of compatibility* refers to the similarity or match between actions with the input device and the reactions the manipulated object. Within the design of ReacTickles MAGIC, there are varying degrees of physical directness, which were explored during the iterative cycle of development.

4   Participatory Design Methods

The Participatory Design movement has been motivated by the substantive role end-user communities play in activities that can lead to the creation and improvement of applications, particularly software and other technologies, and their appropriation in real-world contexts [12].

4.1   Participants

Participatory design for ReacTickles MAGIC was cohered around the involvement of a group of 6 boys aged 15 years with low functioning autism (LFA) and three of their teachers. The boys used no functional verbal language and had very poor concentration. Prior to setting up the project and the MAGIC room, we undertook familiarisation activities with them, blending into the classroom routine, in order to become accepted by the group and to avoid unwanted distractions during the study.

We began the process of developing ReacTickles MAGIC with a four day design workshop, which included the design team - two programmers, a designer, a researcher - the 6 boys and the teachers. Early ideas coming from staff were based on non-digital cause and effect activities that the boys were known respond to. We demonstrated how the motion sensor worked, that it didn't respond to touch and then storyboarded some ideas based on circles that flocked around the user as they moved in front of the Kinect sensor. These became our first ReacTickles MAGIC experience prototypes. Experience prototyping [13] was considered the most effective method for iterative design as it would enable the design team to evaluate whether of not the proposed technology concepts could interest the boys before refining them.

The 6 boys were first introduced to these early ReacTickles MAGIC prototypes as a group. When the ReacTickles shapes tracked their movement, they showed no interest whatsoever. With so much movement in the room the cause and effect was very hard to follow, they were also were distracted by the light from the data projector. They displayed stereotypical behaviours such as hand flapping, erratic movement, and vocalisation, and took only fleeting glances at the projections on the wall. However, the teachers really enjoyed the experience and felt that given time the boys may begin to interact. They suggested that they boys would benefit from being introduced to the room one by one, rather than in a group. The design team responded by rethinking the interface, reducing to one shape that could be controlled by sound. Even though each child's vocal repertoire was limited to very few sounds, we took those as an indication of communicative ability. We progressed our concepts on the basis that if vocal actions or sound inputs provided the trigger for cause and effect, the children may become more aware of their own locus of control, and from this emerging sense of awareness we would gradually introduce more complex responses.

Over the next three days we created prototypes that varied in the degree of physical directness, with the motion sensor offering the least physical directness and the sound inputs offer the most. In relation to this we also varied the complexity of visual feedback, from one monochromatic shape change to a sequence of different shapes and colours, which enabled us to explore the degrees of compatibility necessary to support the children in maintaining interaction beyond the initial experience of discovery.

Periodically, in between intense sessions of programming, the boys came into the room. At the suggestion of one of the staff team, ReacTickles MAGIC was introduced to a group of 4 more verbally able children with Asberger Syndrome. This group were confident in articulating their thoughts and ideas, but were noted as having challenging behaviour and difficulty with concentration, organisation and flexible thinking. For the designers, having the opportunity to observe this group provided real insight into the diversity and complexity of the autism condition. This group became highly animated at being able to control the system through their movement intrigued by the power they seemed to have over the system. They very quickly realised that if they didn't move, they would be able to stop any visual effects, and the motion sensor would make them "invisible". This led to an unprecedented degree of turn-taking as they challenged each other to create and control the visual interface. By the end of the Lab, ReacTickles MAGIC was running from one interface menu and was fully installed in the room on the school computers so that teachers and classroom assistants could continue to use the system.

5   Discussion

Over the following eight weeks the same 6 boys took part in one ReacTickles MAGIC session per week with their teachers and the researchers. The sessions were timetabled at the request of staff, who had seen positive changes in behaviour for each child over time, and a significant reduction in *unwanted* behaviours in the children who were frequently challenging in the classroom. Each child has responded in highly individual ways. One boy, noted as having the most challenging behaviour, enjoyed a clapping game which generated a new small circle with each clap, the circles form a pattern of circles in the shape of a clock and on reaching the twelfth circle, the pattern changes to a square. The application had a clear start and end point to a sequence and the *degree of compatibility* between his actions and the response of the shapes provided a focal point for his attention. The child was observed to need proprioceptive stimulation, he was continuously jumping around and bumping into people. We experimented with offering him a large exercise ball to give him an opportunity to continue to stimulate his proprioceptive sense whilst interacting with the applications. This proved highly motivating for him, he used the ball to interact with the motion sensor, observing how he could change the flocking of circles. He also used the ball as a drum, changing patterns through the volume of sound. Movement and sounds afforded by the ball as an input device enabled a *degree of integration* that was important for his child. After three sessions in the room, his playfulness and flow of concentration increased, he became calmer as he observed his movement and sound projected on the wall. During the 4th session, he began to verbalise shape names. He pointed to his classroom assistant for guidance and verbalised all the shape names in the system: *circle, square, triangle, heart, cross* and *hexagon*. At the most recent session he controlled the interface by altering sound patterns, he articulated the shape names and added colour names. He has also started to use the iPad version of ReacTickles MAGIC, seamlessly transferring his knowledge onto the new platform.

Fig. 2. Exploring the circle of shapes in the iPad

The other boys have made less progress, however, each one is showing signs of individual ability through being able to predict the sequence of interaction. The teaching staff confirmed that some of the reactions observed (copying, observing, participating, taking turns) may seem insignificant to the casual observer, but they represent huge milestones for students with more severe ASC. The data collected during this phase has been used as formative evaluation to ensure that the technology is robust, useful and desirable. The next phase of the project will be to undertake studies that evaluate the effectiveness of ReacTickles Magic in supporting expressive, functional communication. Our hypothesis is that when the child with autism is happy, relaxed and confident in their own ability - through being able to predict a sequence and explore through rewarding interactive play - communication with others may be more desirable. To this end, we are developing methods for observing and analysing highly nuanced experiences in a meaningful, systematic manner. Specifically, we will look for instances of increased concentration and flow, initiating and choosing a sequence of actions, initiating a bid for attention and sharing attention with another person [2] [5]. We are creating a coding scheme for micro-ethnographic analysis using a systematic video performance tagging software tool [15]. Capturing data from multiple angles, we will use the system to observe and monitor children's interactions within each session and over time. This will be complimented by more freeform analysis and interviews with teaching staff.

6   Conclusion

This paper has aimed to provide some insight into the creation of a software interface, ReacTickles MAGIC. From our early observations and from interviews with teaching staff we have noted that the playfulness and predictability of ReacTickles has assisted children in gaining interest and independence through their explorations of the interface. For many children, simply being able to touch, move or make a sound and have that action reflected through the simple abstract graphical output has been motivating. As the possibilities for interaction are discovered through repetitious cause and effect, the children's engagement has increased and become more dynamic, expressive and creative. In adopting a highly responsive, participatory design approach the creators of ReacTickles MAGIC have learned some valuable lessons on designing for this population. Co-designing in the user setting provides vital clues in the early stages of design, but for novel concepts to become usable and desirable, children with autism need more time than their typically developing peers to process new information, and for this new information to gradually become predictable and a source of reassurance. The implementation of new activities needs to be carefully introduced through more familiar routines, which requires the researchers to work at the pace of the children and with the guidance of teachers. Designing in this way we have become interested in the ways in which the whole environment impacts on the children's experience, and realised that interaction with the technology plays a relatively minor role. The other people, physical objects, sensory information, as well as less tangible aspects such as the time of day, all make a difference. Many of these aspects are hard to predict, and in response to this we are developing new artefacts that provide additional physical triggers to provide predictability and to assist interaction. We will continue to work with a number of schools, therapy centres, and with families to identify ways in which real world playful interaction can lead to positive long-term outcomes for individuals regardless of developmental ability.

Acknowledgements. The author would like to thank Autism Cymru, Ashgrove School and the Hollies School, South Wales for their sustained commitment to this work. ReacTickles MAGIC has been awarded funding from the Rayne Foundation and University of Wales Institute, Cardiff (UWIC), Wales, UK.

References

1. Baron-Cohen, S., Scott, F.J., Allison, C., et al.: Prevalence of autism- spectrum conditions. British Journal of Psychiatry 194, 500–509 (2009)
2. Marans, W.D., Rubin, E., Laurent, A.: Addressing social communication skills in individuals with high functioning autism and Asperger Syndrome; Critical priorities in educational programming. In: Volkmar, F.R., Klin, A., Paul, R. (eds.) Handbook of Autism and Pervasive Developmental Disorders, 3rd edn. John Wiley, New York (2005)
3. Bellini, S.: The development of social anxiety in high functioning adolescents with autism spectrum Disorders. Focus on Autism and Other Developmental Disabilities 2(3), 138–145 (2006)
4. Tantam, D.: Psychological disorder in adolescents and adults with Asperger syndrome. Autism 4, 47–62 (2000)
5. Prizant, B.M., Wetherby, A.M., Rubin, E., Laurent, A.C., Rydell, P.J.: The SCERTS Model: A comprehensive educational approach for children with autism spectrum disorders. Paul H. Brookes Publishing Co., Baltimore (2005)

6. Leekam, S., Prior, M., Ularivic, M.: Restricted and repetitive behaviors in autism spectrum disorders: A review of research in the last decade. Psychological Bulletin 137(4), 562–593 (2011)
7. Keay-Bright, W.: ReacTickles: Playful interaction with Information Communication Technologies. The International Journal of Art & Technology 2(1/2), 133–151 (2009)
8. Keay-Bright, W., Howarth, I.C.: Is Simplicity the Key to Engagement for Children on the Autism Spectrum. Journal of Personal and Ubiquitous Computing, Theme Issue on Technology for Autism (May 2011)
9. Keay-Bright, W., Gethin-Lewis, J.: Co-Creating Tools for Touch. Include 2011: The Role of Inclusive Design in Making Social Innovation Happen, Helen Hamlyn Centre, Royal College of Art, UK (2011), http://include11.kinetixevents.co.uk/4dcgi/prog?operation=detail&paper_id=398 (accessed October 2011)
10. Antle, A.N.: The CTI framework: Informing the design of tangible systems for children. In: Conference on Tangible and Embedded Interaction, pp. 195–202. ACM Press, Baton Rouge (2007)
11. Beaudouin-Lafon, M.: Instrumental interaction: an interaction model for designing post-WIMP user interfaces. In: Proceedings of the ACM CHI 2000 Conference, pp. 446–453 (2000)
12. Muller, M.J.: Participatory Design: The third Space in HCI. In: The Human-Computer Interaction Handbook, pp. 1051–1068. Lawrence Erlbaum Associates, London (2003)
13. Buchenau, Fulton Suri: Experience prototyping. In: Proceedings of the Conference on Designing Interactive Systems, New York, pp. 424–433 (2000)
14. Marans, W.D., Rubin, E., Laurent, A.: Addressing social communication skills in individuals with high functioning autism and Asperger Syndrome; Critical priorities in educational programming. In: Volkmar, F.R., Klin, A., Paul, R. (eds.) Handbook of Autism and Pervasive Developmental Disorders, 3rd edn. John Wiley, New York (2005)
15. Jewitt, C.: Editorial. International Journal of Social Research Methodology 14(3), 171–178 (2011)

Towards Augmented Choreography

Diego Bernini[1], Giorgio De Michelis[1], Mauro Plumari[1],
Francesco Tisato[1], and Michele Cremaschi[2]

[1] DISCo, University of Milano-Bicocca,
viale Sarca 336, 20126 Milano, Italy
{bernini,demichelis,plumari,tisato}@disco.unimib.it
[2] Residenza Teatrale InItinere,
via Valmarina 25, 24129 Bergamo, Italy
michele.cremaschi@gmail.com

Abstract. Choreographers are interested in enriched performances where virtual actants play together with live performers. Augmented Choreography can be viewed as the definition of how perceptions generated from the environment turn into commands that influence the environment itself and, in particular, virtual actants. This paper introduces a modular and extensible architecture that supports the flexible and dynamic definition of augmented choreographies and presents an experimental application.

Keywords: augmented choreography, interactive performance, multimodal interaction, performance design, virtual puppetry.

1 Introduction

Choreography [1] is the art of designing sequences of movements (*choreographies*) performed by actants. In ballet and stage dancing choreographies define sequences of dance steps that are synchronized with music beats and, in general, with musical events: for example, choreography might prescribe that during a musical phrase one dancer has to withdraw from another dancer. Choreography may also prescribe how actants behave (for example, moving their arms or jumping) according to the behavior of a coryphaeus. Finally, choreography may prescribe stage effects (for example, lighting) in correlation with music or movements. Ultimately, choreography dictates how perceptions are mapped into performers' actions.

New media technologies enhance the potential of performing arts by introducing virtual actants and by exploiting multifarious sensing technologies. For example, Latulipe et al. [2] explore the design space of dance and technology presenting a specific show of interactive dance "Bodies/AntiBodies". James et al. [3] describe Lucidity, a show of "interactive choreography".

Augmented Choreography is choreography where perceptions, actions and mapping rules are augmented by exploiting hardware and software technologies. For example, one or more virtual actants i.e., computer-projected body animations, move according to music, movements of real dancers and clapping.

A.L. Brooks (Ed.): ArtsIT 2011, LNICST 101, pp. 10–17, 2012.
© Institute for Computer Sciences, Social Informatics and Telecommunications Engineering 2012

A major challenge is how to design and develop cost-effective IT systems that allow artists to realize Augmented Choreography (ITAC). At a first glance, they seem close to widespread real-time and interactive systems, ranging from automation to video-gaming, which ultimately turn input stimuli into output actions. However, these systems are mostly "vertical" in the sense that they are designed and optimized once and for all to perform a specific task and to exploit specific technologies.

Augmented choreographies should adaptively exploit heterogeneous perception and actuation flows, which not only depend on the rapid technological evolution of sensing and actuation devices, but also rely on different conceptual models of the environment and, in particular, of the performance space. This leads to a high degree of technological dependency, which combinatorially explodes as the system must integrate heterogeneous technologies and computational models. On the other side, there is a wide semantic gap between the languages and cultures of technicians and artists. The result is that the design, development and evolution of augmented choreographies involve a close and painful collaboration between artists and technicians.

A sound architectural approach may reduce the combinatorial explosion of complexity by carefully separating technological issues from choreographic aspects. A further step is to devise a technology-neutral language that allows choreographers to define augmented choreographies in a seamless and user-friendly way.

Section 2 presents basic ideas about architecture and linguistic issues. Section 3 presents an experiment in the virtual puppetry area. Section 4 compares our system to significant related work, while Section 5 proposes some conclusions and future developments.

2   Augmented Choreography

2.1   Architecture

The architecture of an ITAC system should carefully separate technological issues, which are wrapped by peripheral software components, from mapping functions, which conceptually define the choreography and are up to a Mapper component.

Sensing Wrappers encapsulate device-specific technicalities and produce Perceptions, i.e., symbolic representations of events localized in Perception Spaces. For example (Figure 1), a Microsoft Kinect wrapper provides perceptions localized in the 3D space of a stage, a camera wrapper provides perceptions localized in the 2D space of an image and a microphone wrapper provides perceptions localized in a 1D space modeling sound loudness.

Actuation Wrappers encapsulate device-specific technicalities and are controlled by Actions i.e., symbolic representations of expected actions localized in device-specific Action Spaces. For example, a screen wrapper receives actions defining where graphical objects must be visualized in the 2D space of the screen.

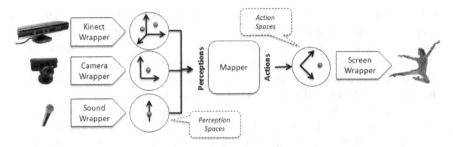

Fig. 1. ITAC architecture

The Mapper encapsulates the choreography i.e., how localized Perceptions are mapped into localized Actions. For example, it defines how the position of a hand of a physical performer, which is perceived in the 3D Kinect space, must be mapped into the position of a foot of a virtual performer in the 2D screen space.

The proposed architecture clearly separates technological issues from conceptual aspects. Therefore it reduces the technology dependency of artists and improves the flexibility and extensibility of the ITAC system. New devices can be added by realizing proper wrappers that generate Perceptions (or receive Actions) expressed in a symbolic and technology-neutral style. Conversely, choreographies can be modified without dealing with technological details.

2.2   Choreography as Translation

Though the proposed architecture enhances the separation between technological and conceptual concerns, defining the behavior of the Mapper is still a complex issue as long as the Mapper is a software component that must be explicitly programmed to realize a specific choreography. The next step is to devise a generalized Mapper, which acts as interpreter of choreographies defined in linguistic, artist-oriented terms. For example, the choreography of a dance should be defined by stating how beats (i.e., perceptions) expressed in musical notation are mapped into movements (i.e., actions) expressed in choreutic notation.

The role of Mapper is to *translate* Perceptions into Actions. This can be generalized in linguistic terms:

- o   An input language L_I is defined by a grammar G_I whose tokens t_I model Perceptions localized in Perception Spaces.
- o   An output language L_O is defined by a grammar G_O whose tokens t_O model Actions localized in Action Spaces.
- o   A choreography $C_{I,O}$ defines translation rules from well-formed strings S_I^i of L_I (i.e., G_I-compliant sequences of t_I tokens) to well-formed strings S_O^j of L_O (i.e., G_O-compliant sequences of t_O tokens).

Established results from the area of Language Theory can be exploited to model more and more sophisticated choreographies. For simplicity and according to the experiment presented in Section 3, in the following "performer" and "puppet" denote a physical and a virtual performer respectively.

Direct Mapping Choreography. In the simplest case both L_I and L_O are context-free languages and the translation rules (i.e., the choreography) just translate perceptions into actions. For example, the positions of the skeleton joints of a performer turn into positions of the corresponding skeleton joints of a puppet. Mirroring or more complex effects can be easily defined. For example, an Action describing the position of a puppet joint can depend both on the Perception of the position of a performer joint in a Performer Space and on the Perception of a sound in a Sound Space.

Behavioral Choreography. More complex behaviors can be achieved by translating an input token into a sequence of output tokens (in Language Theory parlance, L_O is a regular language). For example, the perception of a new position of the performer's hand might turn into a sequence of positions of the puppet's hand. Moreover, if the input language L_I too is a regular language whose legal strings are modeled by a state automaton, performers' behaviors (i.e., specific strings of L_I) can be recognized. For example, a sequence of repeated movements from left to right of the performer's hand can turn into a puppet's movement that causes it disappearing.

Time Sensitive Choreography. Choreography is intrinsically tied to the concept of movement, therefore to the concept of *time* [4]. Timing is relevant both to recognize specific input behaviors (for example, fast movements) and to drive output behaviors.

This implies that both input and output tokes are *time-stamped*. Timestamps are referred to a unique reference time. On the input side timestamps are exploited to recognize specific behaviors. On the output side timestamps are exploited to generate output commands according to a proper timing. For example, like in a physical dance performance, the movements of the orchestra conductor are perceived as timed input tokens and analyzed to recognize beats, whose frequency leads the timing of the commands delivered both to sound sources (be they humans or software) and to dancing puppets. Time sensitivity [4] supports the realization of choreographies that include advanced domain-specific issues. For example, the choreography might include the concept of laziness of a puppet to drive how fast it reacts to a command. The choreography could also include a dynamic model instead of a simple kinematic model to take into account the mass of the puppet.

Choreographers as Performers. The Mapper in the basic architectural scheme of Figure 1 is an interpreter of choreographies that define translation rules from well-formed strings S_I^i of L_I to well-formed strings S_O^J of L_O. Choreographies, though sophisticated, are assumed to be statically defined by a Choreographer *before* the performance takes place. The ultimate step is to lift up the role of the Choreographer to that of a full-fledged Performer. This means that she/he is a Performer that dynamically changes the choreography i.e., the translation rules *during* the performance. Ultimately, the separation between Performer and Choreographer vanishes.

3   An Experiment: Augmented Puppetry

Puppetry is a very ancient form of art [5]. *Computer puppetry* [6] turns in real-time the movements of a performer to the movements of an animated character (*puppet*). Coutrix et al. [7] observe that computer-mediated puppetry has been used extensively for animation production rather than for live public performances.

On December 2010 the InItinere theatrical residency contacted us to realize a system to support their future shows. Quoting their needs: *"We would like to produce a staged theatrical performance, drawing on the tradition of mimes, clowns and visual comedy augmented with digital technologies. One or more virtual puppets will be put on stage through a character that is hand drawn and video-projected rather than physical. The movements of an actor-performer should determine the virtual puppet animation. We imagine different interaction scenarios. First there could be a direct, real-time connection by the performer and the puppet motion. Then the connection could be made less directed introducing time delays...The performer should interact with the puppet through different modalities, even simultaneously...For example by gestures recognized by a camera-based system; or by a tangible cross bar...".*

Starting from these needs, we developed a modular system for augmented puppetry, which is instantiated according to artists' requirements and whose architecture is strongly based on the openness, multiplicity and continuity qualities [8]. The development and experimentation activities allowed us to highlight the problems and to define the architecture introduced in the previous section.

The current implementation includes Sensing Wrappers for Microsoft Kinect, for Nintendo Wii Balance Board and for microphones. Microsoft Kinect provides 2D images with distance information for each pixel. The Kinect Wrapper exploits open source middleware to provide perceptions that model the 3D position of fifteen skeleton points of a performer moving in front of the camera. The Nintendo Wii Balance Board Wrapper computes the projection of the barycenter of the performer in the bi-dimensional Board Space. Finally, the Microphone Wrapper produces the sound intensity detected by a microphone.

The Puppet Visualization Wrapper executes Actions defining positions of puppet joints. It exploits the Animata real time animation software, an open source project maintained by the Kitchen Budapest lab. Puppets are animated according to the *skeletal animation model* [9]. A character is represented in two parts: a surface representation used to draw the character (*skin* or *mesh*) and a set of *joint*s connected through *bones* (*skeleton*) used to animate the mesh. Various computational methods can be exploited to animate the skeleton. Our system exploits inverse (*goal-directed*) methods allowing the position of some joints only to be specified. The positions of other joints are automatically computed by taking into account previous positions, bone lengths and joint angles.

The Mapper component is at the heart of the system. Different versions of Mapper realize different scenarios i.e., different choreographies.

The first scenario realizes a direct mapping choreography by projecting the perceived 3D positions of the skeleton points of the performers into 2D positions on the screen of the corresponding joints of the puppet.

The second scenario too realizes a direct mapping choreography, but the Mapper simulates a cross bar by projecting the 3D positions of the performer hands into 2D positions of the puppet hands; the movements of other puppet joints are computed by Puppet Visualization Wrapper according to the skeleton animation model.

The third scenario realizes a time sensitive choreography, which is similar to that of the first scenario, but actions that control puppet positions are delayed.

Finally, the fourth scenario (Figure 2) simultaneously exploits all the three Sensing Wrappers. The performer wears a microphone and stands in front of a Kinect sensor on a Nintendo Balance Board. Performer hands are mapped to puppet hands as in the second scenario. The position of the performer barycenter perceived by the Balance Board Wrapper is mapped to actions that control the tilt of the boat, thus the position of the puppet foots. Moreover the vocal intensity sensed by the Microphone Wrapper is linked to the character mouth: when the voice intensity overcomes a threshold, the mouth moves.

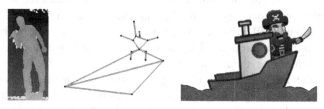

Fig. 2. Multi-modal animation

4   Related Work

Several live digital animation systems have been proposed in literature.

A first class of works aims at translating the interaction of the user/performer with different interfaces to corresponding actions of a virtual character in a virtual world.

Mazalek et al. [10] present an embodied puppet interface that translates the performer body movements to a virtual character, focusing on the fine grained control of the character. Mazalek and Nitsche [11] show a system which exploits a tangible marionette in order to control the correspond virtual one.

Liikkanen et al. [12] present PuppetWall, a multi-user, multimodal system intended for digital augmented puppetry. It provides functionalities to control puppets and manipulate playgrounds including background and puppets. PuppetWall exploits hand movement tracking, a multi-touch display and speech recognition.

Shin et. al. [13] propose an approach to generate realistic motion for a character in real-time while preserving the characteristics of captured performance motions as much as possible.

These solutions are focused on digital animation reproducing human motion. Our approach is more general because it aims to augment the performance through a virtual puppet, whose behavior is influenced by a wide range of perceptions including, as a particular case, the movements of a human performer.

Other systems are more flexible with respect to the correspondence between performer motion and puppet animation. For example, Dontcheva et al. [14] present an animation system where the relation between the animator and the character can be either explicitly defined or inferred from similarities. CoPuppet [15] is a system for multimodal, collaborative puppetry where performers, or even audience members, affect different parts of a puppet through gestures and voice.

Finally, several works share our vision of an open system accessible to artists and choreographers.

Neff et al. [16] propose an approach for mapping 2D mouse input to high-dimensional skeleton space via *correlation maps* which transform the input to meaningful abstract output.

Samanci et al. [17] propose a framework for interactive storytelling. It exploits an interaction technology based on computer vision and full-body tracking. The framework provides a rich set of interactions and supports simultaneous multi-point and multi-user input.

Vasilakos et al. [18] present a system offering to the performance artists a creative tool to extend the grammar of the traditional theatre. Actors and dancers at different places are captured by multiple cameras and their images are rendered in 3D form so that they can play and dance together on the same place in real-time.

Kuşcu and Akgün [19] propose an approach to interactive performance systems which is very close to our proposal. They define a component-based architecture which resembles our architecture, though they do not highlight the possible different kinds of mappings and the role of suitable choreographer-oriented languages. Like us, they highlight the need of taking timing into account and propose a timed state machine allowing choreographers to edit the audiovisual behavior of a choreography system.

5   Conclusions and Future Work

The ITAC framework we developed is a good starting point for radically changing the way technologists interact with choreographers: from trying to realize what is requested by an artist, to providing she or he with the possibility of autonomously defining augmented choreographies.

In order to bring our system to completion, we plan to work on two parallel directions: on the one side, we plan to continue our collaboration with InItinere and to collaborate with other choreographers in order to augment our experience; on the other side, we plan to do an ethnography of choreographers at work in order to deeply understand the nature of their work. In fact, an ITAC system must be evaluated from two viewpoints: its capability of orchestrating movements so that the effects required by the artist are reached and its capability to be directly exploited by the choreographer without distracting them from their way of working.

References

1. Blom, L.A., Chaplin, L.T.: The Intimate Act Of Choreography. University of Pittsburgh Press (1982)
2. Latulipe, C., Lottridge, D., Wilson, D., Huskey, S., Word, M., Carroll, A., Carroll, E., Gonzalez, B., Singh, V., Wirth, M.: Exploring the design space in technology-augmented dance. In: Proceedings of the 28th of the International Conference on Human Factors in Computing Systems - CHI EA 2010, p. 2995. ACM Press, New York (2010)

3. James, J., Ingalls, T., Qian, G., Olsen, L., Whiteley, D., Wong, S., Rikakis, T.: Movement-based interactive dance performance. In: Proceedings of the 14th Annual ACM International Conference on Multimedia - MULTIMEDIA 2006, p. 470. ACM Press, New York (2006)

4. Micucci, D., Oldani, M., Tisato, F.: An Architectural Model for Time Awareness. Aracne editrice (2006), http://www.disco.unimib.it/go/215281425

5. Blumenthal, E.: Puppetry and Puppets: An Illustrated World Survey. Thames & Hudson (2005)

6. Sturman, D.J.: Computer puppetry. IEEE Computer Graphics and Applications 18, 38–45 (1998)

7. Coutrix, C., Jacucci, G., Spagnolli, A., Ma, L., Helin, M., Richard, G., Parisi, L., Roveda, S., Narula, P.: Engaging spect-actors with multimodal digital puppetry. In: Proceedings of NordiCHI 2010, p. 138. ACM Press, New York (2010)

8. De Michelis, G.: The Swiss Pattada. Interactions 10, 44–53 (2003)

9. Murray, C.: A user-based evaluation of skeletal animation techniques in graph interaction. In: Proceedings of the 2005 Asia-Pacific Symposium on Information Visualisation, vol. 45, pp. 7–14. Australian Computer Society, Inc., Darlinghurst (2005)

10. Mazalek, A., Chandrasekharan, S., Nitsche, M., Welsh, T., Clifton, P., Quitmeyer, A., Peer, F., Kirschner, F., Athreya, D.: I'm in the game. In: Proceedings of the Fifth International Conference on Tangible, Embedded, and Embodied Interaction - TEI 2011, p. 129. ACM Press, New York (2011)

11. Mazalek, A., Nitsche, M.: Tangible interfaces for real-time 3D virtual environments. In: Proceedings of the International Conference on Advances in Computer Entertainment Technology - ACE 2007, p. 155. ACM Press, New York (2007)

12. Liikkanen, L.A., Jacucci, G., Huvio, E., Laitinen, T., Andre, E.: Exploring emotions and multimodality in digitally augmented puppeteering. In: Proceedings of the Working Conference on Advanced Visual Interfaces - AVI 2008, p. 339. ACM Press, New York (2008)

13. Shin, H.J., Lee, J., Shin, S.Y., Gleicher, M.: Computer puppetry: An importance-based approach. ACM Transactions on Graphics 20, 67–94 (2001)

14. Dontcheva, M., Yngve, G., Popović, Z.: Layered acting for character animation. In: Proceedings of ACM SIGGRAPH 2003, p. 409. ACM Press, New York (2003)

15. Adams, R., Gibson, S., Arisona, S.M., Bottoni, P., Faralli, S., Labella, A., Malizia, A., Pierro, M., Ryu, S.: Transdisciplinary Digital Art. Sound, Vision and the New Screen. Springer, Heidelberg (2008)

16. Neff, M., Albrecht, I., Seidel, H.-P.: Layered Performance Animation with Correlation Maps. Computer Graphics Forum 26, 675–684 (2007)

17. Samanci, Ö., Chen, Y., Mazalek, A.: Tangible comics. In: Proceedings of ACE 2007, p. 171. ACM Press, New York (2007)

18. Vasilakos, A., Wei, L., Nguyen, T., Thienqui, T., Chen, L., Boj, C., Diaz, D., Cheok, A., Marentakis, G.: Interactive theatre via mixed reality and Ambient Intelligence. Information Sciences 178, 679–693 (2008)

19. Kuşcu, H., Akgün, B.T.: A new approach to interactive performance systems. In: Proceedings of MULTIMEDIA 2005, p. 578. ACM Press, New York (2005)

At the Bottom of the U: Arts-Based Leadership of Creative Learning Processes in Educators and Social Workers' Training

Tatiana Chemi

Centre for Design, Learning and Innovation, Institute for Learning and Philosophy,
Aalborg University
Niels Bohrs Vej 8, 6700 Esbjerg, Denmark
tc@learning.aau.dk

Abstract. The purpose of the developmental project "Dance with the future" is to test a new professional area for educators and social workers, and at the same time to offer teachers within this educational sector a novel opportunity for personal and professional growth. This project is targeted for teachers in education and caregiving at Danish University College North (UCN) and is being evaluated by means of a qualitative case study, which is described in the present paper. The scientific documentation will collect evidence for the application of arts-based facilitation tools in change processes, and on opportunities to foster creativity and innovation at UCN. The social technologies applied draw from Expressive Arts therapy and systems thinking, respectively through means of arts-based coaching and Theory U.

Keywords: innovation, arts-based learning processes, social technologies, coaching, organizational learning, and systems thinking.

1 Dancing at the Bottom of the U

In the present paper I wish to describe an ongoing development-and-research project within the field of organizational learning and the arts. The purpose of the development project "Dance with the future" is to test a new professional area for educators and to offer teachers within the educational sector a novel opportunity for personal and professional growth. During the Spring 2011, the project "Dance with the future" offered a group of teachers at Danish University College North (UCN) the opportunity to know more about arts-based coaching and Theory U. The former framework is based on the application of Expressive Arts therapy's tools to coaching tasks; the latter is the theory and social technology conceived by MIT scholar Otto Scharmer (arts-based coaching and Theory U will be shortened in ABC-U). Both frameworks draw from the practical application of artistic –or arts-based- tools and understandings to facilitation and coaching.

UCN is an undergraduate school for several professions, among the others is the one for "pedagogists" (in Danish: *pædagoger*). Students can aim at becoming

A.L. Brooks (Ed.): ArtsIT 2011, LNICST 101, pp. 18–28, 2012.

educators and social workers, e.g. as pre-school (nursery nurses) or kindergarten educators, social workers or caregivers at public institutions, experts in children and adults with special needs. UCN felt the need for developing new areas of professional application for its students; therefore a group of school leaders got engaged in a deep reflection about the issue of profession-development. The first step the coordination group took was to engage the school's internal resources, which could carry on such an innovative enterprise. Specific assets were found in the innovation group that was already working with practical applications of Theory U in social or organizational contexts and whose teachers were engaged as out-reaching facilitators. In other words, external customers hired the innovation group in order to facilitate change management processes, activity that the UCN innovation group offered besides the group's internal teaching tasks. Since the school leadership wished to try out an innovative approach to the management of learning processes, professional development and organizational learning, this initiative was considered suitable to test new future strategies, and the innovation group's activities were structured and widened in a pivotal project.

The project "Dance with the future" was initiated with the help of an external expert in the field of Expressive Arts and arts-based coaching, and designed as a joint collaboration between the UCN's internal innovator, expert in Theory U, and the external consultant, expert in arts-based coaching. The two experts had the tasks of designing, coordinating and supervising the project, and of teaching the facilitation tools. Both the coordination group and its leadership, expressed the strong wish to link a specific evaluation to this experiment, as they were convinced that follow-up research would strengthen the project's outputs, both at organizational and educational level.

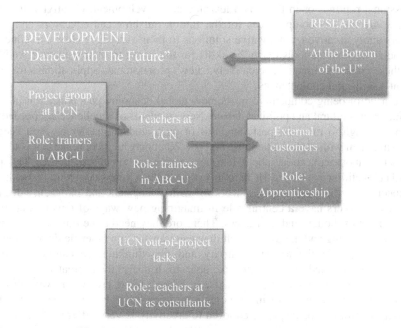

Fig. 1. Relational network of involved stakeholders

The research study "At the Bottom of the U" was kicked-off within this wish. It aims at following and describing the process within "Dance with the future" and at reporting the outputs of this experimental initiative. The research project "At the Bottom of the U" is both the result of strategic thinking underlying the development project and a future tool for internal evaluation. At strategic level, the research project links UCN to a prestigious Danish academic institute: Aalborg University and its Institute for Learning and Philosophy, which I represent. In the present paper I will focus on the description of this research project.

The above figure visualizes the structure of the developmental project and its relationship to the research project. The target group of both development activities and research observation consists of teachers for education and social workers' students at UCN. These teachers take a learner perspective within the frames of "Dance with the future", and act as students within the course and as trainees in their final apprenticeship. At the moment, the study is in its data-collection stage, where ethnographic observations and interviews are being carried on, as described in the section regarding the methodological approach. For this reason, the present paper will describe background, research design and expected findings rather than results, which I expect to publish during the Spring 2012.

2   The Creative Challenge

The background for this study is the need that educators and social workers' schools are in the middle of: on one side the whole professional field meets the modern society's needs –or cravings- for creativity, on the other side educators and social workers have a hard time with the systematic integration of creativity in their professional routines or in their own learning and development. Creativity and new-thinking are the key-competences for the future, but how can educators and social workers apply creative or innovative solutions to their everyday? How can educators and social workers' schools teach the skills for the future to their students? And how can these schools imagine, creatively, new professional applications for their student's skills and competences?

The need of being competitive in the new global economy puts education in a key position in the cultural and political debate. New standards of excellence are needed, but it is not enough to raise the past standards or push students harder or even keep on measuring them with sophisticated instruments. What may be more important is to think differently, about education, about learning, and even about excellence. The push toward competition is what led UCN to investigate how to innovate within its field.

Especially if their job involves working with youngsters and children, educators and social workers have a central role in imagining new ways of developing minds and sensitivities, bodies and awareness. Therefore they need to be trained in the skills of creative thinking and making, which they can transfer into other fields or domains.

Being trained in the art of creativity and new-thinking, educators and social workers are expected to naturally be able to transfer their creative skills into pedagogical tasks or even other contexts. In reality, being creative is very different from being trained to teach or inspire creativity in children; being trained in teaching creativity to children or inspiring children to creativity is very different from leading larger creative processes. The same can be formulated for the social workers' occupation: learning about creativity and innovation doesn't grant the ability to think and act creatively. To fill in the gap, educators and social workers can be guided with specific tools, reflections and meta-reflections. Within the project "Dance with the future" the tools chosen are Expressive Arts (specifically arts-based coaching) and Theory U. I'll describe below how the two are being intertwined and applied. The presumption is that training educators and social workers to apply and reflect upon creative and innovative social technologies would broaden their disposition to new-thinking and build brand-new competences, spendable in innovation tasks.

3   Research Design

Before discussing the theoretical background of the present research, I wish to frame the methodological setting by indicating my considerations about hypothesis, research questions, empirical data-collection, and ethical guidelines.

With a theoretical and empirical background on my specific research interests [1], [2], I designed a research plan focused on the following hypothesis:

- The arts and arts-based processes can inspire, create and implement an optimal innovative and creative approach within the pedagogical field
- Arts and arts-based tools can have a qualitative influence in learning, development and prosperity for the field of preschoolers or kindergarten education and social workers' caregiving
- Arts and arts-based approach can be integrated with optimal outputs in educators and social workers' education and training strategies

In other words, the project "At the bottom of the U" examines whether and how creativity and aesthetic learning processes can foster and implement change within the educators and social workers' institutions at individual, professional (domain) and organizational (field) level. Drawing from Csikszentmihalyi [4] I will portray three levels of organisational learning: individual, field and domain.

I will look at the specific quality of individual learning and development, trying to answer the following research questions:

- Which specific cognitive challenges does the arts-based learning offer to the educators and social workers' field?
- Which specific positive emotions arise in the arts-based learning?

At the level of field interaction, I will describe how organisational gatekeepers facilitate or oppose the new professional opportunities or the arts-based approaches, and how this innovative initiative can open future career opportunities:

- Which consequences for the field of educators and social workers can be observed?
- Can the arts-based processes contribute to create an innovative professional opportunity for the UCN's educators and social workers?

Finally I will involve my informants in reflecting on which qualitative changes can contribute to re-think the whole education for social workers and which concrete propositions can be prototyped for the educators and social workers' careers of the future.

- Which consequences for the domain of educators and social workers can be observed?
- Can the arts-based processes contribute to create a culture of deep thinking and engaging education at the UCN?

Since this is an empirical and case-based qualitative study, the research method selected is ethnographic and participatory [9], [19].

The target group of the qualitative fieldwork is the trainee group (see figure 1.): they are followed by means of ethnographic participant observation and are involved in ethnographic interviews (individual and group). The observation prioritizes the apprenticeship sessions, where the trainees, divided in pairs, are asked to apply the principles of arts-based coaching and Theory U. The pairs freely choose the hosting institution, complete observations and interviews in the field, design and lead arts-based interventions.

As a support to the semi-structured interviews the trainees are invited to focus group interviews (one completed and one still to be held), with the intention of establishing a participatory relationship with the ongoing scholarly research.

Finally the trainees will be asked to respond to a qualitative self-report, in order to provide a reliable triangulation and bias reduction.

One last remark about the research design should be given to the ethical principles that are guiding the study. Special attention to this should be always given when research is with and about people, awareness that led me to contact the participants beforehand. Specifically, the participating institutions and participating trainees were offered the opportunity to accept or decline their contribution to the research project, and were informed about the project's purpose, overall design, time-span, and researcher's expectations to their role and contribution to the project.

4   Theory "ABC-U"

As introduced above, the main theoretical traditions, which are at the background of both the developmental initiative and the research project are the Expressive Arts [11], [12], [13] and Theory U [15], [16], [20]. They are two distinct theoretical frameworks within different domains: the former is therapeutic and phenomenological, the latter organizational and systemic. Nevertheless, they share a common interest for the aesthetic, bodily and ineffable knowledge of the senses, as mediated by arts forms and processes. Especially the Expressive Arts application in coaching, the arts-based coaching, and its "decentering" stage show great similarities with the Theory U stage of "sensitizing". These terms, which will be explained and conceptualised below, constitute the theoretical core of the developmental initiative "Dance with the future".

Theory U is a model, which visualizes individual (individual-in-organizations), collective and organizational learning processes and is targeted to a systemic vision of the future. The essence of the theory is the deep level of learning skills, "presencing" that can be achieved by activating all the known, unknown, forgotten or hidden human resources. This theory was at first developed by a group of academics affiliated to MIT -Otto Scharmer, in collaboration with Joseph Jaworski, Peter Senge and Adam Kahane [20]- and afterwards fully conceptualized by Scharmer [16].

The theoretical background is undoubtedly Senge's systems thinking and approach to organizational learning. To this, the almost 10-year's testing of the theory in organizational practices adds experimental evidence, such as the experience at the Society for Organizational Learning and the many interviews with world leaders and experts in organizational learning within the project "Dialogue on Leadership", which contributed to a clear grounding of theory in real challenges [5].

The U-model can be used both as a theory, e.g. as a description of a new ontological and epistemological perspective on organisations, or as a social technology, e.g. as a tool to generate deeper conversations among individuals in organizations. A special feature is a proactive and cooperative approach that differs from other learning models by its non-linear u-shaped movement from knowledge to action, which is strongly related to systems thinking principles.

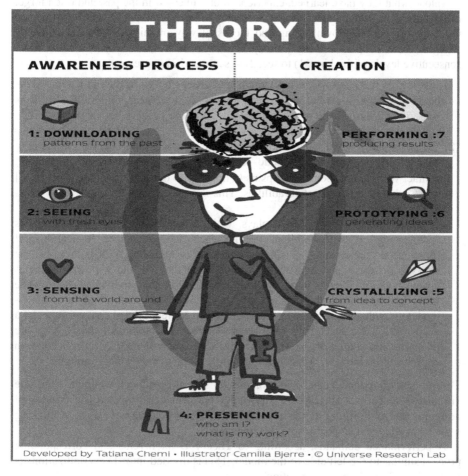

Fig. 2. The U-journey[1]

---

[1] The illustration appears originally in Danish at www.blivklog.dk/page13070.aspx. Scharmer's model can be downloaded at www.ottoscharmer.com.

The above model makes visible the learning journey that we go through or can shape differently when we need to learn optimally. In Scharmer's analysis [16], when we need to learn in organizations, we often activate the usual cognitive processes, based on past learning. We download the usual information, within the usual frames and habits, and then we apply this "old" knowledge by acting uncritically. This non-innovative process results in certain patterns of action that lead us towards a performance that is quick, tangible and manageable, but also "more of the same."

Being an expert, in this perspective, is not always an advantage, since experts specialize in one circumscribed area and exclude new and unusual opportunities or solutions. In a world characterized by rapid change and complexity, creative solutions are a necessity, as well as the need to adapt to a challenging reality. Experts often download what they have learned, experienced or witnessed in the past and often forget to be present in the moment, being so ready to what emerges. Scharmer proposes instead to go beyond downloading and the usual way of thinking and behaving, by engaging in a deeper learning journey. This can be achieved by activating three consecutive levels of thinking: 1) to see, 2) to sense and 3) to pre-sense.

1) "Seeing" is the level where individuals and groups let go of the old habits, take a break and try to see what we see and to hear what we hear, mindfully [10]. This stage is still associated with a traditional cognitive process but its purpose is to slowly work toward an open mind.

2) "Sensing" is the level where individuals and groups activate alternative learning channels by stimulating aesthetic sensitivity; artistic experiences; spirituality; contact with nature. Sensing helps us to open up to our emotional intelligence [8] and to change our perceptive abilities. This is a necessary step toward wholeness and presence.

3) "Presencing" is a word that plays with two meanings. If pronounced as "pre'sencing" it will highlight the presence and attendance to learning; if pronounced "prese'nsing" it will put emphasis on the senses. In both cases, the stress is on the experience of transformation of the self and will. Presencing is always both an individual and a collective process, because individuals learn while being in contact with the personal self and with others. At the bottom of the U-model individuals and groups experience a deep content-related conversation and a deep relational contact with each other. Themes the bottom of the U hosts are related to the source of one's own motivation, which stems from a reflection on oneself ("Who are you?") and about one's role in the world ("what is my job?").

This process of openness can be seen on the left side of the model, while the right side visualizes the various stages of a knowledge-performance process. The process of designing and performing innovative solutions, often based on new ways of thinking or new knowledge, can profit from this openness.

A performance demands, according to Theory U an inverse and corresponding process similar to the left side of the model. This is divided into: 1) crystallization, 2) prototyping, 3) performance or action.

1) When individuals or groups experience a "presencing" state, they often deal with an intrinsic motivation and clarity in the form of a paradox: It is impossible not to act. It is impossible not to "crystallize" one's thoughts on possible actions.

2) Scharmer suggests a rapid prototype of the crystallized actions.

3) Similarly, he suggests acting immediately, before the inner censorship and rationalization castrates every innovative solution or suggestion. It is important to preserve the good and innovative energy that can be the main output of the U-learning journey.

For what is concerning the learning journey through the arts-based coaching setting, the coordination group of "Dance with the future" has chosen the theory and praxis of the Expressive Arts Therapy as practiced and conceptualized by Swiss Paolo Knill.

To illustrate how the theory of Expressive Arts can be applied to coaching I can draw on my own interpretation [1] and on Knill's [13].

Ordinary experience of life		Life of client	
Establishing trust	"Hallo"	Filling in	
Art experience	SERV SENSITISE EXPLORE REPETITION VALIDATING	Decentering	
Alternative context of the world	Reflection through poetic concepts, sentences and mindset	Analysis	
Extraordinary experience of the world		Harvest	

Fig. 3. Arts-based coaching session model

In a coaching situation, the client steps in coming from his/her everyday life, and the related experience of it. He or she (or them, in case of a group or a team) is seeking help: his/her ordinary experience of life has entered a negative spiral. These help-seekers feel restricted by a lack of opportunities, alternatives or solutions and experience a limited play range. They experience a feeling of impotency ("I am not able to do anything"), a lack of resources ("if I only had a job, I wouldn't be depressed"), a blind spot or lack of perspective ("I know better than anyone else about my issue"), loneliness ("no one can help me"), separation of body and mind. This negativity is consistent to what Scharmer defines "the blind spot", and as in Theory U, the Expressive Arts turn to bodily, aesthetic and sensitive experiences in order to switch the focus from helplessness and blindness to mindful presence and relational well-being. As individuals, and as groups, we are experts in our problem; we know everything about it. Yet, in practice - we are experts in setting our own restrictions! When coachees enter an arts-based coaching session, they undergo a concrete process described by the phases visualised in the above figure: 1. filling in, 2. decentering, 3. analysis (or analysing),

4. harvest (or harvesting)[2]. At the end of the session, they might be able to perceive the world differently as plenty of endless and achievable possibilities. The Expressive Arts, similarly to Theory U, achieve this by stimulating our natural feelings towards aesthetic processes and products and by practically engaging coachees in the artistic process of creation. Art consultants or coaches should offer their clients activities, which demand low manual and technical skills, and yet should be meaningful and not trivial. The artistic task must be challenging but not threatening, as in an optimal learning experience, otherwise defined as flow [3]. To stimulate flow experiences within coaching sessions might seem a contradiction in terms, being the coaching activities based on mindfulness and awareness, versus flow experiences enhanced by a sense of deep presence in the task and self-forgetfulness. This apparent contradiction is not conceptualised in the arts-based coaching, for the simple reason that the two different experiences occur in two different stages: flow and self-forgetfulness during the decentering activities, and the coaching reflective activity during the harversting.

As in the Theory U framework, the experience of the senses opens up to a deeper (and often surprising) reflection and conversation. Having completed the creative phase of art making, coachees step into the analytical phase. This is the most difficult stage of a coaching session where an artistic decentering is used. *Decentering* is a specific term used in the Expressive Arts to define the process of forgetting one's own issue or problem and being completely involved and immersed in the alternative experience of art-making. It is the experience of being out of the lack-of-resources-centre, and moving outside of it, building resilience. This experience is induced by the *SERV*. SENSITISE: is the stimulation of the different senses through specific activities. In Theory U terms it corresponds to the "sensing" stage. EXPLORE: is the openness to investigate material reality in a new light. REPETITION: is the repetition of the task given, beyond feelings of boredom and against any inducement to superficiality. In this stage the participants have to face their motivations and self-discipline, being challenged into staying in the task in spite of boredom, in spite of routines and in order to avoid shallowness. VALIDATING: is the corroboration of the work done. This can be done through an evaluation session or a metaphorical activity that makes reflection visible.

When the SERV stage is done, the reflection can begin. The analytical stage is determined by the evaluation of the artistic product (or in Knill's terms: "oeuvre") and has a clear phenomenological approach. "To stay or remain at the surface" doesn't mean to be superficial, but rather not to loose touch with the material truths of the empirical world, as in the etymological sense of the word "sur-face". Observations are guided through reflections on: The "surface" of the work; The "process" of shaping; The "experience" of doing it; "What does the work say? How is it significant?" [13]. After that, a coach has to make sure to harvest as much meaning as possible from the experience of art making, building bridges of meaning and associations between the artistic experience and real-life challenges. This stage hosts unexpected views and clarifications.

5   Future Perspectives and Visions

How the above frameworks are going to be conceptualised within the educators and social workers' understandings and subsequently applied in facilitation tasks is still to

---

[2] All the definitions are borrowed from the Expressive Arts theory.

be documented. By now, it is possible to look at how the expert-trainers make sense of the two theories as one paradigm. In the very dissemination of theoretical concepts the two experts unite arts-based coaching (abc) with Theory U (u) in a new, common synthesis: the abc-u model. This conceptual patchwork is justified by the similarities mentioned above, which make the two theories mirror and complete each other. Within the vocabulary of the project's participants the therapeutic and phenomenological terms and concepts blend consistently with the organisational and systemic ones, the former being used within arts-based coaching, the latter within dialogical social technologies, as Theory U. Specifically, the expert-trainers seem to draw parallels between the left side of the U and the decentering experience. Both learning journeys are described as dialogic, collective (even in case of individual coaching, the intervention is always relational, involving coach, coachee and artwork) and aesthetic. Both imply radical changes and deep learning by means of the meeting with the arts and artistic experiences.

But why should we turn to the arts in order to solve individual or organisational problems at all? The Expressive Arts maintain that art has the power to stimulate imagination and creativity, being among countless means of inspiration for creativity, innovation and personal development. Then why are the arts a privileged tool both within arts-based coaching and Theory U? This discussion falls beyond the purpose of the present article. Nevertheless I will hint at some considerations. The arts have a specific form of logic, which is different from all the others, being bodily, mediated and meaning generating. Introducing this language in learning processes means breaking with the conventional thinking and mindset, and being open to new ways of making sense with the alternative logic of aesthetics. In so doing, individuals unlock the unsaid, the emotional, the opaque [6], and the multi-dimensional in their psychological and social being [14]. Moreover the final artistic product is a material, tangible witness to the creative process. By means of the artistic product we can refer at anytime to the artistic process that led to it, even when the process is finished or completed. The artistic work is a "materialization of imagination" always present and "thingly" [13]. Even though the arts appear in the above theoretical frameworks as just one of the means of stimulating perception, emotion and cognition, it is my opinion that it is no coincidence that both frameworks make use of artistic experiences. The ambition of my research study is to uncover the reasons for this specific preference, conceptualising my reflection within artistic learning processes.

The long-term ambition in the pedagogical field, to build resilience together with skills and dispositions seems to be enacted by the "Dance with the future" project. Here, teachers are students themselves and learn how to challenge their own creative competences, through innovative thinking and profession development. They learn to appreciate, nourish and encourage artistic and aesthetic learning processes in order to cultivate wholeness of learning environments. These processes, being conceptualized within the frameworks of organizational learning and coaching, can be actually applied to lead positive or optimal change. Outputs from this initiative are therefore expected to be promising within several fields and domains, both the pedagogical and the organisational.

References

1. Chemi, T.: Artbased Approaches: A Practical Notebook to Creativity at Work. Fokus Forlag (2006)
2. Chemi, T.: Once Upon a Time, in the Enchanted Kingdom of Denmark: A Fairy Tale on the Meeting Between the Arts and Organisations. In: European Conference for Creativity and Innovation, Copenhagen (2007)
3. Csikszentmihalyi, M.: Flow: The Psychology of the Optimal Experience. Harper Collins, New York (1990)
4. Csikszentmihalyi, M.: Creativity: Flow and the Psychology of Discovery and Invention. Harper Collins, London (1996)
5. Dialogue on Leadership, http://www.presencing.com/presencing/dol
6. Eisner, E.W.: The Arts and the Creation of Mind. Yale University Press, New Haver (2002)
7. Gardner, H.: Frames of Mind: The Theory of Multiple Intelligences. Harper Collins, London (1994)
8. Goleman, D.: Emotional Intelligence: Why It Can Matter More Than IQ. Bantam Books (1996)
9. Heron, J., Reason, P.: The Practice of Co-operative Inquiry: Research 'with' rather that 'on' people. In: Reason, P., Bradbury, H. (eds.) Handbook of Action Research: Participative Inquiry and Practice, pp. 179–188. SAGE, London (2001)
10. Kabat-Zinn, J.: Wherever You Are There You Are: Mindfulness Meditation in Everyday Life. Hyperion (2005)
11. Knill, P.: The Essence in a Therapeutic Process: An Alternative Experience of Wording? Poiesis. A Journal of the Arts and Communication 2, 6–14 (2000)
12. Knill, P., Levine, E.G., Levine, S.K.: Principles and Practice of Expressive Arts Therapy: Toward a Therapeutic Aesthetics. Jessica Kingsley Publisher, London (2005)
13. Knill, P., NienhausBarba, H., Fuchs, M.N.: Ministrels of Soul. Intermodal Expressive Therapy. EGS Press, Toronto (1995)
14. Perkins, D.N.: The Intelligent Eye: Learning to Think by Looking at Art. Paul Getty Trust, Los Angeles (1994)
15. Scharmer, O.: Presencing: Learning from the Future as it Emerges. On the Tacit Dimension of Leading Revolutionary Change. School of Economics, Helsinki (2000)
16. Scharmer, O.: Theory U: Leading from the Future as it Emerges. SOL, Cambridge (2007)
17. Senge, P.: The Fifth Discipline: The Art & Practice of the Learning Organization. Doubleday, New York (2006)
18. Senge, P.M., et al.: The Fifth Discipline Fieldbook. Nicholas Brealey, London (1996)
19. Senge, P., Scharmer, O.: Community Action Research: Learning as a Community of Practitioners, Consultants and Researchers. In: Reason, P., Bradbury, H. (eds.) Handbook of Action Research: Participative Inquiry and Practice, pp. 238–249. SAGE, London (2001)
20. Senge, P., Scharmer, O.C., Jaworski, J., Flowers, B.S.: Presence: Exploring Profound Change in People, Organizations and Society. Nicholas Brealey, London (2007)

TenSeconds - A Collaboration Platform for Distributed Action Painting

Andre Burkovski, Benjamin Höferlin, Michael Raschke, and Thomas Ertl

Institute for Visualization and Interactive Systems, University of Stuttgart, Germany
andre.burkovski@vis.uni-stuttgart.de
benjamin.hoeferlin@vis.uni-stuttgart.de
michael.raschke@vis.uni-stuttgart.de
thomas.ertl@vis.uni-stuttgart.de

Abstract. We present the collaboration art platform "Ten Seconds Art". With this platform art interested people can participate in an art creation process. Up to four people can simultaneously create a piece of action painting art in real time by using an android smartphone app. The platform records accelerator values which are transformed to joint movements of a manipulator arm. This arm splashes color to a canvas and thus produces a picture similar to action-paintings. Users can view this process via webcam stream in real-time. With this work we want to discuss questions of amateur, distributed, everywhere, and bite-size creativity from the point of view of telerobotics.

Keywords: mobile app, amateur creativity, distributed creativity, robot art, action painting, telerobotics.

1 Introduction

Social and technological developments are often reflected by arts. Examples are the invention of new music instruments like synthetic sounds, or graphical techniques, such as intaglio printing plates by copper engravings, as well as contemporary movements in architecture with their specific stylistic elements. With the emergence of new media and wide-spread use of the internet, interesting new paradigms open a broad access to arts and influence the artistic practice. With our work we want to discuss four trends of new media (cf. Fig. 1): amateur, distributed, everytime-everywhere, and bite-size creativity. We describe these four trends and their influence on the development of our platform.

A.L. Brooks (Ed.): ArtsIT 2011, LNICST 101, pp. 29–37, 2012.

1.1 Amateur Creativity

Social media and web 2.0 technologies were a precursor to a participation process that in the end unified consumer and producer of digital artifacts in one person. The mergence sometimes is called the *prosumers* or *produsers* [2]. These emerging technologies provide an architecture of participation, not only by exploiting open source-like volunteering, but by pursuing the users' "selfish" interests to build collective value as an automatic byproduct [6] (e.g., *Napster* defaults the automatic share of data downloaded by its users). The driving force behind this development - Prada terms it *amateur creativity* [7] - is the experience of the user to be part of the collectivity, to participate in emotional interactions. This process is largely driven by service platforms, such as *YouTube, Flickr, Facebook*, or *Wordpress* and leads to a state where the user no longer is solely the target of professionally created content, but also the origin of creative contributions.

As final product of the participation process, the border between artist and consumer fades. According to Alan S. Brown, we may distinguish five modes of participation in arts that can be measured by the level of creative control by the participant [1]:

- *Inventive Arts Participation* engages the mind, body and spirit in an act of artistic creation that is unique and idiosyncratic, regardless of skill level.
- *Interpretive Arts Participation* is a creative act of self-expression that brings alive and adds value to pre-existing works of art, either individually or collaboratively.
- *Curatorial Arts Participation* is the creative act of purposefully selecting, organizing and collecting art to the satisfaction of ones own artistic sensibility.
- *Observational Arts Participation* encompasses arts experiences that you select or consent to, motivated by some expectation of value.
- *Ambient Arts Participation* involves experiencing art, consciously or unconsciously, that you did not select.

While Brown [1] suggests that the predominant emphasis of professional cultural nonprofits is the fourth mode on the list, we present in this paper a participation platform for Jackson Pollock-style action painting, where users can join the creation process at the highest level of creative control (i.e., *Inventive Arts Participation*). The other modes could further be covered as we discuss in future work section.

1.2 Distributed Creativity

Collaboration is an important component in the participatory turn, since the success of participatory projects may depend on a feeling of belonging to a common group or of having a common identity [4]. Nowadays, there is a strong social trend towards collaboration, driven by people's desire to contribute to something larger than themselves [9]. The trend to open collaboration that follows the successful model of open source, can yet be observed in many different fields, such as participatory journalism (e.g., *Slashdot*), or collaborative music sessions (e.g., *Flashmobs*, or the *Youtube symphony orchestra*[1]). In the same way, as in the mergence of consumers and producers, web 2.0 technologies, such as blogs and wikis, play a central role in the development of distributed creativity. Important for the success of contribution platforms are besides the "common interest" technical requirements that have to be met, such as ease of use, ease of contribution, and ease of interaction [9].

In our approach, we facilitate collaboration and distributed creativity by accounting for these requirements. Please note that we use the term collaboration not only in the sense of cooperation, but also to describe potential counteraction that appears by interaction and manipulation of different ideas and conceptions.

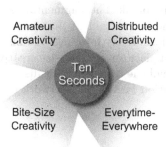

Fig. 1. Newly emerged paradigms build the foundation of the presented action painting platform

1.3 Everytime-Everywhere Creativity in a Virtual Studio

Tremendous increase of information circulation and communication between everyone, at everytime and everywhere shapes the actual and future evolution of our ubiquitous society (cf. [3]). We got used to have all information at our fingertips by using our smartphone's internet connection, no matter where we are. And it is "convenient and cool to carry our entire inventory of media and entertainment in our pocket. No matter if you are at home or on the road, access to your media entertainment library is just a touch of a button away" [10]. Even our office is omnipresent in the guise of Blackberries or Wi-Fi-connected laptops. The same way, technology enables us to be creative everywhere and everytime.

As communication becomes ubiquitous, life becomes virtual, too. Terms such as virtual office, virtual government, and virtual banking describe the abstract and virtual environments derived from real-world places and actions. In this paper we use the metaphor of a virtual studio as the equivalent to the traditional studio. Users remotely control a robot in the virtual studio that becomes their tool to express their creativity. By using the telerobotics methodology, we transform this virtual creativity to a real-world object: an action painting.

---

[1] Youtube symphony orchestra 2011: http://www.youtube.com/user/symphony

1.4 Bite-Size Creativity

A consequence of the everytime-everywhere development is the demand of fast entertainment, and bite-size media. The *Wired* magazine is even convinced that "today, media snacking is a way of life" [5]. "Media snacking" describes the trend towards quick and instant consumption of media, such as a 30-seconds news clip, a one-minute game on the cell phone, or a randomly shuffled 3-minute song on the *iPod*. Similar as the before mentioned trends, this development is also driven by technology and particular platforms. Among the trendsetters are *Youtube* and *iTunes* [10]. Further, the bite-size trend is not only restricted to the snacking of media, but can be found in similar fashion in all kinds of activities. For example, we quickly make a reservation for the cinema, while waiting for the bus; or just communicate our latest thoughts to others using the 140 characters of Twitter messages during a conference break. The fragmentation of our daily life into small pieces of bite-size work and entertainment units is largely supported by apps: small manageable applications, ready for quick and instant execution. Apps also found the way into arts as a platform for bite-size creativity. The ZKM (Zentrum für Kunst und Medientechnologie Karlsruhe) for instance, recently organized the AppArtAward[2], a competition for the best artwork in app format.

2 Ten Seconds

The presented paradigms inspired us to create a new modern art platform – the 'Ten Seconds Art'. This platform provides an easy, bite-size, and collaborative way of creating action art paintings. Technically, the Ten Seconds platform consists of three elements: an Android smartphone app, a painting robot and a connection server. Next, we present the interaction concept and the technical architecture.

2.1 Ten Seconds Interaction and Collaboration Concept

On the one hand our interaction concept has to manage the collaboration of several users spread over different places, while, on the other hand it has to provide intuitive interaction with the connected robot. Since we aim for bite-size creativity, our concept enable users to interact with each other with a minimum of training required. To facilitate amateur creativity, we provide a smartphone app that is accessible to everyone with a smartphone, thus everyone can become an artist. Further, we meet the requirements of the art creation process by four simple and intuitive steps:

1. Connection to the art server that is the access to the virtual studio
2. Staging of collaborating artists
3. Expression of artistic intentions by moving the smartphone for ten seconds
4. Viewing the aggregated movements of the robot via real-time webcam stream

---

[2] http://www.app-art-award.org/

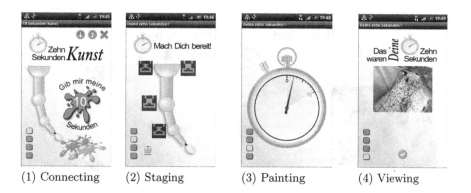

(1) Connecting   (2) Staging   (3) Painting   (4) Viewing

Fig. 2. The four steps of our interaction concept, which are also the four screens (or activities) presented to the users of our app

These steps are repeated with different colors, and different artists, until the final piece of artwork is formed. Particularly notable are the limitations of hardware and time that shape the art creation process and render it exciting and interesting.

2.2   Technical Details

Smartphone App. The app is implemented using the Android operating system for smartphones. Four activities are implemented reflecting the four steps of art creation. The first activity shows the start screen of the app. Users have to push the 'Gib mir meine 10 Sekunden' button (german for "Give me my ten seconds"). When pushing the button the app checks for a free slot for the user on the server. If a slot is available the next activity is shown. In the second activity users can see which axes they are controlling. The axes are assigned by the server. For easy identification of user controlled axes we use *Gravatars*[3]. The user's Gravatar is depicted at the axes the user controls. The text 'Mach Dich bereit' ('Get ready') signalizes that collaborating artists have to pay attention to the start signal which is delivered by the server. This so called 'staging room' was implemented to raise the feeling of a special moment and to increase the concentration for the movement recording process. After the smartphone receives the start signal from the server, it vibrates for a short time and a stopwatch is shown that counts the ten seconds down. During these ten seconds we record the accelerator sensors and finally send the data to the server. In the fourth activity, users get an exclusive view of the robot arm movements via a webcam stream. Finally, the Ten Seconds Art app returns to the first activity and users can start over again.

---

[3] Gravatars (Globally Recognized Avatars) are visual identifiers that generate a small avatar image based on the connection profile (like IP-address or email-address) of the user.

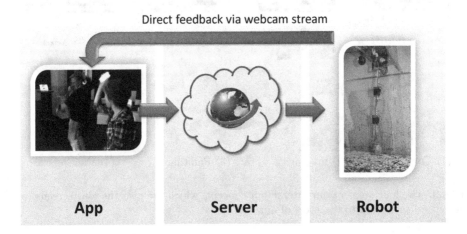

Fig. 3. The art creation pipeline: After login, users move their smartphones. These movements are recorded and sent to the art server which transforms the accelerator sensor values to the movements of the axes of the robot. The art creation process can directly be viewed via webcam stream.

Server System. The Ten Seconds art server is based on a apache web server system. The main functions of the server are user management, handling of the accelerator sensor value coming from the app and sending the webcam stream to the Ten Seconds artist or other viewers. Also, the single steps of the art creation process are controlled with a web-based administration tool.

Painting Robot Platform. The robot manipulator arm is installed upside down on the ceiling of its protected working environment. Fig. 4 shows the painting robot platform. Based on experiences during the development of the robot system JP [8], we have chosen a very simple and robust architecture with four joints driven independently by servo modules. The working environment has a basal area of DIN-A0 paper size. A rubber hose transports the fluid color from outside the working environment to a small color container at the end effector of the manipulator arm which has the possibility to swing freely. Thus, every painting is unique.

The robots' angular history is prescribed by an algorithm which transforms the accelerator sensor values from a three dimensional Cartesian smartphone space to the joint space of the robot system. In case of one user, all three sensor axes of a user are mapped to single robot joints. The angular history of the fourth robot joint is prescribed by a superposition. In case of two users axes with the highest and second highest alteration rates are separately mapped to robot joints. When painting with three users, every user controls one axis, the fourth axis again is a superposition of all users' movements. Four users separately control four axes.

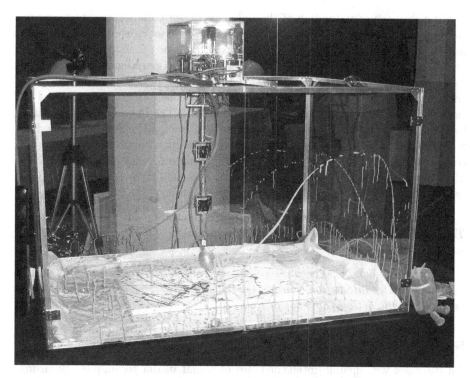

Fig. 4. The painting robot is installed upside down on the ceiling of its protected working environment, has four degrees of freedom, and is driven by servo motors

3   Discussion and Future Work

In this paper we presented the art collaboration platform 'Ten Seconds Art' for creating modern art paintings inspired by Jackson Pollock's action painting. Based on the three elements smartphone app, server and robot, art-interested people are able to create their individual pieces of art in four intuitive steps. A webcam stream gives a direct feedback of the creation process.

Ten Seconds Art was presented at the first AppArtAward of the Zentrum für Kunst und Medientechnologie in Karlsruhe (Center for Art and Media, Karlsruhe) in July 2011. Due to great interest we performed a second time at the Karlsruher Museumsnacht (Open Night of Museums) in August 2011. During both events several hundred people saw the art platform and fifteen paintings were created by visitors (cf. Fig. 5).

We observed that visitors were able to handle the Ten Seconds app after only a short introduction. We ascribe this effect to the high conformity to users' expectations of our app. Further, both children and adults were fascinated and excited to create pieces of art in this technical and playful fashion. This shows that our approach to create art by a collaboration platform for distributed action painting is a broadly accepted way for amateur creativity.

For a deeper understanding of the influence of our collaboration platform on the artistic practice, we conducted a survey with associates of the ZKM that were involved in the AppArtAward. We asked questions to determine if our approach to arts is suitable to cope with the introduced paradigms of new media. In summary, the participants agreed that the bite-size period of 10 seconds suits very well our approach of participatory creativity (one participant suggested an extended period up to 30 seconds for introduction). The impact of collaboration to the experience of the art creation process of our platform was expected to be high, since the final result is a collectively produced artifact with apparent traces of the own contribution (assuming different colors for each participant). Moreover, the robot is considered as a partner in the art creation process. Subsequently, we reflect some relevant feedback of our survey:

"In principle, the robot represents the tool (extended, modified arm with brush). The participant (human) is the artist who generates the painting by his movement."

"On the one hand, it [the ten seconds art] reflects the aesthetic aspect of the human computer interaction concept. On the other hand, the paintings are clearly evocative of the action paintings of Pollock, but as post-modern version."

"[In the future,] I expect that we will be commonly confronted with the combination of Smartphone, human, and some controllable mechanism."

Future work will include intensified use of social media techniques. By using mechanisms for feedback and ranking of created action paintings even more levels of creative control will be introduced to our platform.

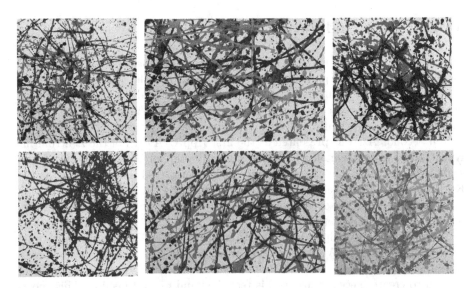

Fig. 5. Action paintings created by Ten Second painters during the ZKM AppArtAward 2011 and KAMUNA 2011 in Karlsruhe

Acknowledgements. We would like to thank all the visitors of our Ten Seconds Art installation during the AppArtAward party and Open Night of Museums in Karlsruhe. Especially, we like to thank all the Ten Seconds artists who created unique and beautiful pieces of robot art.

References

1. Brown, A.: The five modes of arts participation (January 2005)
2. Bruns, A.: Gatewatching: Collaborative online news production, vol. 26. Peter Lang Pub. Inc. (2005)
3. Kunio, T.: Toward the ubiquitous society in which humankind will continue to be the leading actor from "technology trends". NEC Technical Journal 1(1), 143–148 (2006)
4. Milevska, S.: Partizipatorische kunst -Überlegungen zum paradigmenwechsel vom objekt zum subjekt. Springerin - Hefte für Gegenwartskunst 2 (2006)
5. Miller, N.: Minifesto for a new age, Issue 15.03 (March 2007)
6. O'Reilly, T.: The architecture of participation (June 2004)
7. Prada, J.M.: Web 2.0 as a new context for artistic practices. The Fibreculture Journal 14(98) (2009)
8. Raschke, M., Mombaur, K., Schubert, A.: An optimization-based robot platform for the generation of action paintings. International Journal of Arts and Technology 4(2), 181–195 (2011)
9. Scholz, T.: Technologies for distributed creativity: Share, share widely. Interview with Axel Bruns (2004)
10. Craig Watkins, S.: The young and the digital: what the migration to social-network sites, games, and anytime, anywhere media means for our future. Beacon Press, Boston (2009)

Playfulness and Openness: Reflections on the Design of Learning Technologies

Emanuela Marchetti and Eva Petersson Brooks

Centre for Design, Learning and Innovation
Department of Learning and Philosophy
Department of Architecture, Design, and Media Technology
Aalborg University
Niels Borhs Vej 8, 6700, Esbjerg, Denmark
{ema,ep}@create.aau.dk

Abstract. What does it mean to design a playful learning tool? What is needed for a learning tool to be perceived by potential users as playful? These questions emerged reflecting on a Participatory Design process aimed at enhancing museum-learning practice from the perspective of primary school children. Different forms of emergent interactions were evident, both during museum visits and while testing a low-fidelity prototype. Deeper reflections on the meaning of enhancing learning through play from a user's individual perspective was assessed. In this respect, openness and multimodality were evaluated intertwined with design of playful learning tools to enrich non-formal learning and to allow support for individual needs.

Keywords: non-formal learning, playfulness, open-ended design, multimodality, emergent interaction, learning technologies.

1   Introduction

Museums are currently facing a challenging innovation process, including a re-shaping of their role as learning practices. Related work has dealt with this challenge from different angles; from an institutional perspective [1] or from the visitors' perspective considering new design solutions to enhance museum as learning practices [2]. According to our study, mono-directional forms of communication of historical processes during guided tours still appear unexplored. These forms of transferring knowledge result in static interactions between children and adults, and to superficial understanding of abstract historical concepts. Primary school children (age 10) experience museums as an "adults-mediated" activity, in which adults are in control and where children and museum guides do not talk much to each other. The children are often depicted as a pleasant audience, as their behaviour is generally polite, somehow influenced by their school training. Therefore, a Participatory Design (PD) study has been conducted with a group of children (age 10), in order to investigate how museum-learning practice could be enhanced from the children's perspective.

A.L. Brooks (Ed.): ArtsIT 2011, LNICST 101, pp. 38–45, 2012.
© Institute for Computer Sciences, Social Informatics and Telecommunications Engineering 2012

The aim of the PD process was to develop a new playful learning tool, involving a group of 10 years old children as co-designers. Observations conducted during visits in the museum and co-design workshops revealed how children may have different individual needs, in relation to play and to experiencing the museum. Some children tend to prefer more social situations, in which they can talk, laugh and eventually be physically active together with others. Others may choose quiet and solitary experiences, to enjoy by themselves or just together with a few friends.

Based on these findings, a reflection was conducted in relation to what makes a learning tool playful and engaging, from the individual perspective of the learners and their individual needs. It is argued that playfulness should be intended as an intertwining of openness and multimodality, to facilitate different user experiences.

2   Related Work

The field of technologies related to learning and more specifically to the museum context has become incredibly wide. However, some main tendencies can be identified and considered for inspirations when it comes to designing new technologies for museums. The first technological solutions for museums were interactive kiosks showing video audio media about the museum exhibition [2].

Generally, technologies proposed for museum contexts focus on providing visitors with interactive alternative access to information. The aim of this research is to provide visitors with an exciting museum experience, to allow them to learn more about the exhibition, to have fun during their visit, and to motivate them to come again. Many researchers have specifically focused on young audiences (children and teenagers), proposing computer-augmented installations to make their museum experience more fun [3, 4, 5]. Some of these works simply intend to leverage on young people's interest for computer games [4, 5], while others refer more or less explicitly to Prensky's theory about digital natives [3]. According to Prensky [6] young people have been deeply affected by continuous exposure to digital media since a very young age, and accordingly, developed different preferences regarding learning and fun. For example, they prefer a learning-by-doing approach to reading and education, and "random access" to information instead of being guided step by step by adults [6]. Based on these considerations, Prensky proposes a "computer-based" approach to learning, in which young learners may acquire knowledge by playing a computer game [6].

Researchers active in the field of developing technologies generally follow the same approach. Studies such as [3] explicitly refer to Prensky as a source of inspiration in their attempt to bridge teenagers' everyday interests with museums to elicit in them a motivation to visit museums. In order to achieve their goal, Dindler and his colleagues ran a series of participatory workshops which allowed them to find out that in some cases teenagers were not interest to the past itself, but it could be made more interesting by constructing parallels between the past and their own everyday [3]. Other researchers in the same field do not explicitly refer to such theories, but still seem to adopt digital technologies to add elements of fun and play. In the case of the Life Tree interactive table, at the Museum of Natural History in Berlin the researchers intended to provide a more engaging access to information about the different species displayed in the museum [4]. The result is an interactive multi-touch surface; a series of popping-up bubbles allows the users to navigate among different information. Tests conducted in the museum revealed that people developed playful gesture interactions, as they experimented how to touch the surface, for instance by tapping with one or more fingers simultaneously, or even with flat hands [4].

A study conducted by Hall and Bannon [5] about ubiquitous computing within museum space, refers specifically to primary school children and proposes to hide technology to focus on interaction in itself. A new setting was created for the Hunt Museum in Limerick, through a participatory process and tested during an exhibition. An interactive environment was proposed in which children could interact with RFID-augmented copies of the collection items. In this way, they could leave their feedback about the exhibition by talking to a phone and listen to others' activating a radio [5]. Finally, systems such as Kurio introduce play more explicitly, intended as a way to support learning by doing and social interaction [5]. Kurio was designed to enrich families' museum tours, introducing a form of shared-problem solving activity. Families are supposed to pretend they are time travelers, stranded in a different time, and gather information about the current time to be able to come back [7]. Interestingly, this system seems to transform museum tour into a sort of apprenticeship, in which children and adults cooperate together in shared problem solving activities [8].

These works are inspiring and provide new directions to museum innovation. However, a gap was identified in the fact that such works do not discuss guided tours, which are the most common modality for children when they visit museums. Moreover, such approaches, as well as the installations provided by museums, aim at providing an immersive sensorial impressions of the past from a synchronic perspective, neglecting somehow the diachronic perspective, dealing with historical processes. Hence, issues related to guided tours practice and the diachronic perspective constitute the main focus of this study.

3   Methods and Background

The context for our research is *Ribes Vikinger*, the Viking Museum in Ribe, in Southwestern Jutland, Denmark. This museum was chosen because it has a mission in spreading knowledge related to local history to a wide audience, moreover, it displays a small but precious collection of artifacts, dated more or less from Prehistory to the Renaissance, with a special emphasis to Viking and Middle Ages.

In order to gain more meaningful and child-centred knowledge, a Participatory Design process was organized with an after school institution, involving a group of 25 children (10 years of age), in designing a playful learning tool for museums. Several activities have been conducted within the PD process; the children were interviewed about their previous museum experience and asked to carry out a few tasks, such as writing the name of the last museum they visited and detail an adjective to describe it. Furthermore, they should comment on pictures showing artifacts displayed in Ribe. The children were also invited to visit the museum; data collected during this visit were analyzed qualitatively and compared with data from observations conducted during a guided tour with a group of pupils (age 10). Afterwards the children participated in four co-design workshops, in which they had to design and test low-fidelity prototypes of the game. During such workshops and museum visits, individual needs were identified in relation to play and museum experience, which constituted a framework for the reflections presented in this study.

4   Emergent Play and Museum Experience. Design of Micro-Culture and Observational Data

The aim of this study was to investigate how to transpose complex historical processes, specifically urban development through time, into playful interactions, to enhance learning and engagement in museums. Special attention was dedicated to guided tours, as they represent the typical way children experience museum. Moreover, board games, objects-mediated form of play, seemed to offer an interesting framework to enhance social interaction and to provide an experiential/tangible grounding to historical processes. Games such as Monopoly or Risk provided interesting sources of inspiration. Board games practice is a form of social interaction mediated by material objects [9], in which players engage in a peer, face to face, based communication. Moreover, the players often start a theatrical improvisation, staging the game situation and teasing each other, as it was all for real [10]. The material configuration of the games seems to play a central role in eliciting this particular interaction, as the board is placed at a lower level than the players' gaze, defining a circular interaction space with the players sitting around it. Hence players are supposed to place tangibles on the board and in some cases, like in Monopoly, to exchange them with each other. In this way the game play has a natural affordance for eye contact and social interaction, as the players look at each other through the game, then while acting on the tangibles they enter into a closer contact and in that moment a particular form of emergent interaction may occur as the players start staging the game situation [10].

This social dynamics match communication of historical processes, allowing the players to experience how a certain process may unfold through time and what would be the implications for the people involved. However, board games have usually a complicated system of rules that must be learnt before starting to play. Our game intended to be more unstructured and leverage on material affordance of a gaming board and tangibles.

The outcome of this process is *Micro-Culture*, a mixed reality setting composed by a tabletop surface, showing a simulated territory consisting of a population and a set of tangibles, representing infrastructures to be placed on the territory, such as bridges or streets. The Micro-Culture game is based on a biological metaphor with experiments and observations of bacterial cultures. A low-fidelity prototype has been developed and tested twice; a working prototype is currently under development.

The technical set up includes a webcam and a computer. The game is implemented in Python and with ReacTIVision, a system including a set of markers and software to develop tangible interfaces[1]. The markers are placed on Micro-Culture tangibles, so that they can be traced and recognize by a webcam and through the software. In this

---

[1] http://reactivision.sourceforge.net/

way, the simulation and population can be programmed to respond to the tangibles and provide direct feedback to players' actions. For instance, if a player places a bridge on a river, the bridge will appear in the simulation and people may start crossing it.

However, interviews, observations in museums and testing of a low-fidelity prototype showed that children had individual needs to express themselves, both in relation to the museum experience and related to play and playing. Comparisons between observations conducted with a group attending a guided tour and with the group of co-designers during a free tour, revealed different forms of emergent interaction. During the guided tour the children were very quiet, they tended to split into small subgroups, some followed more constantly the guide while others, usually on the back of the main group, moved around and whispered to each other. Other children did not seem to be part of a specific group, but looked at things by themselves. Children participating to the free tour manifested similar tendencies: some actively explored the exhibition space, chatting lively and almost running. Other children preferred a more quiet fruition of the space, walking quietly, talking and laughing at each other, at times even asking questions to us. Finally some children liked to be alone, for example, a girl liked to sit by herself in a niche and when she was asked if she liked the museum, she mentioned that she especially liked the space because "it is silent and I can be alone with my thoughts" (Figure 1).

Testing with the prototype showed a similar differentiation. Some children set up their "settlement" by placing a few tangibles and then started to play as expected; they interpreted the setting as a board game or a role-play game platform. Hence they acted as they were "landlords", competing with each other to conquer the other player's land. They also introduced tanks, a float, and soldiers as new tangibles for the game. Especially girls, considered the game as a design tool, which meant that they spent most of their time in creating their own settlements and in making new tangibles, specifically shops for the market place, animals and farms, ships. Afterward some children from the designer group started to play with the "landlords" group and seemed to enjoy a war-like game (Figure 2).

Fig. 1. Solitary and social museum experience

An interesting interplay emerged when this mixed group of players agreed that they wanted to play the game together. However, one designer girl expressed the desire to have everything ready before playing and she spent a lot of time in settling everything up with another girl. The landlord group asked repeatedly if they were ready and even took initiative attacking their piece of land so that they could play. The designer girl did not appreciate this and she stated: "Stop, I am not ready yet!"

Fig. 2. Emergent play: designing and engaging

Despite the small size of the cardboard board the children managed to arrange different groups playing differently. Interestingly, the mixed group and some individuals expressed forms of so called playful play, defined by Sutton-Smith [11] as a particular form of play in which creative players may define rules for others' play. This happened during the game a few times. The mixed group created tangibles and dynamics related to the tangibles for their play. Two female designers spent their time in making tangibles and playing dynamics related to such tangibles, and then they placed them on the board for the others to play with. Moreover, during a co-design workshop, a girl created a whole narrative framework, in which the player had to go through a quest, in the end a fight with Kraken should have taken place, and if the player survived then he/she would be able to access the Valhalla, otherwise he/she would die and be buried in a cemetery.

Considering these different forms of interaction expressed by the children, a concern emerged in terms of defining the meaning of designing a playful learning tool. In other words, what would be the characteristic of a learning tool to be perceived as playful by different individuals?

5   Playfulness, Openness and Multimodality

Reflections conducted on observational data from Participatory Design and museum visits informed that certain play dynamics might not be appealing for all learners.

Furthermore, considering the communication mode used to convey meanings related to historical processes, it seems as they primarily are based on a verbal mode of communication. This may happen because of the sequential nature of historical processes, as confirmed by interviews conducted with museum practitioners. We propose more tangible and playful communication modes to support understanding of historical processes.

The creation of a playful tool promotes a deeper investigation about how to enrich the current interaction style. Playful and fun experiences were targeted. This means that the children were engaged through different choices of action. The choice in how to do things was in this case closely related to having fun [12, 13, 14]. In this way, the learning tool provided a basis for evolution of playful experiences where the children could find their own ways for interacting.

In this sense it is being claimed that a playful learning tool should be characterized by openness, in the sense that its material affordance should easily support different forms of emergent interaction. This challenge requires multiple opportunities for manipulation and forms of play integrated in an open-ended model for learning [15].

To achieve such openness, the concept of multimodality appears as closely interconnected benefiting from the insight that children have different orientations to modes, specific preferences for temporal or spatial, image or speech, bodily movement [16, 17]. Multimodality combines these different modes providing a framework allowing different forms of sensorial explorations and openness in the form of extended forms and choice of interaction mode.

The board game configuration, Micro-Culture, facilitated social and object-mediated interaction. The absence of specific rules, which are typical in board games, allowed the children to decide for themselves, they could decide to engage with others in cooperative play but also to create some space for themselves and their imaginary world, or even to shift from one modality to another. The relatively small size of the board seemed not to hinder the co-existence of subgroups and their play dynamics. However, it may have created a few issues, for instance social players tended to occupy most of the space, while solitary players were using very little areas of the board. Probably a larger surface, such as a projection on the floor, may have provided a better affordance.

Social interaction is supported basically by hiding the technology and by coupling input and output, players' actions and the simulation responses, on the same playing surface, so that the system is not disrupting players' attention from establishing eye-contact and from the learning content. Audio effects could support tangible interaction and visual animated simulations in order to make the whole simulation even richer and more engaging.

6   Conclusion and Future Work

This study presented reflections about the meaning and implication of designing learning related technologies. The discussion is based on data collected during a one year Participatory Design process, aimed at exploring ways to enhance museum-learning practice from the perspective of primary school children. A group of 25 children, 10 years old, were involved in designing a new learning technology, aimed at enriching learning of historical processes and also social interaction between children and their guides when attending museum tours.

Reflecting on related work and data from the study, we propose a perspective in which playfulness regarding learning related technology should fit individual values of play. During our PD process it was noticed that children expressed distinctive individual needs regarding museum experience and play. Hence our original project was re-shaped to create space for users' needs. In this sense, playfulness is interpreted as strictly interrelated to openness and multimodality, to provide support for richer and more self-driven interaction forms.

References

1. Lang, C., Reeve, J., Woollard, V.: The responsive museum: working with audiences in the twenty-first century, Ashgate (2006)
2. Kidd, J., Ntala, I., Lyons, W.: Multi-touch Interfaces in Museum Spaces: Reporting Preliminary Findings on the Nature of Interaction. In: Ciolfi, Scott, Barbieri (eds.) Rethinking Technology in Museums: Emerging Experiences. University of Limerick (2011)

3. Dindler, C., Iversen, O., Smith, R., Veerasawmy, R.: Participatory design at the museum: inquiring into children's everyday engagement in cultural heritage. In: Proceedings of the 22nd Conference of the Computer-Human Interaction Special Interest Group of Australia on Computer-Human Interaction, OZCHI 2010, Brisbane, Australia (2010)
4. Hornecker, E.: I don't understand it, but it is cool – Visitor Interaction with a Multi-Touch Table in Museum. In: Proceedings of IEEE Tabletop (2008)
5. Hall, T., Bannon, L.: Cooperative design of children's interaction in museums: a case study in the Hunt Museum. CoDesign 1(3), 187–218 (2005)
6. Prensky, M.: Digital Natives, Digital Immigrants. On the Horizon 9(5) (2001)
7. Muise, K., Wakkary, R.: Bridging Designers' Intentions to Outcomes with Constructivism. In: Proceedings of the 8th ACM Conference Design of Interactive Systems, Aarhus, Denmark (2010)
8. Rogoff, B.: Apprenticeship in Thinking. Cognitive Development in Social Context. Oxford University Press (1990)
9. Henare, A., Holbraad, M., Westel, S.: Thinking through Things, Theorising artefacts ethnographically. Routledge (2007)
10. Marchetti, E.: Evocative Objects and Fun. A study about board games practice as objects-mediated social interaction. In: CRESC Conference 2009, Objects – What's Matters? Technology Value and Social Change. University of Manchester (2009)
11. Sutton-Smith, B.: The Ambiguity of Play. Harvard University Press (1997)
12. Göncü, A. (ed.): Children's Engagement in the World. Sociocultural Perspectives. Cambridge University Press, New York (1999)
13. Rogoff, B.: Becoming a Cooperative Parent in a parent Cooperative. In: Rogoff, B., Goodman Turkanis, C., Bartlett, L. (eds.) Learning Together. Oxford University Press, New York (2001)
14. Petersson, E.: Non-formal Learning through Ludic Engagement within Interactive Environments. Doctoral dissertation, Malmö University, School of Teacher Education, Studies in Educational Sciences (2006)
15. Petersson, E., Brooks, A.: Virtual and Physical Toys: Open-ended Features for Non-formal Learning. Cyber Psychology and Behavior 9(2), 196–199 (2006)
16. Kress, G.: Multimodality. A Social Semiotic Approach to Contemporary Communication. Routledge, London (2010)
17. van Leeuwen, T.: Introducing Social Semiotics. Routledge, London (2005)

Improving L-System Music Rendering Using a Hybrid of Stochastic and Context-Sensitive Grammars in a Visual Language Framework

Lim Chen Kim and Abdullah Zawawi Talib

School of Computer Sciences, Universiti Sains Malaysia,
11800 USM Pulau Pinang, Malaysia
chenkimlim@gmail.com, azht@cs.usm.my

Abstract. L-Systems have been extensively utilized in plant modeling and music rendering. However, the music generated was not very pleasant as the grammars used are very simple. This paper describes a hybrid method that generates more complex grammars for L-Systems in a visual language framework for music rendering so that the musical sounds generated can be improved and fine-tuned. The method which uses a hybrid of stochastic and context-sensitive L-Systems grammars is vital in producing harmonious musical sounds and a variety of L-System grammars for L-Systems music rendering. Based on the evaluation, the method has been rated to be useful and effective in rendering harmonious musical sounds using the visual language framework even for anyone who does not have prior knowledge in L-System music rendering.

Keywords: L-System Attributes, Stochastic, Context-Sensitive, Plant Modelling, Music Rendering, Visual Programming Framework.

1   Introduction and Related Work

L-System is a language consisting of a set of strings governed by a set of production rules while a string consists of a sequence of symbols called axioms. When the production rules are applied to the axioms, the string generated can be used to model plants and render musical sounds [1]. This paper focuses on visual generation of musical sounds using L-Systems. Stochastic and context-sensitive grammars are combined to produce a pleasant arrangement of musical notes. Consequently, the production string will render a more harmonious music. In an existing tool for music rendering called LMUSe [2], the production of a string is generated randomly, such as:

$$D<E>F(1/2)=LMNOP \tag{1}$$

which means that 50% of the time if E is between D and F, E will be replaced by LMNOP and:

$$(0.33)Z<G>H=SS \tag{2}$$

A.L. Brooks (Ed.): ArtsIT 2011, LNICST 101, pp. 46–53, 2012.
© Institute for Computer Sciences, Social Informatics and Telecommunications Engineering 2012

which means that there is a 33.33% chance that G will be replaced by SS if G is between and H. As the production rules are performed randomly, the string produced will generate inaccurate and different results each time. Current works in L-Systems music rendering are based on simple grammars since they have to be scripted by the programmers or users. Stochastic and Context Sensitive L-Systems grammars allow complicated grammars to be generated easily on visual language framework. Hence, a system called Visual Language Music Rendering (VLMR) has been developed to provide the flexibility in generating visually harmonious musical sounds using these complicated grammars.

1.1   Stochastic Grammar

Stochastic grammar is vital for reading the rules differently in an effort to meliorate the L-System music rendering [3]. Most of the times, every occurrence of the predecessor is simply replaced by the successor that is bounded by a set of production rules represented by the derivation symbol $\rightarrow$. The derivation of the successor is obtained through probabilities derived from a set of predecessor grammars. The production string is generated by replacing the successor that has a higher probability i.e. a note with the highest occurrences in a set of input rules. The sum of the probability of all musical notes is equal to 1. Let's assume that 'a' is the predecessor for all productions, thus

$$\sum_{i=1}^{N} P_{ai} = 1 \tag{3}$$

Stochastic grammar also allows the representation of its attributes using the Markov model [4]. For example, chord 'D' will be replaced from chord 'E' in the production string as the probability of chord 'E' is higher compared to the other chords as given below:

$$p : D \quad \begin{array}{l} \xrightarrow{3/10} C \\ \xrightarrow{3/10} D \\ \xrightarrow{4/10} E \end{array} \tag{4}$$

At times, it is unavoidable to have equal production probability as given below:

$$p : a \quad \begin{array}{l} \xrightarrow{1/2} b \\ \xrightarrow{1/2} c \end{array} \tag{5}$$

which can also be written as:

$$\begin{array}{l} a(.5)=b \\ a(.5)=c \end{array} \tag{6}$$

which implies that the predecessor 'a' has an equal chance to be replaced by the successors 'b' or 'c'. This particular replacement is randomly determined by VLMR.

1.2   Context-Sensitive Grammar

In order to generate a variety of musical notes, VLMR has been extended to include context-sensitive grammar which is concerned with the other symbols surrounding the symbol to be replaced. The context-sensitivity rule can be portrayed as follows:

$$A<B>C=DEF \tag{7}$$

which implies that B will be replaced by DEF provided that A is on the left of B and C is on the right of B. The rule can also be one-sided at times. For example:

$$J<K=XYZ \tag{8}$$

means that K is replaced by XYZ when J is on the left of K and there is no symbol to the right of K, or at the end of the production string. The same theory applies for:

$$R>S=PQRST \tag{9}$$

which means that R is replaced by PQSRT if R is at the beginning of the production string and there is no symbol to the left of R but there is S on the right.

1.3   Previous Work

Our work is inspired by the previous work of Siew and Talib [5] namely Visual Language Plant Modeling system (VLPM) which is a visual language framework for plant modeling using L-Systems. The user-friendly visual language framework is to cater those users with no prior knowledge in both programming and L-Systems. The user can easily generate plant model by using the framework which consists of the L-System attributes and grammars that are represented by icons. As for LMUSe [2], it is a complete and sophisticated system that is compatible with L-System grammars specifically for music rendering. However, music cannot be rendered if one does not know the L-System grammar that is supposed to instruct the direction, movement, operations of the stack, increment and decrement of musical pitch, and tempo. In LMUSe, as proposed by Worth and Stepney [6], it is possible to produce more 'pleasing' or harmonious musical sounds by using stochastic and context-sensitive grammars. However, it requires the users to key in the L-System grammar and to have extensive knowledge in L-System. In this paper, we propose a visual language framework for creating more harmonious musical sounds that can easily be used by the users who have little or no knowledge on L-Systems. By chance, VLMR integrates parts of VLPM with pieces from LMUSe since VLPM provides iconic representations which match the musical notes with the attributes of plant models [5].

2   Proposed Method

In the visual programming domain, the emphasis of the research depends on the application of visual formalism. From the view of programming it is regarded to be more effective than textual formalism. The overall implementation approach is designed based on the data flow programming model. The usage of data flow model has a few advantages. It results in easier debugging process because it allows immediate access to the program state. Besides, data flow model also supports automatic parallelization which is vital for music rendering. As the processes encountered in the implementation of VLMR involve concurrent processing scenarios, the data flow model is well suited in this case. The data flow model can run repetitively for the next event and this model starts with the string input as shown in Figure 1.

In the method, firstly, the user needs to input the rules (lower and upper scales) using the visual language framework by selecting, and dragging and dropping the icons on the window for defining the rules. The selected icons will be read by the L-System editor that runs behind the interface. The editor then converts the rules by matching them with the L-system grammars and stored the converted rules in an array. As the rules are too short to generate harmonious musical sound, the rules can be mutated using the stochastic L-System grammar. Rewriting the converted rules (mutation) then takes place (if required) so that a longer piece of rules is generated [7][8][9]. The mutated rules are also able to create a plant model. The L-System editor will then pass the rules to the string generator. Then, the string generator which follows the context-sensitive L-System grammar, outputs (interprets) the production rules based on the mutated rules [10]. Finally, harmonious musical sound can be played with the aid of MIDI library [11].

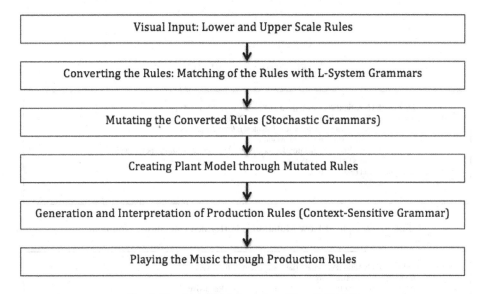

Fig. 1. The Overall Method: Data Flow in VLMR

3   Implementation

The visual language framework was developed using the code that was taken from a functioning Java L-System application. The software is available for public use and so is LMUSe for music rendering [12]. The functioning Java L-System application is created to allow users to draw trees easily in a visual environment [13]. This system is written in Java [14] and the development toolkit used is Eclipse Galileo IDE. The system overview of the architecture of VLMR is shown in Figure 2. The implementation code of Mutator.java where the stochastic grammar is used to mutate the rules is shown in Figure 3 while the implementation code of Production.java where the context-sensitive grammar is used to generate a variety of production rules is shown in Figure 4.

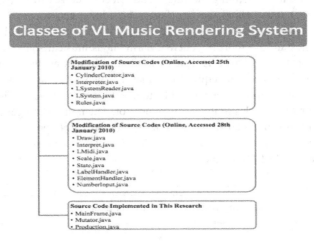

Fig. 2. Classes of VLMR

```
private void makeBTNActionPerformed (java.awt.event.ActionEventvt) {
if (count == 1) {      String backup = convertedrumeATXT.getText ();
                       Vector rulesVector = textToRules(); //mutate process
                       Mutatormutator = new Mutator();
                       rulesVector = mutator.do_mutation(rulesVector,0,1); //one-point swap
                       rulesToText(rulesVector); }
convertedruleATXT.setText(backup);
count++;}
```

Fig. 3. Example of How Mutation is Performed (Stochastic Grammar)

```
private void makeBTNActionPerformed (java.awt.event.ActionEventvt) {
        InString = MainFrame.axio;
        Production p = new Production(inString,3,"[]<>"); //Recursive
        intnumrecursionsdone = 0;
        numrecursionsdone += p.run();
        p.interruptime = true;
        p.run();
        outString = p.getProduction();
        productionruleATXT.setText(outString);}
```

Fig. 4. Example of How Production Rules are Obtained (Context-Sensitive Grammar)

Based on L-System, the plant modeling can then be interpreted for music rendering [6] through the interpretation of the L-Systems grammars. A snapshot of the VLMR system is shown in Figure 5. The visual language framework is implemented with musical icons that can be dragged and dropped and is written in Java [14] using Netbeans IDE in order to integrate with the context-sensitive and stochastic L-Systems grammars that were taken partially from LMUSe system. As shown in Figure 5, the VLMR system consists of the Rules (Upper Scale and Lower Scale), Music Toolbox (Key, Transpose Up, Transpose Down, Play, Posh and Pop), Tree's Attribute (Angle, Left Branch's Size and Right Branch's Size), Converted Rules and Production Rules. The rest of the method is implemented under Functions Menu of the interface namely ConvertRule (Converting the Rules: Matching of the rules with L-System Grammars), Mutate (Mutating the Converted Rules (Stochastic Grammars)), Make (Creating Plant Model through Mutated Rules), Interpret (Generation and Interpretation of Production Rules (Context-Sensitive Grammar)) and Play (Playing the Music through the Production Rules). The music can be easily rendered by clicking 'Play' button on VLMR as shown in Figure 5.

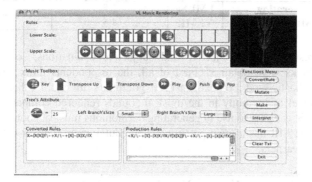

Fig. 5. A Snapshot of the VLMR System

4   Evaluation and Discussion

A survey together with a set of experiments were carried out to determine the acceptability and the quality of the techniques and methods derived in this research. The respondents were required to listen to the musical sounds rendered by LMUSe as well as VLMR and then make comparison between both sounds based on the level of harmony. The harmony of the musical sound is defined as the complication of note played per tab on the instrument. Ten respondents who are experts in music as well as ten respondents who are non-experts in music who mainly originate from the School of Computer Sciences and the School of the Arts, USM were asked to complete the questionnaires. In addition, a total of twenty respondents who are neither experts in L-System nor have any experience with L-System were also surveyed subjectively on the ease of using both systems.

Table 1 shows the results of the evaluation of LMUSe and VLMR by the respondents. The rating is based on a scale of 1 to 5 where 5 is the highest. The mean rating is calculated as follows:

$$\text{Mean Rating} = \frac{\text{Rating of Respondent 1} + \ldots\ldots + \text{Rating of Respondent 10}}{\text{Number of Respondents}} \qquad (10)$$

For the level of harmony of the musical sounds generated, the musicians and non-musicians have rated 3.7 and 3.1 respectively for LMUSe, and 4.3 and 4.8 respectively for VLMR. On the ease of generating the harmonious musical sounds, the musicians and non-musicians have rated 2.5 of and 1.7 respectively for LMUSe, and 4.5 and 4.2 respectively for VLMR. The 20 respondents who are neither expert in L-Systems nor have any experience with L-Systems also wrote down some feedbacks on their opinion about the systems.

Table 1. Result on the Evaluation of LMUSe and VLMR

Question	System	Mean Rating	
		Musicians	Non-Musicians
Level of Harmony in the Musical Sounds	**LMUSe**	3.7	3.1
	VLMR	4.3	4.8
Ease of Generating Harmonious Musical Sounds	**LMUSe**	2.5	1.7
	VLMR	4.5	4.2

From the results of the objective and subjective evaluations, some useful and effective feedbacks were obtained. First of all, the respondents think that the hybrid method of stochastic and context-sensitive grammars in VLMR has significantly enhanced the level of harmony in the musical sounds rendered compared to LMUSe. Secondly, VLMR is easier to use in generating harmonious musical sounds compared to LMUSe. Thus VLMR has a great potential as an edutainment tool for both L-Systems and basic music learners.

5   Conclusion and Future Work

As compared to the previous research on L-Systems music rendering, this research has provided a variety of L-Systems grammars by combining stochastic and context-sensitive L-Systems. Firstly, the hybrid models allows rendering of a more harmonious musical sound for music rendering. Secondly, it is found that VLMR is easy to use in producing harmonious musical sounds. Thus, the visual language framework used in VLMR is well-suited to allow non-experts to understand, learn and use L-Systems in particular for L-System music rendering [15].

In order to further improve the method, the use of accurate deterministic and non-deterministic L-Systems should be investigated.

Acknowledgments. This work presented is supported by USM Short Term Grant No. P3710 and scholarship from Mini Budget 2009 for Malaysian researchers.

References

1. Lim, C.K., Talib, A.Z.: A Visual Language Framework for Music Rendering Using L-System. In: Proceedings of the 3rd WSEAS International Conference on Visualisation, Imaging and Simulation (VIS 2010), Portugal, pp. 47–52 (2010)

2. Sharp, D.: LMUSe, Available from World Wide Web,
   http://www.geocities.com/Athens/Academy/
   8764/lmuse/lmuse.html (accessed on January 28, 2010)
3. Stepney, S., Beaumont, D.: Grammatical Evolution of L-Systems. In: Proceedings of 11th
   Conference on Congress on Evolutionary Computation, Trondheim, Norway, pp. 2446–
   2453 (2009)
4. McCormack, J.: Grammar Based Music Composition. In: Stocker, et al. (eds.) Complex
   Systems 1996: From Local Interactions to Global Phenomena, pp. 321–336. IOS Press
   (1996)
5. Hwa Siew, B., Zawawi Talib, A.: Visual Language Framework for Plant Modeling Using
   L-System. In: Badioze Zaman, H., Robinson, P., Petrou, M., Olivier, P., Schröder, H.,
   Shih, T.K. (eds.) IVIC 2009. LNCS, vol. 5857, pp. 696–707. Springer, Heidelberg (2009)
6. Worth, P., Stepney, S.: Growing Music: Musical Interpretations of L-Systems. In:
   Rothlauf, F., Branke, J., Cagnoni, S., Corne, D.W., Drechsler, R., Jin, Y., Machado, P.,
   Marchiori, E., Romero, J., Smith, G.D., Squillero, G. (eds.) EvoWorkshops 2005. LNCS,
   vol. 3449, pp. 545–550. Springer, Heidelberg (2005)
7. Majherová, J.: Virtual Plants in High School Informatics. In: Conference (ICL 2007),
   Villach, Austria, pp. 1(7)–7(7) (2007)
8. Pradal, C., Dufour-Kowalski, S., Boudon, F., Fournier, C., Godin, C.: OpenAlea: A Visual
   Programming and Component-Based Software Platform for Plant Modelling. Functional
   Plant Biology 35(10), 751–760 (2008)
9. Prusinkiewicz, P., Lindenmayer, A.: The Algorithmic Beauty of Plants. Springer-Verlag
   New York Inc. (1990)
10. Sato, K.: Design Information Framework, Context Sensitive Design and Human-Centered
    Interactive Systems. In: Conference on Human Factors in Computing Systems, Vienna,
    Austria, pp. 1588–1589 (2004)
11. Bresson, J.: OpenMusic MIDI Documentation. Ircam Software Documentation (2004)
12. Teresi, S.: Scott Teresi's Website, Available from World Wide Web,
    http://teresi.us/html/main/programming.html
    (accessed on January 25, 2010)
13. Ijiri, T., Owada, S., Igarashi, T.: The Sketch L-System: Global Control of Tree Modeling
    Using Free-Form Strokes. In: Butz, A., Fisher, B., Krüger, A., Olivier, P. (eds.) SG 2006.
    LNCS, vol. 4073, pp. 138–146. Springer, Heidelberg (2006)
14. Java Technology, Available from World Wide Web, http://www.sun.com/java
    (accessed on January 20, 2010)
15. Menzies, T.: Evaluation issues for Visual Programming Language. Handbook of Software
    Engineering and Knowledge Engineering 2, 93–101 (2000)
16. Bruno, F., Jose, C.L., Marcio, C.P.: L-Systems, Scores, and Evolutionary Techniques. In:
    Proceedings of 6th Sound and Music Computing Conference, Portugal, pp. 113–118
    (2009)
17. Prusinkiewicz, P.: Score generation with L–systems. In: Proceedings of the International
    Computer Music Conference, Den Haag, Netherlands, pp. 455–457 (1986)
18. Bresson, J., Agon, C.: Sound Writing and Representation in a Visual Programming
    Framework. In: DMNR 2006 Doctoral Research Conference, Digital Music Research
    Network, Goldsmiths College, University of London, United Kingdom (2006)

Computer Mediated Visual Communication in Live Musical Performance: What's the Score?

Sudarshan Balachandran and Lonce Wyse

Arts and Creativity Lab, Interactive and Digital Media Institute,
Communications and New Media Department,
National University of Singapore
{sudarshan,lonce.wyse}@nus.edu.sg

Abstract. The document on the music stand in front of performing musicians has become reterritorialized by dynamic and interactive notation enabled by computational and communications technologies. The implications are far reaching for how we create, how we play, and how we listen to music. Considering the mediated musical score as a collaborative workspace, issues of awareness and structural relationship models that were latent in traditional scores now become foregrounded. A survey of current practices illustrates different score-based collaboration and communications strategies and provides motivation for a new "anticipatory" interactive scoring system.

Keywords: visual communication, real-time scores, improvisation, computer supported collaborative workspaces.

1   Introduction

Some of the conventions defining the activities and the relationships between composers, performers, and audiences are so deeply embedded in our musical culture as to seem beyond question. Composers write music before a performance. Performers follow instructions encoded in notation to render a performance while communicating with each other through the sounds they make as well as through body movements and eye contact. Audiences experience music primarily through the sound the performers create with added understanding that comes from watching performers perform. Improvisational music shifts much or all of the musical decision making power to the musicians, but the paradigm outlined above remains essentially intact.

The most audible of the 20th century upheavals to music was the radical expansion of the sound palette from the pitched and percussive sounds of acoustic instruments to the theoretically unlimited palette of sounds made available via new recording, signal processing, sensor, and electronic and digital synthesis techniques. Although scores and performers were sometimes circumvented entirely in studio-based electroacoustic practices, the activities and roles between composers, performers (when present), and audiences remained essentially as it always had been for traditional ensemble music whether composed or improvisational.

A.L. Brooks (Ed.): ArtsIT 2011, LNICST 101, pp. 54–62, 2012.
© Institute for Computer Sciences, Social Informatics and Telecommunications Engineering 2012

Communications, particularly in conjunction with computer-based visualization strategies, are playing a role in the deconstruction of the tripartite structure of traditional musical relationships. By changing the way composers, performers, and audiences engage with each other (both within and across the group boundaries), sense-making and the experience of music are also altered.

In this paper, the focus is on visualizations that trace their lineage back to the traditional score in that they are comprised of graphical elements meant to communicate information to performers to help them understand what their fellow performers are (were or will be) doing, and/or are interpreted as encoded instructions that influence the performer's musical behavior.

2   Awareness

One of the key elements in skilled musical performance whether composed or improvisational is awareness. This includes awareness of what fellow performers are doing, and awareness of where the music is going. In traditional western orchestral music, the score, musical "parts", rehearsals, body movement and eye contact all contribute to the awareness a musician needs to play their role effectively. In electronically mediated music making, awareness is more of a challenge because of what Simon Emerson has called the "three electroacoustic dislocations"[1]. Sound can be dislocated from original musical gesture in space (by being electronically transmitted to remote speakers), dislocated in time (delayed through digital algorithmic processes or recording and retransmission), and dislocated in causality (since the mapping between gesture and sound is arbitrary and changeable in electronic music).

While awareness in electroacoustic musical practices is undermined by the dislocations that result from multiple stages of electronic mediation, computer-supported communications between performers through instruments, notational representations, and interfaces can help restore it. Networks digitally linking musicians began appearing in live musical performance in the 1980s. The League of Automatic Composers, for example, collaborated in their networked performances using audio and message passing between programs running on their different machines, but without visual support for insight into the digital exchanges. These programs relied on the control data flowing back and forth within the network to determine their behavior [2]. A limited view into the workings of the algorithms and communications could be gleaned from messages scrolling over text-based displays. In *Vague Notions of Lost Textures* (1987) [2], the Hub implemented computer-supported visual communication strategies in the form of text based communication to coordinate the creation of an improvised shape for the musical performance.

Dynamic visual graphic scores go considerably beyond screen dumps of text in creating awareness among performers, even when they are precomposed animations on fixed media. Luke Harris made use of a three-dimensional space to display the graphical notations in his piece titled *Animated Graphic Score for Quartet*. Four musicians played simultaneously by interpreting motion graphics (flying notes and rotating staffs) in a pre-recorded video projected on a large screen (Figure 1).

The musicians had no prior rehearsal or exposure to the graphics. The projected score contains four conjoint spaces, one part for each of the musicians. Animated notational elements enter the projection space, and move back and forth between the four component spaces. Such a visual technique provides separate areas as "parts" for each musician individually, while also connecting the individual performers informationally as well as visually. The audience also views the entire score which serves as an aid to understanding the performance.

Fig. 1. Animated Graphic Score for Quartet by Luke Harris showing a four-panel shared-view dynamic score for four musicians (http://vimeo.com/2625318)

Computer Supported Co-operative Working (CSCW) with real-time collaborative graphical spaces for work [3] and play [4] make awareness a central issue, and so it is when visual representations of musical activity are shared by musicians[5]. Typically different subsets of the visual representation are directly relevant to the different individual performers' activity, while the rest of the information is used for understanding the activity of others. In *Density Trajectory Studies* [6], Nick Didkovsky employed a shared visual space on which the notations are projected for all the musicians to see. The projection is divided into four equal quadrants, with each quadrant displaying instructions assigned to one of the musicians (or subgroups in a larger ensemble). Such a strategy of dividing up a shared visual space into individual segments that is meant for each of the performers is also observed in the real-time networked music environment called *Quintet.net* [7]. In this piece, the conductor controls the performance by constantly sending out text messages and performance parameters as settings to the shared space.

ChucK ChucK Rocket by Ge Wang and Scott Smallwood uses a checkered game board representation [8] where sound objects are placed and "mice" move creating sound when they encounter the objects. For this piece, each performer is assigned one spatial region to which his/her musical gestures are restricted though the whole space of other performer regions are visible to all. Knowledge of layouts on other performer regions can be used to make musical decisions such as "teleporting" a mouse between regions. A special role is played by a "conductor" who can change aspects of the entire system behavior. This shared space engages performers in a way that blurs the boundary between compositional and performative roles.

3   Relationship Models

Scores as mediated collaborative workspaces embody models of interaction between and among composers, performers, and audiences. Notational strategies can be seen as existing on a scale from prescriptive leaving relatively little freedom for performance time flexibility, to interpretive where graphical elements may come with almost no preconceived rules or shared knowledge about their intended influence on performance behavior. In this sense, notational conventions establish a balance of decision making power between the notator and the performer.

Luke Harris's *Animated Graphic Score for Quartet* is an example of an interpretive score. It demands quick responses from the musicians that are dependent on the musicians' improvisational experience and creative thinking abilities. The flexibility in interpretation defines the musical indeterminacy of the piece by virtue of the balance it establishes between the structure provided by the composer and the freedom vested in the performer.

Textual notation animated in position, shape, and color, have been used as an interpretative performance score for unpracticed audience/performers. Shane McKenna makes use of this technique in one of his unnamed compositions in the *Graphic Score Experiment* series. Familiar iconic symbols such as letters are freely interpreted by audience/participants using their voices (Figure 2). Although, multiple interpretations are possible, there is a subtle and natural way in which performance rules are conveyed incrementally by the composer to the participants using motion graphics during the course of the performance. This score occupies a position somewhere between a fully interpretative and a fully prescriptive score.

Fig. 2. Textual graphic score in Graphic Score Experiment by Shane McKenna are freely interpreted by audience members to make vocal sounds (http://vimeo.com/10140889)

Another dimension in the establishment of relationships between musical participants is when notation is created during performance. While composers traditionally create scores in advance of performances, there is a proliferation of new works using dynamic and real-time scores in music performances by composers such as Jason Freeman [9] and Christopher McClelland and Michael Alcorn [10] and on open-form scores by David Kim-Boyle [11].

Justin Yang's *Webworks I* is representative of a score that is generated live during the performance through composer-performer interaction and is also rendered as dynamic motion graphics. It is a network based performance that also demands the need for a shared visual space to ensure that there is mutual awareness amongst the geographically distributed musicians. A shared and consistent representation is important to the cooperative engagement of performers [12]. In this performance, the traditional role of the composer as sole notation generator is seen once again.

Fig. 3. Webworks *I* by Justin Yang is a networked piece that uses a shared clock-like scrolling score element to which the composer adds dynamic elements in real-time (Image: Justin Yang)

4   Temporal Representation

The representation of time in a score has important implications for the kind of awareness that performers can develop. Although there may be examples of alternative time representations in 20th century graphical works (c.f. [13],[14]), dynamic and interactive scores where time moves or is moved through create fundamentally new paradigms. In this section, we outline three broad categories of temporal representations based on a study of a wide variety of current practices. McClelland and Alcorn previously identified *pages, scattering,* and *scrolling* as three basic modes of display [10]. Our categorization maintains McClelland and Alcorn's scrolling type, but specifies two other categories that seem more generally applicable to current practices such as those surveyed herein.

In a *scrolling* score, the notations move across the screen (usually horizontally) and the performers act when the notation comes in contact with a fixed vertical cursor indicating the 'present' moment. The scrolling score representation typically provides a view of both the past and the future in a way similar to traditional printed score notation. Smule's commercial iPad applications such as *Magic Piano* and *Magic Fiddle* [15] make use of a scrolling visible future so performers can anticipate actions.

MIMI by Alexandre François et al.[16] is an interactive music-improvisation software system that engages a human improviser in an interactive loop with machine as a partner (Figure 4). The scrolling score is projected and enables anticipatory activity by the performer by providing visual access to the future activity of the computer partner, as well as visual access to past events. Despite tradition, it is not immediately obvious why it might be important to have visual access to recent history. However, previous research [17] found that electroacoustic improvising musicians in particular may find information about who made which sound helpful.

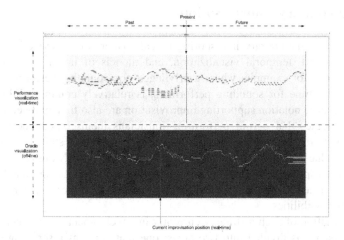

Fig. 4. MIMI score in which the bottom window contains musical material used by the machine improviser, and the top window is a scrolling view of the machine-generate music to the right of the cursor (the future), and both human and machine-generated to the left (the past). (Image from [16], with permission).

Another variant of the scrolling score can be observed in *Webwork I* by Justin Yang where the "present" time indicator is not fixed, but rotates like hands on a clock within a circle. Like its horizontally scrolling cousin, a window of time extending in both directions around the present is visible. The notational elements generated in real-time by the composer also have independent animated behavior. This makes this representation a kind of hybrid of both the scrolling and filmic view categories (discussed below).

The *filmic* view is one that uses two spatial dimensions, neither of which is time. The visualization changes with time, and the view always represents a notational "now". Animated scores are almost always filmic, but interactive scores may be as well. Shane McKenna's composition, *Three for Four* is an example using the filmic temporal view[18]. The performer generally has no access to either the past or the future (though there are examples that do represent a temporal window with, for example, graphical fades).

Navigational strategies were developed for printed scores long before computers were used. Stockhausen's *Klavierstuck XI* (1956) and John Cage's *Fontana Mix* (1958) are two such examples. Navigational scores embody a very particular balance between precomposed structure and performance-time flexibility. At any given time, the "present" is represented by the specific location of the performer. Notational objects that are spatially more distant represent musical states or events that would take more time to reach than those close by. The performer is aware of many *potential* actualizations of music which are determined by the particular path the performer chooses to navigate. Two representative examples are Tarik Barri's *Versum*[19] and Jason Freeman's *Flou*.

5   Anticipatory Improvisation

This survey of contemporary live scoring reveals patterns of practices dealing with awareness support, temporal visualization, and models of interaction. The central composer model for example, where a privileged non-sounding performer generates notation in real-time for sounding performers, is relatively common. Filmic scores with interpretative notation supporting improvisation are also frequently employed.

Score strategies that permit performing musicians themselves to be engaged in generating notation for others to use is a relatively neglected strategy. The neglect may well be due to the fact that many instruments keep hands busy. However, for platforms that support both notation and a performance interface for sound synthesis (for example a tablet computer), this strategy enables novel performer relationships and musical possibilities.

One incarnation of such a strategy currently in development can be seen in Figure 5. The workspace is divided into two areas; one that contains a scrolling score that includes a "now" indicator dividing the time window into a visible past and a visible future. The future area supports notation of a performer's own performance intentions or compositional elements designed for other performers. The other section of the workspace is the performer's own instrumental interface. The multi touch screen permits simultaneous activity in both the future (on the score) and the present (on the instrument).

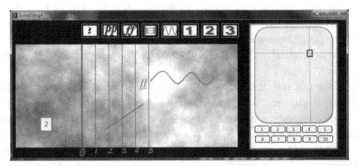

Fig. 5. Anticipatory improvisation. On the right is a private instrument interface. On the left, a shared graphical space includes a scrolling score (cloud background) with a stationary temporal "now" indicator (marked '0'). The area to the right of the "now" indicator is used by performers to communicate performance intention or prescriptive notation by drawing or positioning icons.

One relatively unexplored musical dimension this design supports is what we term "anticipatory improvisation". Improvisation is typically either structured around a musical "chart", in which case awareness of the structure permits synchronization of musical activity (e.g. simultaneous key changes), or unstructured in which case coordinated activity grows out of the awareness that musicians build through listening, memory, and visual communication. "Anticipatory improvisation" represents a hybrid of these two paradigms where coordinated activity is facilitated by structured notational material planted in the future "just in time" during performance.

6   Summary

Computer-supported musical performance has developed in tandem with notational techniques that take advantage of newly available graphical, dynamic, and interactive capabilities. Notational, spatial, and temporal representations affect the musicians' ability to anticipate upcoming events, they affect the various performer/performer interactions such as mutual engagement, awareness, cooperation, consensus building, and they determine the balance of decision making between composers and performers. The model of a central conductor or composer still remains prominent in contemporary practices of dynamic scores. A novel system for "anticipatory improvisation" was presented that puts tools for scoring into the hands of the performers themselves. Relationships between musical participants embedded in visual communication and notational strategies are still rapidly evolving. The notational and communications approaches we have discussed are certainly not exhaustive of current practices, and even less so of future possibilities.

Acknowledgments. This work was supported by project grant NRF2007IDM-IDM002-069 from the Interactive and Digital Media Project Office, Media Development Authority, Singapore.

References

1. Emmerson, S.: "Live" versus "real-time". Contemporary Music Review 10, 95–101 (1994)
2. Brown, C., Bischoff, J.: Indigenous to the Net: Early Network Music Bands in the San Francisco Bay Area, http://crossfade.walkerart.org/brownbischoff/IndigenoustotheNetPrint.html
3. McCarthy, C., Bligh, J., Jennings, K., Tangney, B.: Virtual collaborative learning environments for music: Networked drumsteps. Computers & Education 44, 173–195 (2005)
4. Ishii, H., Wisneski, C., Orbanes, J., Chun, B., Paradiso, J.: PingPongPlus: design of an athletic-tangible interface for computer-supported cooperative play. In: SIGCHI, pp. 394–401 (1999)
5. Fencott, R., Bryan-Kinns, N.: Hey Man, you're invading my Personal Space! Privacy and Awareness in Collaborative Music. In: NIME, Sydney, Australia (2010)
6. Didkovsky, N.: Density Trajectory Studies: Organizing Improvised Sound. Contemporary Music Revs. 29, 75–80 (2010)

7. Hajdu, G.: Quintet. net: An environment for composing and performing music on the Internet. Leonardo 38, 23–30 (2005)
8. Smallwood, S., Trueman, D., Cook, P.R., Wang, G.: Composing for laptop orchestra. Computer Music Journal 32, 9–25 (2008)
9. Freeman, J.: Extreme sight-reading, mediated expression, and audience participation: Real-time music notation in live performance. Computer Music Journal 32, 25–41 (2008)
10. McClelland, C., Alcorn, M.: Exploring New Composer/Performer Interactions Using Real-Time Notation. In: Proceedings of the International Computer Music Conference, Belfast (2008)
11. Kim-Boyle, D.: Real-time Score Generation for Extensible Open Forms. Contemporary Music Revs. 29, 3–15 (2010)
12. Bryan-Kinns, N., Healey, P.G., Thirlwell, M.: Graphical Representations for Group Music Improvisation. In: IGC, London (2003)
13. Sauer, T.: Notations 21. Mark Batty Publisher, New York (2009)
14. Vickery, L., Hope, C.: The Aesthetics of the Screen Score. In: CreateWorld 2010, Brisbane, Australia, pp. 48–57 (2010)
15. Smule: Experience Social Music, http://www.smule.com/
16. François, A.R.J., Chew, E., Thurmond, D.: Visual Feedback in Performer Machine Interaction for Musical Improvisation. In: NIME, New York (2007)
17. Merritt, T., Kow, W., Ng, C., McGee, K., Wyse, L.: Who makes what sound?: supporting real-time musical improvisations of electroacoustic ensembles. In: CHI, pp. 112–119 (2010)
18. McKenna, S.: Animated Graphic Notation. In: ISEA 2011, Istanbul (2011)
19. Barri, T.: Versum: Audiovisual Composing in 3D. In: ICAD, pp. 18–21 (2009)

Assistive Technology and Performance Behaviours in Music Improvisation

Ben Challis and Rob Smith

Cardiff School of Creative and Cultural Industries, ATRiuM,
University of Glamorgan, 86-88 Adam Street, Cardiff, CF24 2FN, UK
{bchallis,rksmith}@glam.ac.uk

Abstract. The findings from three trial workshops with a group of music-learners with physical disabilities have culminated in an initial design for a novel interactive music-generation system. Using a variety of commercially available music-technologies in a synchronised set-up, the target group identified those aspects of both music production and accessible interaction that were most appealing and productive. The proposed design places equal emphasis on improvisation and accessibility, generating rhythmic, harmonic and melodic patterns that an individual can trigger and manipulate. The system will also allow a group of improvisers to work together offering variable levels of synchronization based on individual need or preference. A prototype system is currently under development.

Keywords: Accessibility, disability, music, improvisation, technology.

1 Introduction

Though there have been a number of research projects exploring the design of new and novel musical instruments and music systems within a context of accessibility, there has been little focus within these on the relationship between assistive technology and self-expression through improvisation. The work being presented here aims to contribute to the beginning of an on-going dialogue on the concepts and challenges that are likely to arise when the relationship between performer, instrument and creativity is considered against a backdrop of individual needs. By observing and presenting music workshops to a group of adults with a variety of physical challenges, a small research team from the University of Glamorgan, has been able to document a range of issues and opportunities relating to the practical application of a number of potentially quite accessible electronic musical instruments. The overall aim of the project is to design one or more new musical 'tools' that will build upon the best of these opportunities whilst aiming to lessen the impact of the more profound challenges that have been acknowledged along the way.

There are two phases to the project and the first of these is now complete. This has been a process of close observation and analysis with the aim of identifying the key challenges for enabling improvised musical activities. The second phase is one of

A.L. Brooks (Ed.): ArtsIT 2011, LNICST 101, pp. 63–70, 2012.

proposing and testing alternative or assistive means for achieving these same creative outcomes. The key researchers are active performers with a shared interest in the use of novel technologies in improvised music. Smith is an experienced practitioner and tutor in Community Music with a research background in free-improvisation and Challis has a background in human-computer interaction and the design of novel technologies for music performance. Although this article represents the completion of the first phase of the overall project, the second phase is in progress and aspects of the design 'brief' are included alongside the closing conclusions.

2   Improvisation, Novel Technology and Community Music

It is vital, when contemplating using a potentially liberating new musical tool, or devising and testing a novel approach to an existing instrument, to consider how and to what ends the tool might be utilised in the context envisaged. Of course, outcomes and goals frequently predate, shape and guide the creation of tools, but once the tool is in use new avenues and possibilities can be discovered. Some of these new possibilities may be discovered by accident, by a process of play and, in some cases, by wilful abuse or subversion of the tools themselves. All these three areas of activity (celebrating and working with accidents, play, subversion of rules) can easily be viewed as sitting comfortably within the area of activity widely known as *free improvisation.*

If *improvisation* is the creation of musical utterances in the moment (often, in the case of experienced and dedicated improvisers, in the moment of performance), and this activity can encompass different genres (folk, Indian classical music) and rule based improvisational systems (bebop) as well as more abstract forms including *free improvisation,* then we would appear to have in free improvisation a powerfully liberating area of musical practice. Of course reality is more fluid than this. Improvisers can create music of great excitement and beauty entirely from within a genre or set of rules, seemingly working in a mind-space oblivious to any such constraints, or indeed from instinctive syntheses of rule-breaking and rule-keeping strategies: indeed many stable, freely improvising groups (AMM, Supersilent, The Necks) seem to mutually discuss and delineate their own rules or at least areas of interest for exploration when playing.

However, the nature of *free improvisation* is notoriously difficult to define. Bailey [1] comes down approximately defining free improvisation being free of genre and rules. Others prefer to avoid definitions and contribute to the on-going discussion of improvisation and its uses by action. Stevens [2] divides his work broadly into *rhythm* and *improvisation.* Rhythm, in Stevens' methodology (as propounded in *Search and Reflect* but also in his performances and recordings with groups such as the Spontaneous Music Ensemble) is necessary for group cohesion and finding one's place in a dynamic group statement without destroying that dynamic or the group's coherence. In his introduction to the *Improvisation* section of *Search and Reflect,* Stevens tells us that he is building on the preceding rhythm work in dealing with 'specific processes and skills which help to prepare the way for a sensitive, concentrated approach to creative group interaction and individual spontaneity' [2].

The fact that Stevens' 'Music Workshop Handbook' is widely used throughout the international improvised music communities is testament to the power and potential of this model. Stevens and *Search and Reflect* were both frequently cited as both starting points and a continuing resource during a previous research project into Free Improvisation Pedagogy in the UK and Norway [3].

Improvisation is also a potentially powerful methodology when trying to overcome the problems that people with special needs have in accessing music-making. It is an important tool in the work of music therapists and related disciplines (such as running music-making sessions with people with physical and/or learning disabilities). Music therapists often need to elicit musical expressions from their clients and make open improvised responses to these utterances and establish a (albeit non-semantic) dialogue with the patient whilst clinically assessing the patients' responses to the therapy. An attitude of watchful patience and the responsive skills of the improviser are key here.

In working with novel technologies in a community or special needs context [4], [5] we have deployed similar improvisation skills as those used in free improvisation performance *and* musical therapy and related quasi-therapeutic contexts. It is particularly true for instruments where small physical movements can make big dynamic musical changes, that the feedback loop of action-sound-response requires a long learning period where the interface is tested through improvisation and it is here that the improvising-searching-reflecting axis of skills are particularly useful in demonstrating and allowing new users with varying levels of musical skill and manual dexterity to learn to create their own musical expressions using experimental interfaces. If we are in danger of becoming swept away by enthusiasm for the potential power of improvisation, we must not turn our back on the notion of *composition*.

Composition is a complex and multi-faceted task in itself. At one level however (and this is especially true of electro-acoustic composition) it can be the selection of sounds to form a palette of sounds which can be shaped, manipulated, varied and combined to create a piece or musical performance. Improvisation may be the watch-word for creating surprising musical expressions with new-technology but there is a necessary process of careful selection and creation of soundfiles to create the raw materials with which to improvise.

On the other hand, a free musical context, where it can be agreed that there is no right or wrong, and therefore all musical gestures are valid, can free up the user to explore the potentials of a configuration of, maybe, new instruments and interfaces that are perhaps only new to that particular user or group of users. Alongside these new and novel interfaces can be used traditional instruments such as percussion or keyboard instruments which could not be synchronised by an external clock or time-code generator, but could operate happily alongside such a community of interfaces. Indeed, this might serve to tighten-up or reinforce the participants' existing time-keeping skills on acoustic instruments.

3   Methodology

The first phase of the project has centred around three contrasting workshop experiences. To provide the project team with an opportunity to fully appreciate the kind of activities that could be regarded as 'typical', a workshop was arranged with a group of adult music-learners with physical disabilities in the South Wales area; the researchers were accommodated within the group as active observers. The group have been together for a number of years and engage in various musical activities using fairly traditional resources (e.g. hand percussion and electronic keyboards). There is a broad spectrum of individual challenges represented within the group with most of the members experiencing some form of difficulty with upper limb movement and/or dexterity; some of the members are also wheelchair users.

Based on the observations from this preliminary workshop, a series of two follow-up workshops was proposed that would allow the group to work in a different way using a selection of accessible technologies. The first of these workshops was focused on training the group to use the technology (some of which was relatively unfamiliar) and the second workshop was focused on bringing different members of the group together into a number of short improvised music sessions.

4   Performance Behaviours and Ownership

This study is ultimately concerned with the design of new 'instruments' to assist with or enable improvised performance. With this in mind, it is of considerable interest as to how assistance can be introduced that does not erode the performer's feeling of musical-involvement and control. Healey [6] refers to this as 'ownership' and stresses that within a context of community music and new technologies this concept is particularly important. A given assistive technology might be quite successful in terms of enabling an individual to produce musical fragments whilst perhaps being relatively disabling in terms of the breadth of originality, contrast, creativity etc. that is on offer. In some ways relating to this, Malloch et al. [7] have proposed a model for referencing and potentially 'placing' some of the limitations and constraints that a digital musical instrument might contain. The model is essentially a continuum that extends between two extremes of performance behaviours. Where the performer is responsible for forming or triggering individual notes, the performance behaviour can be regarded as *skill-based*. Where the performer has no control over the system beyond starting and stopping playback of a predetermined piece, the performance behaviour can be regarded as *model-based*. A third performance-behaviour (*rule-based*) sits partway between these two extremes and encompasses systems and instruments that allow the performer to trigger and perhaps manipulate patterns based on predetermined rule-sets.

This model is a useful tool for helping to define the performance opportunities that any given system might offer, however, it does not appear to immediately consider the nature of systems that are being manipulated by performers with additional individual needs. For example, it could be argued that the skill required by an able-bodied performer to play, for example, a chord shape on a keyboard at a specific time is comparable to another performer with physical and dextrous challenges pressing a single (and possibly quite large) switch within a quantised time-scale. With this in mind, the model will be used within discussion to help define the performance behaviours in use but the notion of *skill* will be kept within a context of individual needs and abilities.

5   Workshops and Observations

The aim behind the preliminary workshop was one of sharing activities that could be regarded as typical across the group's history. The main musical activity was one of creating group-based rhythms by starting with a single repeating pattern on one or more instruments and then adding further patterns on different instruments. This use of layered rhythms is really quite an effective workshop technique to adopt where there are a large number of players within the group with little or no instrumental training. At a fundamental level, hand-percussion will generally allow even the least experienced of players to contribute something whilst still offering additional complexity through the rhythmic patterns that might be attempted. Percussion instruments also suit the physical needs of many of the group some of whom have quite restricted finger movement such that working with a traditional melodic instrument could be particularly challenging.

Perhaps the most significant observation from the initial workshop these was that although the rhythm-based approach to creating group-music was effective in allowing everyone to contribute, it was also quite restrictive; offering little opportunity to create melodies and/or harmonies. It was also recognised that for quite a number of the group, it would be difficult to engage with many traditional musical instruments that might enable such melodic opportunities. For some of the group, maintaining rhythms on an instrument for any prolonged period could be quite demanding either in terms of physical effort or in terms of maintaining timing-accuracy. However, it was also clear that the various members very much enjoyed functioning as a 'group' musically even though the more members that were involved in any given activity, the harder it became to maintain a sense of rhythmic clarity.

With these key observations in mind, a series of two workshops was proposed to that would allow the group to work with electronic instruments that could suit their specific needs; these would allow them to interact with each other in harmonic and melodic ways as well as rhythmic. Building on the familiarity of working with hand percussion, a Roland Handsonic was the first instrument to be included within this selection. This is a *skill-based* electronic percussion instrument that offers ten velocity sensitive pads that trigger pre-recorded sounds. Other than offering a wide variety of percussion sounds, the Handsonic also offers melodic instruments (e.g. steel drum) and, though it can sit on a stand or table, it can also be placed quite easily on a performer's lap. In addition to the Handsonic, a Korg Kaossilator Pro was also selected. Primarily aimed at the DJ market, this offers a small touchpad that maps the XY position of a finger tip onto a specific sound program. Gently touching the pad will trigger either an individual note or a pattern of notes depending on the nature of the chosen sound and some additional settings. Moving the finger around the screen will then either move to another note within a predefined scale or alter the nature of the pattern being sounded. At a *skill-based* level, individual notes can be targeted and triggered but changing to a pattern generating sound quickly allows the performer to interact with *rule-based* behaviours (e.g. drum rhythms or changing harmonies). The device also allows the results of actions to be sampled as repeating loops such that it could be suggested that it also offers near *model-based* behaviours. The last instrument to be considered was a synthesiser that offers arpeggiated harmonic patterns. In total, two Handsonics, two Kaossilator Pros and two arpeggiators were used for the workshop. Although the intention for the next workshop would be to have some of these instruments synchronised such that their rhythms and patterns would stay together in tempo, this was not demonstrated at this point. Instead, the function of each instrument was demonstrated and members of the group were then given the opportunity to individually experiment with the various sounds and textures that could be achieved. As opportunities arose, the group was encouraged to use their familiar hand-percussion instruments to build rhythmic accompaniments to the sound being created such that short improvised pieces were achieved within the session.

Comments from the group after individual practice with the various instruments were positive across the board and suggested that all three technologies had something to offer to at least some of the group. Observation of individuals at work with each device appeared to show that the range of sounds and 'textures' on offer was both appealing and engaging and this was confirmed by additional feedback offered by the group. It was suggested that the Handsonic offers access to a broader range of percussion sounds at one sitting than might ordinarily be accessed and that it is particularly responsive and therefore not overly demanding to play. A specific comment was offered on the responsive nature of the Handsonic being easy to reach different volumes with little physical demand adding that "you could modify it [the volume] to suit, I thought it was good". General observation of members of the group using the arpeggiation function of the two synthesisers showed that the generative nature of this function was appealing with the players being able to create and control quite complex harmonic patterns. The Kaossilator Pro proved to be particularly effective for those members of the groups who have very restricted hand and finger movement. One member commented on the nature of the interaction, saying that "it's easy for me to touch the screen, and go along, get difficult beats because, with my hands, I can't do that for long". Another member of the group is a competent keyboard player but still expressed great enthusiasm for the device, commenting that it was particularly easy to interact with and that it produced more complex musical ideas and patterns than might easily be achieved using conventional playing techniques on a traditional keyboard. This same group member offered a comparison between the Handsonic and Kaossilator in terms style of interaction method commenting that "I get tired out with my wrists ... I found that one easier [kaossilator pro], that one [handsonic] was good as well but I think with that one [kaossilator] I could do longer".

The aim with the final workshop was to bring together the same technology that was used previously but within small group-based improvisations. In an attempt to hold together the collective improvisations rhythmically some of the instruments were synchronised using an external MIDI clock. Both Kaossilator Pros and both arpeggiators were synchronised in this way such that whenever a pattern was triggered it would always match the tempo of the others. However, if an instrument were to be triggered slightly out of phase in terms of pattern or rhythm it would remain out of phase but still in tempo. So improvisation would be synchronised but not quantised, if a player missed the beat, the pattern would stay off-beat. This would maintain a sense of *skill-based* behaviour even though the patterns being produce would effectively be *rule-based.* To help maintain a sense of tonality, each of the Kaossilator Pros was set to work within the key of C Major. This set of notes corresponds to the white keys on a standard keyboard and is relatively easy for even a novice player to identify. The same was true of the sounds on the Handsonic if the sound set happened to be pitched (e.g. steel drums). Adopting approaches similar to those suggested by Stevens [2], small groups of players were arranged where one player would be encouraged to create a musical idea that could be continued over some time using one of the synchronised instruments. The rest of the small group would be encouraged to listen for some time and to then take the opportunity to introduce a musical idea of their own. Using this concept, a simple structure for improvisation could be achieved where layers would gradually be added and then gradually stripped away using different combinations of instruments, players, patterns and sounds.

Other than further supporting the observations from the previous workshop in terms of ease of access and generative potential, comments were also offered with specific regard to the synchronised nature of the musical system. Most significant within this was a general reassurance that the various players did maintain a sense of musical control whilst interacting with the elements that were to some extent generative and/or rule-based. By way of example, one member of the group commented on the synchronised nature "how all the different instruments could link with each other, I enjoyed that". When asked whether he still had a sense of control within this, he confirmed that he did. Additional comments were made in regard to the synchronised timing being helpful in sustaining a sense of rhythmic 'togetherness'. One of the more able musicians within the group commented on this aspect in conjunction with a feeling of control "yes, it's just finding the right beats - at first I was pressing anything - then I was listening to where the beast were - then trying to remember them to get a rhythm".

6   Discussion and Design Conclusions

The overall concept of coordinating and synchronising a number of contrasting music-technologies has been shown to have considerable potential for assisting with group based improvisational activities. A combination of observation and individual comments suggests that this kind of approach could be highly enabling whilst still offering the individual players meaningful sense of control and therefore 'ownership'. Personal and professional experience also suggests that, though the general model of working with predefined musical patterns and textures in the ways described earlier can produce meaningful and rewarding results, the overall concept could be further enhanced. At a fundamental level, this might be achieved by facilitating composition within the system such that new rhythmic, harmonic and melodic patterns can be introduced by the user-composer. During the workshops, it was convenient to coordinate the various musical streams to share tonal and harmonic relationships. This was not the only compositional choice as it was also decided to not specifically follow a particular harmonic progression, instead allowing the harmonies to emerge organically within the chosen key. As these are compositional choices or constraints that will ultimately affect the nature of the improvisational experience it would be desirable to hand this aspect over to the control of the group. With this in mind, it could be both creative and empowering to implement a system that allows for compositional rules and constraints to be created or applied centrally in contrast to being reliant on those that are contained within specific instruments. This will create a central music-engine unit that is responsible for the generation and manipulation of an expandable library of musical ideas and patterns, effectively providing multiple (synchronised) instruments within a single unit.

The means by which any individual will engage with the system can be designed around the specific needs of that individual. An example was given earlier of an individual who expressed their pleasure over engaging with particular sounds but observation showed that the interaction required was not always easy. In contrast, there were other users for whom this mode of interaction was most effective. If the types of patterns and sounds that are produced by this type of technology are divorced from any specific interface and brought under control of the central music-engine, then specific and adaptable interfaces can be designed to allow any given individual to engage with the system. As suggested earlier, the concept of performance-behaviours for digital instrument perhaps needs to accommodate individual needs more than it currently does. With this in mind, the user-performer should perhaps be able to adjust the level of synchronisation to suit their physical and/or coordination challenges such that the timing assistance achieved still allows the performance experience to be meaningful. A prototype is now being developed that will bring together these various desirable design considerations into a working system. Though this is likely to be relatively basic in terms of its initial functionality, the aim will be to apply the system within an iterative series of workshops and redesigns, introducing additional functionality in a relatively organic way.

References

1. Bailey, D.: Improvisation: Its Nature and Practice in Music, 2nd edn., pp. 83–85, 140-142. British Library National Sound Archive, London (1992)
2. Stevens, J.: Search and Reflect, pp. 1–2. Rockschool, UK (1986)
3. Smith, R.: Teaching and Learning Free Musical Improvisation in UK and Norway. In: Improvisation Continuums Conference (2007)
4. Challis, B.P., Smith, R.: Inclusive Technology and Community Music. In: Proceedings of Accessible Design in the Digital World 2008 (2008)
5. Challis, B.P.: Octonic: an accessible electronic musical instrument. Digital Creativity 22(1), 1–12 (2011)
6. Healey, R.: New technologies in music making. In: Moser, P., McKay, G. (eds.) Community Music: A Handbook, pp. 161–179. Russell House Publishing Ltd. (2005)
7. Malloch, J., Birnbaum, D., Sinyor, E., Wanderley, M.: Towards a New Conceptual Framework for Digital Musical Instruments. In: Proceedings of 9th International Conference on Digital Audio Effects, pp. 49–52 (2006)

From Network to Research – Ten Years of Music Informatics, Performance and Aesthetics

Søren R. Frimodt-Møller[1], Cynthia M. Grund[1], and Kristoffer Jensen[2]

[1] University of Southern Denmark,
Nordic Network for the Integration of Music Informatics, Performance and Aesthetics
[2] Aalborg University Esbjerg,
Nordic Network for the Integration of Music Informatics, Performance and Aesthetics
soren@frimodt-moller.dk, cmgrund@ifpr.sdu.dk,
krist@create.aau.dk

Abstract. This article briefly chronicles the history of the Nordic Network for the Integration of Music Informatics, Performance and Aesthetics (NNIMIPA) and its roots in previous research networks and milieus. It explains how a cross-disciplinary network works and gives rise to research projects that bridge the gap between the disciplines involved. As examples, three thematically linked projects within NNIMIPA are presented. These projects all have performance interaction (between musicians and between musician and audience) as their nexus.

Keywords: Music Informatics, Music Performance, Aesthetics, Philosophy, Interaction, Logical Models, Game Theory, Decision Theory, UML, Gesture, Motion Capture, Research Network.

1 Introduction

Research projects which have artistic endeavor as their area of examination will typically require cooperation between different disciplines: If, for example, investigators are interested in the expressive power of a painting, this may lead them to consult not only theorists of art, but also with practitioners - in this case, the painters themselves – as well as with curators, museum-goers etc. For the members of the Nordic Network for the Integration of Music Informatics, Performance and Aesthetics (NNIMIPA), which has its origins in local research networks and milieus dating back to 2001 (see section 2 below), cross-disciplinarity has been a given condition from the start. A prominent field in current music research is the development of models for how we interact with music (whether as listeners or as performers). Such research calls upon the insights of, among others, musicians, composers, musicologists, philosophers and computer scientists (the latter sometimes with the development of specific products in mind). NNIMIPA has from the start tried to combine the insights of the various disciplines and professions dealing with music performance in order to develop a better foundation for discussing questions related to how we interact with music. In the following, some of the research conducted within NNIMIPA will be presented in order to show how the cross-disciplinary nature of a network can benefit the specific research projects of individual researchers.

A.L. Brooks (Ed.): ArtsIT 2011, LNICST 101, pp. 71–79, 2012.

Section 2 contains a history of the network, while section 3 and its subsections consider three different aspects of performance interaction: The expressive means a musician has at his disposal via his gestures when interacting with an audience (3.1), ways of modeling interaction between musicians during rehearsals and performances when these are recorded on video (3.2), and formal schemes (borrowing methods from epistemic logic, game theory and decision theory) for describing the cognitive background of the decisions made by musicians during the process of coordination in the performance (3.3).

2   The History of NNIMIPA

The driving motivation behind the establishment of NNIMIPA has been to explore the voltage field that is created when music informatics, performance and areas traditionally dealt with by philosophical aesthetics interact. It complements and supplements two Danish networks devoted to interdisciplinary studies involving music – NTSMB – Netværk for Tværvidenskabelige Studier af Musik og Betydning/ Network for Cross-Disciplinary Studies of Music and Meaning (www.ntsmb.dk, established in 2001 with funding from the Danish Research Council for the Humanities) and *The Aesthetics of Music and Sound: Cross-Disciplinary Interplay between the Humanities, Technology and Musical Practice*, a research program based at the University of Southern Denmark as part of the Institute of Philosophy, Education and the Study of Religions since 2006 (www.soundmusicresearch.org). In addition, many NNIMIPA members are active as contributors, peer reviewers and members of the editorial board and/or staff of *JMM: The Journal of Music and Meaning,* www.musicandmeaning.net, an international, peer-reviewed online journal. *JMM* was founded in 2003 as an outgrowth of the activities within NTSMB.

NNIMIPA was officially established during the 2007-2008 academic year, when funding provided by the University of Southern Denmark at Odense was matched by Nordplus in order to establish this Nordic cooperative initiative. The charter members were (1) University of Southern Denmark; (2) Academy of Music and Music Communication, Esbjerg, Denmark, as of 1/1-2010 renamed Academy of Music and Dramatic Arts, Southern Denmark after merging with the Carl Nielsen Academy of Music, Odense and The School of Dramatic Arts Odense; (3) Aalborg University Esbjerg; (4) University of Tampere, Finland; (5) Sibelius Academy, Helsinki; and (6) Royal Institute of Technology, Stockholm, Sweden. Nordplus continued to provide funding for NNIMIPA activities held during the 2008-2009 and 2009-2010 academic years in the form of grants which were matched by the participating institutions. The University of Oslo became a member in 2009. NNIMIPA became a research network under NordForsk (www.nordforsk.org) on September 1, 2010, with funding during 2010-2013. In 2010 Bifröst University, Iceland, and University of Iceland, Reykjavik, Iceland came on board, as well as Malmö Academy of Music, Lund University, Sweden, and Grieg Academy, Bergen University College, Norway. The decision to award the grant was made by the director of NordForsk following an evaluation carried out by a panel of independent experts.

The educational, lecture and research activities are documented through the website www.nnimipa.org which was launched in February 2010.

3   Research

The following three subsections present some of the research projects conducted within NNIMIPA. All of them have performance interaction (whether between musicians or between musician and audience) as their nexus.

3.1   Music, Meaning and Movement

One area of investigation that engages all who are active within NNIMIPA is that which deals with the ways in which music may be regarded as meaningful.

A low-tech approach to the exploration of the relationship between music, meaning and movement took center stage together with a high-tech motion capture approach during the NNIMIPA coordination meeting held at The University of Oslo, February 18-19, 2010. William Westney, Paul Whitfield Horn Professor of Piano, Browning Artist-in-Residence, School of Music, Texas Tech University demonstrated techniques he has been developing for over 25 years in order to encourage musicians to find ways of keeping their playing (or singing) fresh and invested with personal engagement.

Westney's workshop is known as *The Un-Master Class* (UMC) [1] and was originally intended to address the problem that many musicians, despite high levels of training, deliver performances that come across as rather lifeless and generic. While it still functions in this way, it has become increasingly apparent that the presuppositions behind the UMC raise deep questions involving the locus of meaning in music and what the character of this meaning might be.

Westney's work is thus of key interest to Cynthia M. Grund, Associate Professor of Philosophy, Institute of Philosophy, Education and the Study of Religions (IFPR) University of Southern Denmark (SDU) at Odense, Project Manager for NNIMIPA, and Editor-in-Chief for *JMM: The Journal of Music and Meaning*. The two have embarked upon an extensive research cooperation, which became woven into the fabric of NNIMIPA when Westney was named Hans Christian Andersen Guest Professorial Fellow at IFPR-SDU for a six-month period during the 2009-2010 academic year. Grund and Westney write:

> One of the signature features of the UMC is the innovative integration of the audience within its pedagogical and aesthetic framework, which is constructed in stepwise, interactive fashion during the first hour of the two-hour session. All participants listen to instructions about the forthcoming "warm-up," during which audience and performers will be on equal footing as they participate in carefully constructed and sequenced exercises. The warm-up is designed to create a specific experiential context for the second hour, when instrumental and vocal musicians will offer live performances.
>
> The exercises consist largely of expressive, gestural activities. Their conceptual basis owes much to the seminal theories of Emile Jaques-Dalcroze, to which Westney was introduced as a child. Later, as a university professor and performer, Westney revisited the Dalcroze approach to education with a specific question in mind: how to teach rhythm in a more integrated and effective way in the studio. After reacquainting himself with the work of Dalcroze as an adult, however, Westney began to develop new

ways in which similar techniques could be applied in broader contexts involving authenticity in interpretation and the performer-audience dynamic ([2] pp. 34-35).

An important part of Westney's approach thus involves movement and gesture, which function as non-verbal embodied vehicles for capturing and remembering nuances of interpretation and performance. This emphasis dovetailed in a very relevant fashion with the high-tech approaches being developed and employed in the fourMs laboratory by, among others, Professor Rolf Inge Godøy and postdoctoral researcher Alexander Refsum Jensenius. These approaches employ a complete state-of-the-art Qualisys motion capture system. This consists of a nine-camera Oqus 300 system, a MEGA ME6000 Wireless EMG and a 200 fps grayscale Point Grey camera. Data can be streamed in real time through OSC-protocol via UDP/IP to MAX/MSP/Jitter software and synchronized through a MOTU time piece allowing synchronous playback of analog, motion, video and audio data [3], [4]. (For those interested in this type of research, Rolf Inge Godøy and Marc Leman, professor at the University of Ghent, present a body of work on the implications of an array of IT-approaches to the study of the connections between sound, movement and meaning in [5], as does Alexander Refsum Jensenius in [6].)

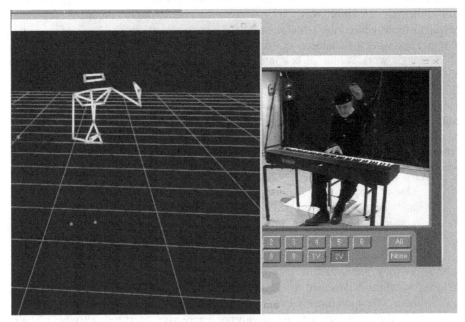

Fig. 1. William Westney (right) performing wearing point-light markers, and the resulting digital model of his movements (left). Point-light display filmed by Alexander Refsum Jensenius and Ståle A. Skogstad at the FourM's Lab, UiO, Oslo, Norway. Filmclip rendered and sound-and-video synchronized by Kristian Nymoen. Still photo from [7].

Grund produced an online multimedia document [7] assisted by and with input from Alexander Jensenius, Kristian Nymoen, Ståle A. Skogstad and William Westney in order to provide some perspectives on where an approach combining state-of-the-art IT, concerns attendant to issues of live performance and concerns from philosophical aesthetics might lead. Grund and Westney are also looking forward to exploring the investigative possibilities afforded by markerless motion capture in the study of movement as it relates to musical meaning, and they are still analyzing the implications of the data provided by the February 2010 Oslo session, aided by Josué Moreno and Dāvis Ozoliņš, who through their affiliations with the Sibelius Academy have had occasion to attend courses offered by NNIMIPA at the Master's level (see www.nnimipa.org) and to do NNIMIPA-funded work at the fourMs laboratory.

3.2   Models of Interaction

One of the aspects of the interaction of musicians that is important within the NNIMIPA network is how musicians communicate during performance. Three different modes of communication may occur: *verbal*, i.e. when musicians talk to each other; *non-verbal, but non-musical* e.g. when musicians nod, smile etc. at each other, and *musical*, i.e. when the musicians give each other signs via their instrumental sound production. It is assumed that musicians act in a manner similar to the belief-desire-intention paradigm of Bratman [8], in which beliefs and desires combine to form intentions. Of course, decisions and planning steps must be included if a full model is to be described, but these steps are usually not externalized to a level where they can be observed. Only the individual musician can know the exact nature of her own belief-desire-intention process, but musicians may obtain knowledge about the belief-desire-intention processes of other musicians via information gathered in the interaction process, i.e. by observing the other players.

Several experiments have been performed by Kristoffer Jensen, Associate Professor, Department of Architecture, Design and Media Technology, Aalborg University Esbjerg, in order to observe and describe the interaction between musicians. One important conclusion has been made from the initial observations: at the level of professional performance, a performance of music based on notation (scores, parts etc.) contains very little visible communication. Therefore, subsequent observations have been made in connection with either improvised music, in collaboration with guitarist Fredrik Søgaard during his improvisation classes at the conservatory in Esbjerg, or with the rehearsals of amateur musicians.

Unified Modeling Language (UML) [9] is used in the field of object-oriented software engineering. UML diagrams are graphic notations of systems, and many different diagrams exist. In the case of interacting musicians, *Use Cases* model the dependencies between the musicians and their goals. *Use Cases* can be further developed to *State Machine Diagrams*, and *Class Diagrams*, if the goal is to implement the system, but for observation and modeling studies, however, the *Sequence Diagram* is of particular interest. In the *Sequence Diagram*, the vertical lines correspond to each musician or other agent, and the arrows correspond to the messages between the musicians and other agents.

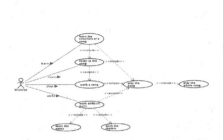

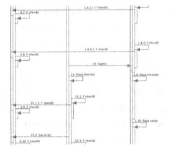

Fig. 2. Use *Case* of a musician learning to play music

Fig. 3. Sequence *Diagram* of musicians in a rehearsal (detail)

In fig.2 an example of a *Use Case* is shown, in which the musician rehearses a song alone, and in fig. 3 a detail of a *Sequence Diagram* is shown in which three musicians rehearse a jazz tune. A UML diagram is useful and easy to access, as many software systems exist for this purpose, and software students and engineers often have knowledge about UML and may gain further experience through the modeling of musicians interacting through UML. It is clear that the information obtained through UML modeling can be used to corroborate the formal logic models described below in section 3.3. For instance, in the *Sequence Diagram*, the decision as to who will play the next solo can be observed. This is done either through verbal communication or through unilateral decision by one musician.

3.3   Formal Models for Decision Processes in the Performance

As stated at the beginning of 3.2, the interaction between musicians during a performance is not only dependent on verbal and non-verbal signalling between musicians, but also on the 'signs' communicated via the music being performed by the individual musicians. A large part of this communication process rests on whether or not the other musicians actually receive the 'message' inherent in another musician's phrasing. This means that the interaction process is dependent on the individual musician's ability to interpret the situation in a way that will promote coordination. As part of his PhD dissertation [10], Søren R. Frimodt-Møller, Managing Editor of *JMM: The Journal of Music and Meaning*, has discussed how performing musicians make decisions not only as a result of their individual intentions for the performance, but also as a result of their assumptions regarding the intentions of the other performers, and of how they conceive of the norms inherent in the performance context at hand. In order to describe these decision processes, Frimodt-Møller has considered three different yet associated modeling schemes which will be briefly described in the following.

1) Coordination based on *common knowledge*: Common knowledge of some fact p in a group of people G involves not only that everyone in G knows that p, but also that everyone in G (potentially) knows that everyone in G knows that p, that everyone in G knows that everyone in G (potentially) knows that everyone in G knows that p and

so on ad infinitum. Common knowledge as described by e.g. Fagin et al ([11], 9) is typically approximated following a situation where p is a public announcement to G. In the music ensemble, a type of information that might attain the status of common knowledge is that consisting of the agreements that are verbalized (and thus made 'public') during the rehearsals. Should a coordination problem occur, that is, should the musicians suddenly not be synchronized in accordance with their initial plan for the performance, the musicians will by default try to follow the general strategies they consider to be common knowledge in the ensemble, based on how they remember the rehearsals. Using classical epistemic logic as a modeling tool, it can be shown that in situations where common knowledge in G of p, notated $C_G p$, has not been established before the performance, $C_G p$ is actually unattainable during a performance due to the unreliable nature of non-verbal communication and symbolic communication through the music itself.

2) Game Theory with Variable Frames: In situations where common knowledge of anything is unattainable, musicians may still be able to make decisions when facing a coordination problem, if they consider how their co-players are most likely to act in the situation at hand. In the branch of game theory developed by Bacharach et al [12] called *variable frame theory*, coordination games (e.g. where two people who are not allowed to communicate will get the highest pay off when simultaneously choosing the same alternative when a choice of several alternatives is possible) are described as a reasoning process where one considers how the opponent 'frames' or, in other words, categorizes the different options at hand, and thereby how likely she is to consider particular choices more 'salient' than others. The more the participating players know about each other in advance, the more accurate their expectations for each others' choices will be. This seems to be paralleled by the fact that musicians often are more comfortable playing with musicians whom they already know well.

3) Decision Theory with Intentions: As has been mentioned in 3.2 above, intentions play an important role in a musician's decision-making process. Olivier Roy [13] has discussed - with regard to decisions in general - the role a person's intentions play in the formation of plans. Transferred to the domain of music performance, the general idea is that in a given situation, the musician can choose to follow a strategy in line with a strategy profile (a combination of strategies, one for each musician in the ensemble) chosen from a limited set of possible strategy profiles. The musician chooses a strategy profile that has one or more possible outcomes that she intends to achieve. If the musician has reason to believe that the other musicians are not following the same strategy profile, she will have to search for a new profile that is in accordance with what she considers to be the possible intentions of the other musicians, but *ceteris paribus* still in accordance with her own intentions. What the formal model based on these ideas shows is that if we disregard the possibility of unintended actions, the musicians should gradually better their chances of coordination with each new step of searching for a new profile (as they will be able to rule out certain strategy profiles at each step).

The general point of exploring the formal models above is to highlight the importance of following rules during the performance and especially the importance of remaining sensitive to the actions of the other players. In short, this research project provides a set of formal descriptive tools to capture some of the intuitive insights regarding interaction that performers already possess. Combined with the insights gained through Kristoffer Jensen's research described in 3.2, this project may be a step towards a comprehensive understanding of performance interaction in general.

4   Conclusions and Further Perspectives

NNIMIPA has, as the title of this paper suggests, indeed moved from being a research network in the sense of a group of researchers networking (e.g. meeting and discussing their products) to being a research network in the sense of a network that works together to conduct research. Grund and Westney's philosophical and practice-based approaches to the investigation of music, meaning and movement have been enriched by the insights gained thanks to the pioneering work of Godøy and Jensenius and the group at the fourM's laboratory at the University of Oslo augmented by the NNIMIPA-funded assistance of Moreno and Ozoliņš. The collaborations between Jensen and Frimodt-Møller concerning the interaction process of performing musicians may similarly lead to an extended platform for discussing matters related to musical interaction.

In the future, NNIMIPA members will continue to explore not only interpersonal interaction within the setting provided by music performance, but also the interaction between musician, listener and environment, or, more broadly speaking, context. The various ways in which the specific context (encompassing physical as well as social and cultural aspects) of the performance affects the audience's experience and the immediate decisions of the musician, provides a rich field of theoretical problems that necessitate further collaboration between performing musicians and researchers in music philosophy and technology.

References

1. A documentary about William Westney's Un-Master Class, filmed at Alsion Concert Hall in Sønderborg November 24, 2009 was broadcast for the first time on ALT-Aabenraa Lokal TV during the week of February 8 (2010), to view the documentary, please see http://vimeo.com/channels/musikmedalt
2. Grund, C.M., Westney, W.: Music, Movement, Performance & Perception: Perspectives on Cross-Disciplinary Research and Teaching within NNIMIPA - Nordic Network for the Integration of Music Informatics, Performance and Aesthetics. An essay in words and pictures recounting the NordPlus-sponsored Coordination Meeting for NNIMIPA held at the University of Oslo (February 18-19, 2010); Text: Grund, C.M., Westney, W.: Photography: Cynthia M. Grund. Odense: The Institute of Philosophy, Education and the Study of Religions at the University of Southern Denmark and NNIMIPA: Nordic Network for the Integration of Music Informatics, Performance and Aesthetics, a network supported by NordPlus (2010), http://www.nnimipa.org/CM.html

3. FourMs - Music, Mind, Motion, Machines: How Can Knowledge About Movement & Sound Create Better Technologies? Qualisys Newsletter, Issue One, Cover and p. 4 (May 2010), http://www.qualisys.com/wp-content/uploads/2011/05/Qualisys_newsletter_2010.pdf

4. Jensenius, A.R., Glette, K.H., Godøy, R.I., Høvin, M.E., Nymoen, K., Skogstad, A.v.D., Tørresen, J.: FourMs, University of Oslo - Lab Report. In: Rowe, R., Samaras, D. (eds.) Proceedings of the International Computer Music Conference, New York, June 1-5 (2010), http://www.duo.uio.no/publ/IMV/2010/103430/103430-fourms.pdf

5. Godøy, R.I., Leman, M. (eds.): Musical Gestures: Sound, Movement, and Meaning. Routledge, New York (2009)

6. Jensenius, A.R.: Musikk og Bevegelse. Unipub, Oslo (2009)

7. Jensenius, A.R., Nymoen, K., Grund, C.M., Westney, W., Skogstad, S.A.: Video Suite – in Three Movements: Jensenius-Westney-Grund on Motion-Capture, Music and Meaning. Multimodal webpage presentation of original motion-capture video with accompanying audio, including original documentary-and-interview video-and-audio about the motion-capture labwork, http://www.nnimipa.org/JWG.html, finalized on April 25, 2010, on the website for NNIMIPA. NNIMIPA Webmaster and Network Coordinator: C.M. Grund (2010)

8. Bratman, M.: Intentions, Plans and Practical Reason. CSLI Publications (1999)

9. Larman, C.: Applying UML and Patterns: An Introduction to Object-Oriented Analysis and Design. Prentice Hall (1997)

10. Frimodt-Møller, S.R.: Playing by the Rules. A Philosophical Approach to Normativity and Coordination in Music Performance. PhD dissertation, Institute of Philosophy, Education and the Study of Religions, University of Southern Denmark, Odense (2010)

11. Fagin, R., Halpern, J.Y., Moses, Y., Vardi, M.Y.: Reasoning about Knowledge. The MIT Press, Cambridge (2003)

12. Bacharach, M., Sugden, R., Gold, N.: Beyond Individual Choice: Teams and Frames in Game Theory. Princeton University Press, Princeton (2006)

13. Roy, O.: Thinking Before Acting. Intentions, Logic, Rational Choice. PhD thesis, Institute for Logic, Language and Computation. Universiteit van Amsterdam, Amsterdam, The Netherlands. ILLC Dissertation series DS-2008-03 (2008)

Violin-Related HCI: A Taxonomy Elicited by the Musical Interface Technology Design Space

Dan Overholt

Department of Architecture, Design and Media Technology
Niels Jernes Vej 14 , Room: 3-107
9220 Aalborg Ø, Denmark
dano@create.aau.dk

Abstract. Acoustic instruments such as the violin excel at translating a performer's gestures into sound in ways that can evoke a wide range of affective qualities. They require finesse when interacting with them, producing sound and music in an extremely responsive manner. This richness of interaction is simultaneously what makes acoustic instruments so challenging to play, what makes them interesting to play for long periods of time, and what makes overcoming that difficulty so worthwhile to both performers and listeners. Such an ability to capture human complexity, intelligence, and emotion through live performance interfaces is the core of what we are interested in salvaging from acoustic instruments, and bringing into the development of advanced HCI methods through the Musical Interface Technology Design Space, MITDS [12, 13].

1 MITDS – The Musical Interface Technology Design Space

Viewed as a whole, the MITDS is a framework that consists of a combination of three major areas: Music performance, Human-Computer Interaction, and the incorporation of modern technologies such as multimodal sensor interfaces and Digital Signal Processing. The MITDS is a conceptual framework for describing, analyzing, designing and extending the interfaces, mappings, synthesis algorithms and performance techniques for advanced musical instruments. It provides designers with a theoretical base to draw upon when creating new interactive performance systems. In this paper, we look primarily at just one component of the MITDS: a taxonomy of design patterns for musical interaction based on existing research and instruments.

1.1 A Taxonomy of Modern Musical Interface Design Patterns

Societies throughout history and around the world have developed formal or informal systems for classifying musical instruments, a broad field known as organology [9]. We look here at only a very small subset of the puzzle, in an attempt to clarify our understanding of how musical interfaces have developed since the separation of the controller from the source of sound became possible through various HCI methods.

A.L. Brooks (Ed.): ArtsIT 2011, LNICST 101, pp. 80–89, 2012.

Although any attempt to classify new digital musical instruments will inevitably include nebulous zones, where a controller crosses boundaries between the categories, many studies have nonetheless proposed a set of three different types of controllers. Wanderley [20] distinguishes between 1) *Instrument-like* controllers, 2) *Augmented* controllers, and 3) *Alternate* controllers. *Instrument-like* controllers do not have any acoustic capabilities, but their interfaces resemble existing acoustic instruments. *Augmented* controllers add new gestural sensing capabilities to existing acoustic instruments, and *Alternate* controllers use electronic sensors directly, not related to any existing acoustic instrument.

1) Instrument-like controllers (interfaces resembling existing instruments)
   a. Instrument-simulating controllers (mirroring playing techniques)
   b. Instrument-inspired controllers (abstractly derived techniques)
2) Augmented controllers (traditional instruments augmented with sensors)
   a. Augmented by capturing traditional techniques
   b. Augmented through extended techniques
3) Alternate controllers (interfaces not resembling existing instruments)
   a. Touch controllers (require physical contact with control surface)
   b. Non-contact controllers (free gestures – limited sensing range)
   c. Wearable controllers (performer always in sensing environment)
   d. Borrowed controllers (VR interfaces, gamepads, etc.)

As shown above, these categories can be broken down into sub-categories in the MITDS. Distinctions are made between instrument-like controllers that attempt to *simulate* existing instruments as much as possible, and those that use existing instruments only as *inspiration* (and can be closer to alternative controllers in some cases). Within the augmented controllers category (traditional instruments enhanced with sensors), sub-categories include those that use sensors to primarily digitize a player's *existing* technique on the traditional instrument, and those that require the learning and practice of new, *extended* playing techniques through the use of sensors in non-traditional roles for that instrument. For alternate controllers, the MITDS uses categories similar to those proposed by [15], which relate to the sensing functionality of an interface relative to the human being. *Touch* controllers do not react until physically manipulated, and therefore provide haptic feedback to the performer. *Non-contact* controllers do not require contact with a physical control surface, but may have a limited range of free-air gestures (the performer can move into and out of the sensing area). *Wearable* controllers are interfaces that capture body movement, turning a performer's limb motions into potential sonic events. Finally, *borrowed* controllers are those not originally designed to be musical interfaces, such as virtual-reality motion capture systems, game controllers, etc.

2   Violin-Related HCI – Elicitation of the Taxonomy

This section investigates recent design approaches in violin-related HCI, as related to the MITDS categories above. It specifically elicits the following sections of the taxonomy: instrument-inspired controllers (category 1b above), augmented controllers capturing traditional techniques (2a), and augmented controllers capturing extended techniques (2b). Category 3 is not relevant in the context of violin-related HCI, and category 1a is not covered in detail here, as the author has been personally frustrated with instrument-simulating controllers such as MIDI violins, due to their lack of musical expressivity. The final section of this article examines the development of the Overtone Violin, which communicates with the computer via USB directly, using a protocol with much higher bandwidth and better dynamic range and expressivity than allowed by the MIDI specification. The Overtone Violin and Overtone Fiddle cross between the boundaries of this taxonomy, as they are augmented instruments that are designed to capture both traditional and extended techniques. It is nonetheless hoped that the exploration of this taxonomy will help elucidate the various design elements and tradeoffs when choosing feature sets and capabilities of an instrument's interface.

2.1   Violin-Related Instrument-Inspired Controllers

Many sensor-based interfaces have been inspired by the violin. This could be due to the fact that the violin is one of the traditional instruments that many people consider to be very expressive, giving rising to their inspiration to model newly designed instruments after it. While the physical form of the violin is not often kept, at least some portion of the player's gestures and technique are preserved.

Dan Trueman's Ph.D. dissertation titled 'Reinventing the Violin' [19] resulted in the "Bowed Sensor Speaker Array" or BoSSA, a violin-inspired controller that has many playing techniques borrowed from his background as a violinist (figure 1). A set of pressure sensors mounted between flexible material (sponges) replaces the strings, and performances usually involve a sensor-equipped violin bow, the "R-bow", which has a two-axis accelerometer and two pressure sensors between the hair and wood on the bow. This is used to play the sensor-sponges while manipulating a sensor-fingerboard called the "Fangerbored." The Fangerbored has four pressure sensors for the left hand fingers. Overall, BoSSA and the R-bow together offer performers an impressive fourteen real-time sensor data-streams, though due to practical considerations and human limitations, the number of playable dimensions is effectively reduced to nine.

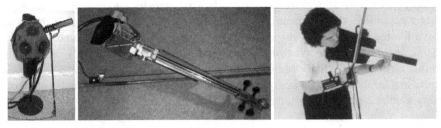

Fig. 1. Violin-inspired controllers: Dan Trueman's Bowed-Sensor-Speaker-Array (BoSSA), NealFarwell's "funny-fiddle", and Suguru Goto's SuperPolm

Neal Farwell's "funny-fiddle" project was inspired by the violin as well, and used four sensors as inputs – a sonar distance sensor between the violin and the frog on the bow, a home made linear position sensor along the neck of the violin, a tape-head from a reel-to-reel tape recorder, and a strip of magnetic tape in place of the bow-hair.

Suguru Goto's Superpolm [5] substitutes electronic sensors for strings and parameter-driven synthesis algorithms for acoustics (figure 1). The instrument is equipped with four touch-strip sensors on the fingerboard and a bow that works as a resistor ladder pressed against a voltage sensor on the bridge, plus a chin squeeze sensor for an added dimension of control. While it is impossible to use strictly traditional playing techniques on the Superpolm (since it doesn't have strings), the gestures it requires are closely related to those of a traditional violin.

2.2   Violin-Related Augmented Controllers Capturing *Traditional* Techniques

We use the term *traditional* here to refer to any instrument having strings that can be played with conventional techniques. Tod Machover's Hyperinstruments research group at the MIT Media Lab began work on this area in the early 1990s. The overall goal of the Hyperinstruments project is to provide virtuoso performers with a means of amplifying their gestures, affording supplementary sound or musical control possibilities [11]. The project resulted in several tailor-made instruments for famous musicians such as the Hypercello for Yo-Yo Ma, the Hyperviolin for Ani Kavafian, and the Hyperbow and next generation Hyperviolin for Joshua Bell. All of the Hyperinstrument's sensor systems focused on capturing *traditional* techniques.

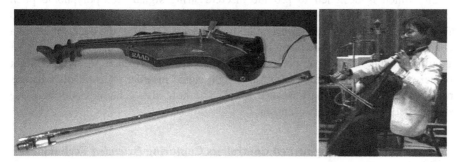

Fig. 2. The original Hyperviolin from the MIT Media Lab, and Yo-Yo Ma performing Tod Machover's *Begin Again Again...* on the Hypercello

Stanford's CCRMA has been instrumental in developing some of the early augmented violin-family interfaces, including Max Mathews' series of electronic violins (figure 3) and Chris Chafe's Celleto (figure 4). Mathews made a number of electronic violins, all of which were closely related to normal electric violins, in that they did not have resonating bodies. Using custom electronic pickups, the sound from their strings was used as the input to electronic circuits that resonated and filtered the sound in various ways. Some of these circuits were based on the resonances of acoustic violins which were analyzed in an effort to "replace" the missing body of the instrument with electronics, while other circuits tuned the resonances to completely change the timbre of the original source of vibration, making the strings sound more like a brass instrument or a human voice [16].

Fig. 3. left, one of Max Mathews' early electronic violins, and right, the IRCAM Augmented violin project by Emmanuel Flety, et al.

Emmanuel Flety, et al. have been developing the "Augmented Violin" (figure 3) project since 2003 at the 'Institut de Recherche et Coordination Acoustique/Musique' in Paris. Their system uses capacitive sensing to determine bow position, and is focused only on capturing gestures that are part of a *traditional* violinist's technique. Other parts of the same IRCAM project focused on software that utilizes multimodal sensor input [18], combining accelerometer and data from a video camera focused on the player in order to analyze traditional bow-strokes, and categorize them into the different techniques (martele, spicatto, detache, etc). The augmented violin project also includes the development of a reflective optical pickup system for acoustic violins, which is designed to provide discrete string signals for polyphonic pitch detection algorithms [10]. Although the pickup system they developed proved effective for its intended use (conversion of pitch to MIDI data), the decision to use a reflective rather than an occlusion based optical design resulted in a poor quality of amplified sound. Reflective designs are subject to interference from other light sources, and require a modulated infrared light signal in order to avoid disturbances from ambient light in a performance space. The bow also generates audible noise when it is above the reflective sensors.

2.3   Violin-Related Augmented Controllers Capturing *Extended* Techniques

Composer, researcher, and performer Chris Chafe developed his Celleto (figure 4), an augmented electronic cello, in collaboration with Max Mathews. The Celleto is used for both performance and research into interactive composition, where the performer controls the computer's musical flow from the sensors on the instrument. The Celleto bow uses a strain gauge sensor mounted at the mid-point, and an accelerometer placed at the frog end of the bow. Additionally, in some configurations a modified Buchla Lightning interface is used for determining the location of the bow in 2D space, allowing traditional gestures alongside extended gestures such as shaking the bow in mid-air to send accelerometer and position data.

Curtis Bahn has also developed a highly *extended* instrument, and a set of new techniques to go along with it, called the Sensor Bass, or SBass (figure 4). The SBass is used with a laptop computer and other external gear, such as the spherical speaker array developed by Dan Trueman and Perry Cook. Many sensors are attached to the electric stand-up bass, such as the pressure strips Bahn is seen playing in figure 4 [2].

Fig. 4. left to right, Chris Chafe playing his Celleto, Curtis Bahn playing his SBass, and Chad Peiper playing the eViolin made by Camille Goudeseune

The eViolin project was started by Camille Goudeseune in 1998 with the idea of "taking advantage of existing performance skill to play sound synthesis algorithms" [6,7,8]. Rather than designing new input methods, the eViolin focuses on mapping systems and software synthesis methods. The sensor technology used is an Ascension SpacePad, a device commonly used in Virtual Reality systems that measures the position of several wired sensors relative to an antenna transmitting a DC magnetic field (seen behind the player in figure 4). This system is used to capture the position and orientation of both the violin and the bow.

In the late 1980s, Australian Jon Rose collaborated with STEIM researchers on the construction of a sensor-bow, a project in which the SensorLab was used (as shown in figure 5) to capture data from a pressure sensor under the index finger and a sonar sensor to detect bow position. Rose's goal was to "bring together the physicality and dynamics of improvised music with the quick change and virtual possibilities of computer music" [17]. More recently, Rose has been utilizing the K-Bow system from Keith McMillen Instruments.

Fig. 5. left to right, Jon Rose with his MIDI Bow, CNMAT's augmented cello for Francis-Marie Uitti and a close-up of its wheel encoder (driven by the bow)

The CNMAT augmented cello [4] (see figure 5) was developed by Adrian Freed, David Wessel, and other researchers at UC Berkeley in collaboration with Francis-Marie Uitti, cellist. The sensors added to the instrument include several pressure sensors, one of which extends along the side of the neck of the instrument, a button matrix underneath the bridge, and a wheel rotary encoder below the strings that can be driven by the bow. The wheel is analogous to the "short string" extended bowing technique (bowing the strings below the bridge), as it is located below the instrument's body. All of these sensors are driven by Uitti as the performer, captured and digitized by the CNMAT connectivity processor [1]. The sensor data is used to control a software environment in Max/MSP/Jitter that the researchers have developed for her real-time performances.

3   Design of the Overtone Violin and the Overtone Fiddle through the Musical Interface Technology Design Space

While the author's Overtone Violin may not look very much like a traditional instrument, it is considered an augmented instrument within our taxonomy. This is because all of the standard violin playing techniques can be used due to the use of normal strings. Such augmented instruments can potentially include the best of both worlds through sensor-based augmentation that preserves customary performance techniques while adding powerful new possibilities for musical expression.

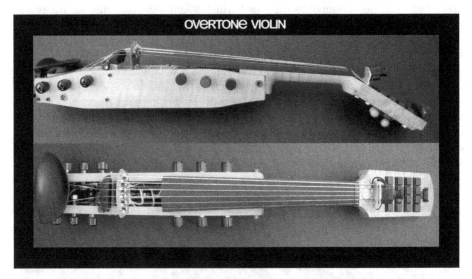

Fig. 6. The Overtone Violin

The Overtone Violin (figure 6) is an entirely custom built, radically augmented musical instrument that preserves the traditions of violin technique while adding a completely new set of gestural possibilities for the musician. The rationale behind the development of the instrument was to keep the expressive elements of the expert violinist, while incorporating the added benefits of gestural controllers via embedded sensors. As we have discussed, any instrument can be augmented to different degrees through the addition of extra sensors; such hybrid instruments offer musicians the familiarity and expressivity of their chosen instrument along with the extended control afforded by the sensors.

There are two ways, however, in which the Overtone Violin differs from most hybrid instruments. First, the extra sensors are used to capture a completely separate (yet complementary) set of gestures, rather than just acquiring traditional skills of the performer. Second, it is designed and built from scratch to be an entirely new, specialized instrument that continues the evolution of the violin, rather than retrofitting an existing instrument. One of the primary motivations behind the Overtone Violin is to put real-time signal processing under direct expressive control of the performer, thereby pushing the envelope of violin performance and composition into completely new areas.

There are many possibilities for using signal processing to mirror/modify the string sounds from the Overtone Violin. The instrument has independent audio outputs from each string, which help in this process by providing clean signals for pitch detection/feature tracking, and allowing different effects algorithms and spatialization techniques to be applied to each string. Signal processing is a very powerful way to enhance the violin using the traditional violin gestural vocabulary, as it preserves the nuances and subtleties of a skilled performer. But traditional instrumental techniques are not well suited for certain parametric controls needed for signal processing algorithms, so gestural controllers are needed as well. The Overtone Violin is a powerful research tool to investigate innovative approaches to combining signal processing of traditional violin sounds with gestural control of synthesis, using combinations of audio effects, synthesis techniques, and algorithms that blur these boundaries. As we have seen, there are many people who have worked on augmenting the violin in different ways, but most have focused exclusively on only a subset of these capabilities.

The Overtone Violin is an ongoing research project that has continued evolving in all three areas of musical performance, HCI, and hardware / software technologies. While this discussion focused on the technical details and development of the Overtone Violin itself and its associated software, the author has been focusing recent efforts towards the development of a new instrument called the "Overtone Fiddle"; a description of the first prototype of this instrument can be found in [14]. The Overtone Fiddle takes many of the lessons learned from the research behind the Overtone Violin, and incorporates it into a new hybrid acoustic/electric instrument in which the design has evolved to include sonic actuators inside the acoustic body of the instrument. Many new performance practices with these instruments have been explored by the author in his musical composition and performance. It is definitely long-term research, as one must allow years to fully develop new playing techniques. It is hoped that this work represents a significant step towards formulating an integrated approach to new violin development and performance; given the versatility and expressive performance possibilities of these instruments, it is impossible to foresee the far-reaching effects they may or may not have on future violin performance and composition. Audio/video clips of the Overtone Violin and the Overtone Fiddle can be found on the author's website.

4   Conclusion

The advancements in violin-related human-computer interaction described herein have taken place through the use of the author's Musical Interface Technology Design Space, MITDS. While the particular design of the author's instruments and their interfaces, interaction mappings, custom technologies, and musical performance practices emerges uniquely from personal desires and musical motivations, the overall approach is influenced by, and plays a part in the discourse of current and recent developments by others in the field. The MITDS is used to inform design decisions, resulting in the contribution of example instruments – the Overtone Violin and the Overtone Fiddle – developed through this methodology. This article has examined the use of the MITDS as a set of design patterns that are understood through the examination of existing methods of violin-related HCI. The taxonomy of research trends in the area influences the development of new systems that combine emerging technologies with musical performance and practical considerations. Ultimately, it is hoped that these considerations will be useful to others interested in pursuing similar approaches to the development of future instruments, be they violin-related or not.

References

1. Avizienis, R., Freed, A., Suzuki, T., Wessel, D.: Scalable Connectivity Processor for Computer Music Performance Systems. In: International Computer Music Conference, Berlin, Germany, pp. 523–526 (2000)
2. Bahn, C., Trueman, D.: Interface: electronic chamber ensemble. In: Proceedings of the 2001 Conference on New interfaces For Musical Expression (NIME 2001), Seattle, WA, pp. 1–5 (2001)
3. Bevilacqua, F., Rasamimanana, N., Fléty, E., Lemouton, S.: The augmented violin project: research, composition and performance report. In: 2006 Conference on New Interfaces for Musical Expression (NIME 2005), pp. 402–406 (2006)
4. Freed, A., Wessel, D., Zbyszynski, M., Uitti, F.M.: Augmenting the cello. In: Proceedings of the 2006 Conference on New Interfaces For Musical Expression, IRCAM — Centre Pompidou, Paris, France, pp. 409–413 (2006)
5. Goto, S.: Virtual Musical Instruments: Technological Aspects and Interactive Performance Issues. In: Wanderley, M., Battier, M. (eds.) Trends in Gestural Control of Music, IRCAM - Centre Pompidou, Paris (2000)
6. Goudeseune, C.: Composing with Parameters for Synthetic Instruments. Ph.D. thesis, University of Illinois at Urbana-Champaign, Urbana, IL (2001a)
7. Goudeseune, C., Garnett, G., Johnson, T.: Resonant processing of instrumental sound controlled by spatial position. In: Publications of the 2001 Workshop on New Instruments for Musical Expression, Seattle, USA (2001b)
8. Goudeseune, C.: Interpolated mappings for musical instruments. Organised Sound 7(2), 85–96 (2002)
9. Kartomi, M.: On Concepts and Classifications of Musical Instruments. The University of Chicago Press, Chicago (1990)

10. Leroy, N., Fléty, E., Bevilacqua, F.: Reflective Optical Pickup For Violin. In: Proceedings of the 2006 International Conference on New Interfaces for Musical Expression, Paris, France (2006)
11. Machover, T.: Hyperinstruments – a Composer's Approach to the Evolution of Intelligent Musical Instruments. In: Jacobson, L. (ed.) Cyberarts: Exploring Arts and Technology, pp. 67–76. MillerFreeman Inc., San Francisco (1992)
12. Overholt, D.: Musical Interface Technology: Multimodal Control of Multidimensional Parameter Spaces for Electroacoustic Music Performance. Ph.D. dissertation, Dept. of Media Arts and Technology, University of California, Santa Barbara (2007)
13. Overholt, D.: The Musical Interface Technology Design Space. Organised Sound 14(2), 217–226 (2009), doi:10.1017/S1355771809000326
14. Overholt, D.: The Overtone Fiddle: An Actuated Acoustic Instrument. In: Proceedings of the 2011 International Conference on New Interfaces for Musical Expression (NIME 2002), Oslo, Norway (2011)
15. Paradiso, J.A.: Electronic Music: New ways to play. IEEE Spectrum 34(12), 18–30 (1997)
16. Roads, C.: An Interview with Max Mathews. Reprinted in Roads, C. (ed.) The Music Machine, pp. 5–12. The MIT Press, Cambridge (1989)
17. Rose, J.: Improvisation and Interactive Technology, a Letter to LMC Magazine, http://www.sysx.org/soundsite/texts/CHAOTIC.html (accessed November 3, 2011)
18. Schoonderwaldt, E., Rasamimanana, N., Bevilacqua, F.: Combining accelerometer and video camera: reconstruction of bow velocity profiles. In: Proceedings of the 2006 International Conference on New Interfaces for Musical Expression (NIME 2002), Paris (2006)
19. Trueman, D.: Reinventing the Violin. Ph.D. dissertation. Princeton University (1999)
20. Wanderley, M.M.: Performer-Instrument Interaction: Applications to Gestural Control of Music. Ph.D thesis. University Pierre et Marie Curie - Paris VI, Paris (2001)

Artistic Rendering of Human Portraits Paying Attention to Facial Features

Mahdi Rezaei

Dept. of Computer Science, The University of Auckland, New Zealand
mrez010@aucklanduni.ac.nz

Abstract. Artistic painting of human portraits are more challenging than landscapes or flowers. Challenges are eye and nose areas where we need to avoid alterations from their natural appearance. Shades or darkness around eyes, or shininess at the nose tip may negatively impact the rendering result if not properly dealt with. The proposed computerized method attempts to be adaptive to those sensitive areas by utilizing a face analysis module. First, the program detects meaningful face segments, and then it utilizes a blending of various filtering parameters to make the final portrait as clear as possible while still supporting an 'artistic painting' in overall.

Keywords: Non-photorealistic rendering, artistic filter, pointillism, Glass pattern, curves and strokes style, facial features.

1 Introduction

Photorealistic rendering aims at creating digital images that look like a photograph. In contrast, *non-photorealistic rendering* (NPR) produces images of simulated worlds, in styles that are different to realism [1]. An artistic filter implements a non-photorealistic rendering technique for transforming a given image with some 'artistic effect' (Fig. 1). Those effects aim to emulate the styles followed by painters, such as impressionism or cubism. Digital NPR bring together art and image processing [2]. Nevertheless, a real painter is normally better at determining what visual style has the best artistic effect, since creativity itself cannot be easily simulated by a computer.

NPR rendering for a flower, a building, or a landscape are considerably easier than a human face. NPR program easily fails on facial features. A program may

Fig. 1. A portrait photograph and a digital NPR example of this photo [1]

A.L. Brooks (Ed.): ArtsIT 2011, LNICST 101, pp. 90–99, 2012.

have difficulties in understanding why a shade around one eye should not lead to a different representation compared to the other eye,or a specularity on a nose should not lead to bended 'brush strokes' around the specularity. The paper proposes an NPR approach that combines options for creative artistic rendering (based on prior work [4]) with a new focus on human portrait particularities, resulting altogether in an artistic painting style.

2 Related Works

A variety of painterly rendering techniques were developed in the early 1990s, starting with Haeberli's pioneering work in [6], which introduced computerized paintings with an ordered collection of strokes described by size, shape, colour, and orientation. The method tried to simulate an impressionistic style. Hertzmann et al. described a two-phase framework called 'image analogies' [3]. In the first phase (the 'design phase'), they used a pair of images, one original image and one filtered image as the training data. Then, in the second phase (the 'application phase'), and following by texture synthesis, the learned filter is applied to some new target images to develop analogous filtered images.

Papari and Petkov [5] proposed an idea to replace natural texture in an input image, with a synthetic painterly texture that is generated by means of a continuous Glass pattern, while its geometrical structure is controlled by the gradient orientation of the input image.

Valente and Klette [4] developed a triangular user interface that allows the user to select different styles of painting according to the users taste (Fig. 2). Each corner of the triangle represents one style, and any point inside the triangle means a combination of two painting style.

DiPaola provided an interdisciplinary method that uses a parametrised approach to approximate a knowledge domain for painterly rendering of portraits [7]. The knowledge domain uses fuzzy knowledge rules gained from interviews with oil portrait painters, data from the traditional 'portrait painter process' combined with human vision techniques and semantic models of the face and upper torso. Except Dipaola's, none of the other NPR works focused on sensitive facial features so far.

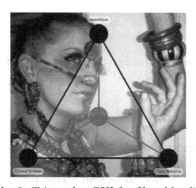

Fig. 2. Triangular GUI for filter blending

3   Painting Styles and Filter Design

As the first step we briefly review on simulation of three painting styles namely *curves-and-strokes*, *pointillism*, and *Glass pattern* which are provided by [4]. Then in section 4, we go for facial feature detection (eye and nose regions), and finally we apply a softened filtering approach in eye and nose regions to generate a more pleasant and sensible artistic renderings.

3.1   Curves-and-Strokes Filter

This filter generates an output image with an appearance of hand-painted brushes. The important point in this method is how to put strokes on the canvas by an appropriate brush size in different areas of images. The algorithm is a three layer painting, takes the source image, and then determines the following information:

- Image size (W_i, H_i)
- Face detection and then detecting face width (W_f)
- Proportional size of detected *face* to the entire *image size* $(p\%)$

Details of face detection and localization are described in Section 4. Based on the p value and inspiring by [3], we select three brush sizes $R_1 = 0.02 \cdot W_i$, $R_2 = 0.01 \cdot W_i$, $R_3 = 0.006 \cdot H_i$. With those brush sizes we got a satisfying appearance. The method starts putting the strokes on the canvas with the largest brush (R_1). To a painter, a painting seems more artistic and professional, if we use mainly larger brushes and just use smaller brushes only in sensitive regions to show details. Therefore, at first, we paint the whole image with the largest brush R_1. Then, applying a convolution of the created painting with the source image, the algorithm determines the mean colour difference to the source image. If the difference is greater than a threshold T, then next smaller brush repaints the canvas, otherwise it remains unchanged:

```
function paint(sourceImage, R m ... R n)
        {
            canvas = a new constant color image
            // paint the canvas
                for (i=n ; i > m ; i--)
                from largest brush to smallest do
                    {
                        // Apply Brush R i
                        Canvas = sourceImage * I(R i);
                        // Threshold in painted layer
                        Threshold (canvas, SourceImage, R i, T i)
                            If (T i <= T) then
                                Exit (loop);
                    }
            return canvas;
        }
```

Following the above algorithm, we will have two benefits of having a more artistic appearance, as well as a logarithmically decrease in computational cost. Figure 3 shows a sample result. The overall output looks pleasant, however, the eyes seem abnormally deviated from their natural appearance, and the nose also a

Fig. 3. Curved brush strokes on a sample portrait with bright eyes and light skin

bit bended. a simple way to fix this problem, is using a smaller brush sizes for the whole painting, to sustain more similarity to the reference image. In spite of the fact that this basic solution can solves the eye and nose problem, but the overall level of artistic painting decrease. As a better approach we tried to keep painting the images at first with larger brushes, then using smaller strokes and brushes *just* for the eye region, as well as applying some image enhancement in the nose area. Section 4, provides the detail for eye and nose detection method.

3.2 Pointillism

For emulating pointillism, it is helpful to apply Seurat's theoretical work [9]. There are two main reasons for computerizing pointillism. The painting process of pointillism is highly exhausting, so unloading the main proportion of the manual painting task is very desirable. Secondly, we are able to approximate pointillism by simpler point-like strokes. For emulating pointillism, we break up the image into three layers, each of which distributes the points in different ways.

The background layer fills up the canvas with large points which have minimal colour distortion. The middle layer adds smaller dots of stronger colours to areas where the brightness of the picture differs from the original by a threshold T_p. The final layer provides some edge enhancement to prevent details so far hidden by the larger dots. At each layer, dots are painted in a random order by using a Z-buffer, where each point's Z-value is initialized by a random number.

Fig. 4. Illustration of a naive emulation of a pointillistic painting. Defected eyes and nose issues (e.g. 'holes') can be seen on the right.

As an advantage comparing to curved strokes method, this filter uses only two parameters that need to be altered. The values that need to be defined is the brush size R and the decreasing rate of size for each layer (default $d = 25\%$). To make it simple, uniform circles of plain colours are used in the implementation. The filter emulates Seurat's painting style by breaking the image into a series of points, restricting the colour palette, and incorporating the idea of divisionism. Figure 4 shows a pointillistic painting. In this sample we have multiple faces, so we consider the average width of detected face as W_f.

3.3 Glass Patterns

This filter generates impressionistic images in the style of Van Gogh; inherent geometric structures are modeled as Glass patterns and transformed into the target image via a random point set. The geometric transformation uses information about the image's gradient to create an effect of impressionistic whirls around image contours. The algorithm is a modified version of the work by Papari and Petkov [5]. Similar to curves-and-strokes and pointillism, we implemented a code based on OpenCV that defines two parameters of Glass patterns (GP), the step size (h) and the standard deviation based on the proportion of the face size to the image size, $\rho = \frac{W_f}{W_I}$, and a grid histogram deviation, respectively. The initial step in the Glass pattern method is an edge preserving smoothing (EPS), which eliminates small textures from the input image while keeping the main object contours. We denote the output of EPS by $I_{EPS}(r)$. The next step is the generation of synthetic painterly textures (SPT) which simulates oriented brush strokes. Assume $\nabla_\sigma I_{EPS}$ as the scale-dependent gradient of I_{EPS}, which is created by convolution of I_{EPS} with the gradient of the Gauss function g_σ:

$$\nabla_\sigma I_{EPS} = I_{EPS} * \nabla_{g_\sigma}$$

Finally we apply a typical Glass pattern such as shown in Fig. 5 at random locations of the image with different strengths of S between 0 to 1. The whirl value θ_w can be a random or a fixed value equals $\pi/4$, $\pi/2$, $3\pi/4$, or π.

The implemented filter gives the look of an impressionistic oil painting by shifting pixels around the canvas in a pattern of impressionistic whirls. The Glass pattern is successful in providing 'pleasant' visual effects for small images, but, because colour values rotate around some fix points, it does not apply well to large portraits, and again some refinements in eye areas are compulsory (Fig. 6).

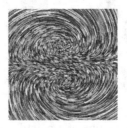

Fig. 5. A sample whirled Glass pattern

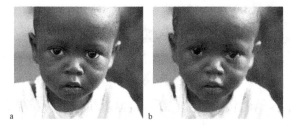

a   b

Fig. 6. Naive impressionistic-style emulation for dark skin subject, showing distortion in the eye regions

4   Haar Classifiers for Face, Eye and Nose Detection

For the facial component detection, we apply Haar-like feature matching based on the Viola-Jones object detection ideas [8] and our previous work [10]. Figure 7 shows mapping the Haar wavelet into a 2D image processing concept and a corresponding Haar feature in common black-white representation.

4.1   Detector Structure

The detector combines three techniques: (1) the use of a comprehensive set of Haar-like features that are in analogy to base functions of the Haar transform (Fig. 8), (2) the application of a boosted algorithm to select a limited set of appropriate Haar features for classifier training, and (3) forming a cascade of strong classifiers by merging week classifiers.

The detection process of a query object (e.g. a face) is based on some important characteristics of the object and the value distributions in dark or light regions of a feature that models expected intensity distributions. For example, the feature in Fig. 9, left, relates to the idea that in all faces there are darker regions of eyes compared to the bridge of the nose. Similarly, Fig. 9, right, models that the central part of an eye (the iris) is darker than the sclera.

4.2   Integral Image

To determine the presence or absence of Haar-like features, we use *integral images*. For pixel $p = (x, y)$, the *integral value*

$$I(p) = \sum_{1 \leq i \leq x \wedge 1 \leq j \leq y} P(i, j)$$

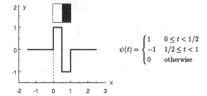

$$\psi(t) = \begin{cases} 1 & 0 \leq t < 1/2 \\ -1 & 1/2 \leq t < 1 \\ 0 & \text{otherwise} \end{cases}$$

Fig. 7. Haar wavelet specification

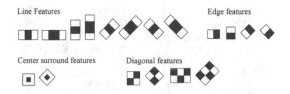

Line Features   Edge features

Center surround features   Diagonal features

Fig. 8. Main categories and shapes of Haar-like features

is the sum of all pixel values $P(q)$, where pixel $q = (i, j)$ is above and left of p.

Considering $p_1, \ldots, p_4$ as the corners of rectangle D, the sum of all pixel values for D equals (see Fig. 10)

$$I(D) = I(p_4) + I(p_1) - I(p_2) - I(p_3)$$

Then, we follow with a Haar-like feature such as $R_1 R_2 R_3$. After calculating $I(R_i)$, values at rectangular regions are weighted by reals $\omega_i > 0$, defining regional values $\omega_i \cdot I(R_i)$. In combination, regional values define the *feature value* for a given *Haar-like feature*. For the above example, we have that $I(F_k) = \omega_1 \cdot I(R_1) - \omega_2 \cdot I(R_2) + \omega_3 \cdot I(R_3)$. Since the region R_2 is black, thus the weight ω_2 is negative, opposite to those of R_1 and R_3.

5   Cascaded Classifiers and Experimental Results

In order to classify object regions of a face such as eye and nose, we use a sliding window to search the image area in different sizes to match different Haar-like features. Figure 11 shows the structure of a cascaded classifiers. We used AdaBoost machine learning to select appropriate Haar-like features among thousands of possible Haar-like features, for each stage of the classifier. Applying an image data set of positive face images, the machine learning algorithm analyses the provided features F_k and adjusts weights W_k, thresholds T_k, and other parameters to maximize the performance according to the goal of detecting the faces. Heavily weighted filters come first, to eliminate non-face image regions as quickly as possible. The initial classifier simply rejects non-object (none-face) regions, if the basic predefined features do not exist.

If an image region includes this feature set with a value greater than the predefined threshold τ, then the system goes for the next stage, otherwise it rejects the region as being a non-object. more details in our previous work [10].

Fig. 9. Application of two sample rectangular features for face and eye detection

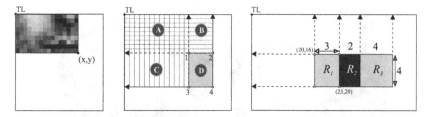

Fig. 10. Calculating integral values for a pixel, a rectangle, and a Haar-like feature

6 Filter Blending

Assume $Img1$ as the input portrait. Before applying an artistic filter, we run the face, eye and nose detector. Then we save an unchanged copy of these detected regions as $Eye1L$, $Eye1R$, $Nose1$ (original eyes and nose). We also save the position ans size of these regions as (x_i, y_i, w_i, h_i). Then, we apply artistic rendering with default parameters set of A to the original image ($Img1$) and we save the new image as $Img2$. afterwards, we apply artistic rendering with modified parameters set of B (as defined in 3.1., 3.2., and 3.3.) on three regions of $Eye1L$, $Eye1R$, $Nose1$ and save the resulted regions as $Eye2L$, $Eye2R$, and $Nose2$. Parameters set of B actually applies smoother effects than parameters set of A. Finally, we remove harsh regions of eye and nose from $Img2$, and replace new smoothed eyes and nose at the same places of x_i, y_i. The final result is $Img3$.

7 Experimental Results and Conclusions

Figures 12, 13, and 14 show the final images for three discussed artistic rendering. The paper utilized a hybrid approach of artistic rendering and facial feature detection to emulate portrait painting in NPR style. The experimental results for three techniques of curves-and-stokes, pointillism, and Glass patterns are satisfying in terms of eye and nose improvements while keeping the overall painting interesting in appearance. As future work, the method could be expanded for other artistic styles. Also, developing a method to ensure 'non-uniform' borders would make the rendered image more similar to a real painter's artwork.

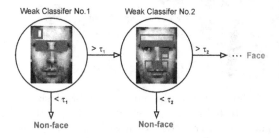

Fig. 11. Haar-feature matching inside the weak classifiers

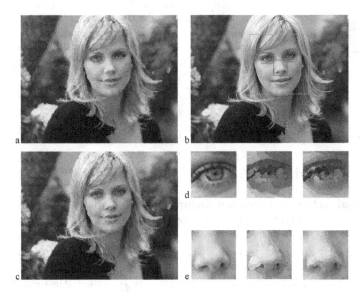

Fig. 12. Curve and Stroke Painting. (a): Initial output with max brush size $R_M = 7$, min brush size $R_n = 3$. (b): Detected face/eye, and, blurred nose with Gaussian aperture width of $p = 11$ (d), (e) centre: Before modification. (d), (e) right: Eye and nose modification with $R_{f_M} = 0.85R_M$ and $R_{f_n} = 0.33R_n$. (c): Final result.

Fig. 13. Pointillistic Painting. (a): Initial output with brush size of $R = 5$ and stroke strength of $s = 1$ (b): Detected faces, eyes and noses (d), (e), (f) centre: Before modification. (d), (e) right: Eyes after modification with $b_e = 0.58R$ and $s_e = s$. (f) right: Nose modification with $b_n = 0.7R$ and $s_n = 0.8s$. (c): Final result.

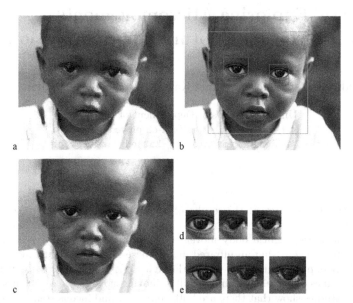

Fig. 14. Glass pattern painting. (a): Initial output with GP step size of h=0.4, $\theta_w = \pi/2$, and s= 0.5 (b): Detected face and eyes. (d), (e) centre: Before modification, (d), (e) right: After modification with $h_f = 0.3h$ and $s_f = 0.8s$. (c): Final result. Note: no nose detection and modification is required in Glass pattern painting.

References

1. Mignotte, M.: Unsupervised Statistical Sketching for Non-photorealistic Rendering Models. In: International Conference on Image Processing, Barcelona, Spain, vol. III, pp. 573–576 (2003)
2. Gooch, B., Gooch, A.: Non-Photorealistic Rendering. AK Peters Ltd. Publisher (2001)
3. Hertzmann, A., Jacobs, C., Oliver, N., Curless, B., Salesin, D.: Image analogies. In: Proc. SIGGRAPH, pp. 327–340 (2001)
4. Valente, C., Klette, R.: Artistic Emulation - Filter Blending for Painterly Rendering. In: Proc. Fourth Pacific-Rim Symposium on Image and Video Technology, Singapore, pp. 462–467 (2010)
5. Papari, G., Petkov, N.: Continuous Glass patterns for painterly rendering. IEEE Trans. Image Processing 18, 652–664 (2009)
6. Haeberli, P.: Paint by numbers: Abstract image representations. In: Proc. SIGGRAPH, pp. 207–214 (1990)
7. DiPaola, S.: Exploring a Parametrised Portrait Painting Space. Int. Journal of Art and Technology 2, 82–93 (2009)
8. Viola, P., Jones, M.: Rapid object detection using a boosted cascade of simple features. In: CVPR, pp. 511–518 (2001)
9. Yang, C.K., Yang, H.L.: Realization of Seurat's pointillism via non-photorealistic rendering. The Visual Computer 24, 303–322 (2008)
10. Rezaei, M., Klette, R.: 3D Cascade of Classifiers for Open and Closed Eye Detection in Driver Distraction Monitoring. In: Real, P., Diaz-Pernil, D., Molina-Abril, H., Berciano, A., Kropatsch, W. (eds.) CAIP 2011, Part II. LNCS, vol. 6855, pp. 171–179. Springer, Heidelberg (2011)

Exploring Micromovements
with Motion Capture and Sonification

Alexander Refsum Jensenius[1] and Kari Anne Vadstensvik Bjerkestrand[2]

[1] University of Oslo, Department of Musicology
[2] Bjerkestrand(self-employed)
a.r.jensenius@imv.uio.no, ka@bodymindflow.com

Abstract. We present the results of a pilot study on how micromovements may be used in an interactive dance/music performance. Micromovements are subtle body movements that cannot be easily seen by the human eye. Using an infrared marker-based motion capture system we have explored micromovements through 15x10 minutes long observation studies of ourselves standing still or moving slowly. The results from these studies show that there are both consistent and inconsistent movement patterns to be found at various temporal levels. Experimentation with three different types of realtime sonification shows artistic potential in using micromovements in dance and music performance.

Keywords: micromovement, dance, motion capture, sonification.

1 Introduction

Is it possible for humans to stand absolutely still? What types of micromovements are found when standing still? How can such micromovements be used in interactive dance/music performance? These are some of the questions we wanted to answer in the pilot project *Sverm* that we report on in this paper.

Our interest in, and methodological approaches to, the topic of micromovement are based on our backgrounds in music (first author) and dance (second author). Body movement is at the forefront in both music and dance, although for different reasons. The body movements of a musician are mainly *sound-producing*, while the movements of a dancer are often *sound-accompanying*. This traditional separation between musician and dancer is currently being challenged (see, e.g., [1]) with the increasing use of *motion capture* technologies that allow a dancer to create sound in realtime while moving, or for musicians to move more freely when playing.

The pilot project *Sverm* grew out of an interest in creating an interactive dance performance that would focus on the absence of movement: *standstill*. In our experience remarkably little is known about standstill in the fields of dance and music. Standstill is often regarded as uninteresting or the "fill" between actions or gestures, similar to how musicians and musicologists do not spend much time talking about *silence*. But in the same way that silence can be very

A.L. Brooks (Ed.): ArtsIT 2011, LNICST 101, pp. 100–107, 2012.

powerful in music, as perhaps most famously documented in Cage's 4'33", we believe that standstill can be an interesting concept to work from in dance.

But what is standstill? As living human beings, physical standstill is not possible to achieve. Most life processes, including in plants, in animals and in human beings, are carried out in recurring cycles [2]. The periods of such cycles vary greatly: from the "nanomovement" of atoms in our cells, breathing and pulse cycles every few seconds, 24 hour sleep/wake cycles, yearly cycles in nature, and up to light-year cycles in the movement of planetary systems. Within this physical world, temporal coordination and adaptation are required for all living beings for survival, and this is the field of study in *chronobiology*. But how does the different chronobiological levels influence the performance and perception of music and dance?

We find it useful to differentiate between three different temporal levels: *micro*, *meso* and *macro*, which coincide with the three main levels of our memory [3]. The *micro* level describes events at the scale of milliseconds. Human experience within these ranges typically falls within the limits of the sensory memory, and is the basis for the experience of the other levels. The *meso* level falls within the boundaries of our short-term or working memory and constitutes most of human utterances (spoken words, musical phrases, etc.) and most everyday actions (opening a door, etc.). Finally, the *macro* level is founded in the long-term memory and is here used as a general term for all activities that are longer than the meso level. We should not forget that in the physical world there is a continuum from the smallest perceivable units to the largest. The experience of the micro, meso and macro levels is based on the limitations (and possibilities) of the human perceptual and cognitive system.

In dance and music the meso and macro levels are often the focus of attention: actions, gestures, phrases and large-scale form. The micro level, both spatially and temporally, is usually regarded more as fine-tuning of technique than as a meaning-bearing component in itself. However, there are some examples of composers and researchers that investigate microlevels in music, e.g., the exploration of microsound using granular sound synthesis techniques [4], and microrhythmic patterns and effects [5]. In the world of movement there are long traditions of *slow* movement in, e.g., Tai chi chuan, which inspired the second author's performance in the piece *10:50–11:00* [6]. But although such practice may also include micromovements to some extent, there are to our knowledge few examples of exploring the micromovements themselves, or standstill, in dance performance. Also *interactive* dance performances seem to focus mainly on large-scale movement, e.g., [7,8]. This has made us curious to see how micromovements, as observed in standstill, can be used in an interactive dance performance.

This paper starts by presenting a series of observation studies on standstill and slow movement that we have carried out to learn more about micromovements. This is followed by a presentation of some sonification strategies that may be used when working with such movements in creative practice. Finally, we suggest some possible directions in our future research and artistic activities.

2   Observation Studies of Micromovements

To learn more about micromovements, we decided to carry out a series of observation studies where we would stand still or move slowly for 10 minutes at a time, as summarized in Table 1. First we did five standstill sessions, each with a slightly different mental strategy: attempting to stand physically still (1), mentally still (2), and two different types of imagined movement (3–4). All of these studies were done standing straight with the arms hanging down, but we also did one session with the arms straight in front of us (5). Next we did five recordings where we moved slowly in different patterns: shifting the weight back and forth between the legs (6), rotating the upper body (7), bending the knees (8), and head (only) movement in the three different planes (9–11). Finally, we did four more standstill studies (12–15) with the same mental strategies that we had used in the first recordings (1–4).

Table 1. Overview of the 15 different 10-minute observation studies conducted

#	Standstill	#	Movement	#	Standstill
1	Physical standstill	6	Weight shift (pendulum)	12	Physical standstill
2	Mental standstill	7	Rotation (upper body)	13	Mental standstill
3	Mental movement	8	Knee bending	14	Mental movement
4	Mental movement	9	Head movement (sagittal)	15	Mental movement
5	Arms in front	10	Head movement (pendulum)		
		11	Head movement (rotation)		

2.1   Method

All sessions were carried out in the *fourMs* motion capture laboratories at the University of Oslo, and were recorded using an infrared marker-based motion capture system from Qualisys (9 Oqus 300 cameras) running at 100 Hz. For the first sessions we only used a few markers each (on the neck, head and on the feet and hands), but added more markers in some of the later sessions. After each 10-minute recording session we talked about the experience, and took notes of each other's immediate and subjective comments. These notes, together with analysis of the motion capture data carried out in Matlab using the MoCap toolbox [9], form the basis for our analysis of the material.

Before we started the study we thought that the standstill recordings would not be particularly interesting, and that they would mainly serve as a reference point for the recordings of movements. However, we have found the standstill recordings to be very interesting, so the following sections will mainly focus on some of these recordings (1–3 and 12–14). Furthermore, to constrain the analysis, we will mainly focus on the marker placed on the neck, at the cervical spinal #7 (C7). The neck marker is particularly relevant, since it represents a point on the body that is fairly stable (more so than the head or hands), yet it reveals micromovements of the body very well.

2.2   How Much Movement?

How still is it possible to stand? Our subjective experience was that we did move quite a lot: shifting weight between the legs, swaying, breathing, swallowing, etc. These movements were small, but they were easily noticeable to ourselves and to each other during the sessions.

Table 2 shows a summary of the distance travelled for two markers per person: one placed on the right foot (rFoot) and one placed on the neck (C7). As a reference of the precision of the motion capture system, we have also included the distance travelled for a static marker placed on the floor next to us. Since this marker did not move at all, its value can be seen as the error margin of the recordings. This error is based on a combination of the resolution of the cameras and the calibration of the system. By comparing the movement of the feet to that of the reference marker, we see that the feet moved very little, and only marginally more than the reference. For recording 12, A-rFoot even moved less than the reference marker, but this is within the error margin of the system.

Table 2. Summary of the distance travelled (in meters) for markers on the right foot and at C7 for each of the 6 standstill studies

#	Static	A-rFoot	A-C7	KA-rFoot	KA-C7
1	1.10	1.15	2.85	1.19	5.89
2	1.01	1.06	2.90	1.49	5.02
3	1.09	1.25	2.76	1.41	5.39
12	1.10	0.99	2.45	1.40	4.20
13	0.95	0.99	2.72	1.17	3.79
14	1.00	1.11	2.85	1.81	4.96

If we look at the results from the markers placed on the neck, A-C7 and KA-C7 respectively, we see that there is considerably more movement. Here we see that the results for the first author (A-C7) are generally quite low for all 6 recordings. The results for the three last recordings are slightly lower than for the first recordings, but not more than could be explained by the error margin. Even though the variation is larger for the second author (KA-C7), we see that she was standing more still in the three last recordings than in the first ones. This could be due to a heightened awareness developed over the course of the sessions, but it is difficult to draw any conclusions from this limited study.

By plotting the cumulative distances travelled for the above-mentioned markers, we see that the movement was more or less evenly distributed over the course of the 10-minute long sessions (Figure 1), as expected.

2.3   Micro, Meso and Macro Level Activity

Let us know turn to investigate the movement of a single marker for all sessions. Figure 2 shows plots of the neck marker (A-C7 and KA-C7) for recordings 1–3 and 12–14. The most important finding at the micro level is that there are, indeed, no signs of standstill: there is continuous movement at the scale of millimetres in all recordings.

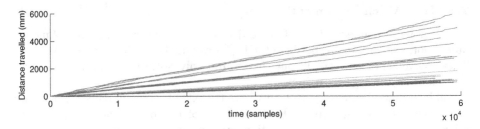

Fig. 1. Cumulative distances travelled for markers Static, A-rFoot, A-C7, KA-rFoot, KA-C7 for recordings 1–3 and 12–14

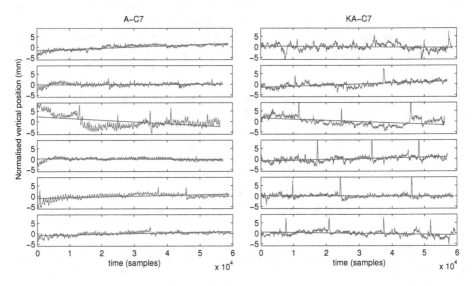

Fig. 2. Plots of the normalised vertical position of the neck marker (C7) for recordings 1–3 and 12–14 for the two authors (A and KA). The straight line indicates the slope of the data set.

At the meso level we can see from the plots that there are peaks in the signal approximately every 5–10 seconds. Estimating the periodicity of the signals, using the *mcperiod* function in the MoCap Toolbox [10], reveals average periodicities in the vertical dimension at 6.0 ± 1.4 seconds and 9.1 ± 2.5 seconds for the two authors respectively. This periodicity most likely corresponds to the breathing pattern, and is something that it will be interesting to explore further in a performance setting.

At the macro level we see that linear regression gives a positive slope in 4 of 6 of the first author's sessions and 3 of 6 for the second author. We believe this can be explained by tension and/or fatigue, something we discussed several times in our post-recording talks. Sometimes we felt that we raised the shoulders because of fatigue, other times we worked towards lowering the shoulders as we straightened the back. This is also something that can be used as a feature in performance.

The most surprising finding from the quantitative analysis is the "spikes" that can be seen in each recording. These are particularly prominent in the recordings of the second author, happening every 2–3 minutes in all recordings. These spikes can probably be explained by postural readjustment, and we are very curious to see whether similar spikes can be seen also in other people standing still.

2.4   Movement Patterns

What types of rotational movement patterns can be found? As the XY plots in Figure 3 show, more movement is happening along the Y-axis (front–back) than on the X-axis (left–right). This can be explained by the feet stabilising the sideways movement more than the front–back movement.

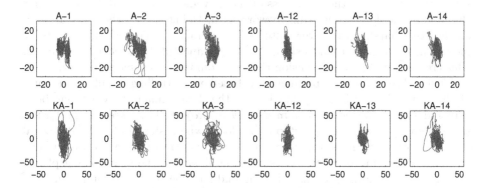

Fig. 3. XY movement patterns of the C7 marker from recordings 1–3 and 12–14 for the two authors (A and KA). The plots can be seen as the left–right (X-axis) and front–back (Y-axis, face pointing upwards) movement of the neck marker.

3   Sonification of Micromovements

The subjective experience of the recording sessions, and subsequent analytical work, made us eager to start exploring how the micromovement data could be turned into sound through, i.e., *sonification* of the data. Since the aim of this work is to create an interactive dance performance, this exploration was mainly driven from an artistic point of view. Using the Qualisys motion capture system in realtime mode, we explored three different types of sonification:

- Sine tones controlled by the vertical position of individual markers.
- Noise controlled by the quantity of motion, with two different mappings: a) more motion produced more sound, b) less motion produced more sound.
- Sample playback using granular synthesis controlled by horizontal position.

We started out by controlling a single sine tone with the vertical position of one marker. The aim was to see if we could "hear" the micromovements happening when standing still. For that reason we created a mapping from a small region (5 cm) to a large frequency range (200–5000 Hz). The effect was dramatic, as, e.g., breathing and heartbeats could easily be heard. We expanded the concept by adding more markers coupled to individual sine tones. This way it was possible to hear how different parts of the body moved at different paces (hands, shoulders, head). We also found it particularly interesting to place markers in close vicinity of each other, e.g., two markers on each hand, something that made it possible to play with interference patterns when the frequencies of the sine tones were close to each other.

For the second experiment, with white noise, we explored two strategies: either the level of noise would increase when there was more movement, or it would decrease. We found both of these approaches conceptually challenging to work with. Coupling sound level to quantity of motion is a logical mapping, as the sonification heightens the awareness of the movement. But we did not feel that this was particularly interesting to work with. Doing it the other way around, on the other hand, led to a very interesting interaction: the performer starts by moving in silence, and then as she approaches standstill the noise level increases. This created an interesting tension that we would like to explore further.

The third sonification experiment was based on controlling the playback point of short sound recordings by moving on the floor, similar to what has been explored in the *Embodied Generative Music* project [11]. Here the performer would move to a specific point on the floor, where she would spend several minutes working with micromovements to explore subtleties in the sound. The intuitive connection between location on the floor and the sound being played back gave the performer a sense of being in direct control of the sound, and was very inspiring to work with.

4   Conclusions

From the analysis of six of our standstill recordings we can conclude the following:

- It is not possible to stand still. Micromovements can be felt by the performer, can to some extent be seen by an observer, and can easily be picked up by a motion capture system.
- The level of standstill that it is possible to achieve is fairly stable and reproducible for one person.
- Different mental strategies for standing still did not change the quantitative results, but they changed the performer's own experience. Whether the mental strategy could be experienced by an observer should be investigated further.
- Breathing is the most important factor for movements at the temporal meso level, and postural adjustment at the temporal macro level. Periodicities at the temporal micro level need to be investigated further.

The analytical findings will be used as the basis for creating movement–sound mappings in our interactive dance performance. Through our preliminary exploration of sonification strategies we can conclude:

- The standstill–noise mapping was the most interesting for exploring stand-still, since the presence of sound heightened the sensation of standing still.
- It was interesting to explore beating patterns of sine tones when using two or more markers in close vicinity.
- The granulation experiment made it possible to explore microsound through micromovements very intuitively.

Future work include:

- conducting more standstill studies of ourselves, movement experts (musicians/dancers) and non-experts. The aim will be to discover more movement features that reliably can be used in performance.
- exploring how the different sonification strategies work with multiple performers, including testing out various types of sound spatialisation algorithms.
- exploring how our current ideas and technologies can be used in real performance in a theatre setting.

Acknowledgments. The project has been supported by Arts Council Norway, Norwegian Research Council, and University of Oslo.

References

1. Jensenius, A.R., Johnson, V.: Performing the electric violin in a sonic space. Computer Music Journal (in review)
2. Klein, G.: Farewell to the internal clock: a contribution in the field of chronobiology. Springer, New York (2007)
3. Snyder, B.: Music and Memory: An Introduction. The MIT Press, Cambridge (2000)
4. Roads, C.: Microsound. The MIT Press, Cambridge (2001)
5. Danielsen, A. (ed.): Musical Rhythm in the Age of Digital Reproduction. Ashgate, Farnham (2010)
6. Jacobsson, S., Bjerkestrand, K.A.V.: 10:50–11:00 (video) (2005), http://youtu.be/y3gecc2_4xy (last checked: 10.11.2011)
7. Dobrian, C., Bevilacqua, F.: Gestural control of music: using the Vicon 8 motion capture system. In: Proceedings of the International Conference on New Interfaces for Musical Expression, Montreal, pp. 161–163 (2003)
8. Downie, M.: Choreographing the Extended Agent: Performance Graphics for Dance Theater. PhD thesis, MIT, Cambridge, MA (2005)
9. Toiviainen, P., Burger, B.: MoCap Toolbox Manual. University of Jyväskylä, Jyväskylä (2010)
10. Eerola, T., Luck, G., Toiviainen, P.: An investigation of pre-schoolers' corporeal synchronization with music. In: Proceedings of the 9th International Conference on Music Perception & Cognition, Bologna, pp. 472–476 (2006)
11. Peters, D.: Enactment in listening: Intermedial dance in EGM sonic scenarios and the bodily grounding of the listening experience. Performance Research 15, 81–87 (2010)

Generating Time-Coherent Animations from Video Data

Javier Villegas and George Legrady

Experimental Visualization Lab,
Media Arts and Technology Department,
University of California Santa Barbara, Santa Barbara CA 93106, USA
jvillegas@umail.ucsb.edu
http://www.mat.ucsb.edu/jvillegas

Abstract. In this paper, a series of techniques for the creation of time coherent animations from a video input is presented. The animations are generated using an analysis-synthesis approach. Information of the scene is extracted using only a 2D RGB image. No markers or depth images are needed. After the analysis, the image is drawn again using the extracted information. To guarantee temporal coherence when redrawing the image, different alternatives have been explored: Interpolation on the parameters' domain and gradient descent parameter update. The different methods are described and illustrated with images.

Keywords: Computer animation, analysis-synthesis, time coherency.

1 Introduction

Music composers have been using analysis synthesis (A/S) techniques for years. In this set of approaches, a signal is decomposed into different parts and then the set of parts is used to rebuild the signal. In between the two A/S processes, the constituent parts of the signal can be manipulated creatively to generate significant alterations of the original sound while keeping its identity. With this strategy, different manipulation of the audio signal are possible: independent pitch and duration modification, dispersion, robotization , whispering or automatic pitch tunning[19]. An (A/S) approach can also be used on images. Some of the art works of Knowlton [11], Silvers [17], Levin [13,12] or Rozin [4] are examples of A/S techniques applied to still images with creative purposes. Figure 1 shows the output of different A/S processes when the input is the picture of a face.

If A/S strategies are extended to moving images simply by independent processing of every frame, coherency problems will occur. Synthesis objects can suddenly appear, disappear or their parameters can change abruptly. A distracting flickering artifact that is often non desirable will be present. Although this paper focuses on finding strategies for temporal coherency on animations created with an A/S process, similar problems had been explored by the academic community interested on generalize the stylized rendering of still images

A.L. Brooks (Ed.): ArtsIT 2011, LNICST 101, pp. 108–117, 2012.

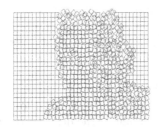

Fig. 1. Different examples of A/S processes applied on a still image

to animations. Bousseau et al [5] presented a technique to create time coherent watercolorizations. They applied deformations to the watercolor textures, using optic flow information from the input sequence. Meier [16], used particles over 3D surfaces to keep track of the position and direction of brush strokes in consecutive frames of pure synthetic non photorealistic scenes. Litwinowicz [14] developed a technique to create hand-painted-looking image animations. He used the edges map of an input image to constrain the length of strokes, then he used optical flow to ensure coherence of the strokes between successive frames. A similar approach but oriented to interactive real-time application was created by Hertzmann and Perlin [10]. Bernard et al had explored the use of dynamic textures and Gabor noise primitives to create time coherent stylizations [1,2]. Finally, in Animosaics [18], Smith, Liu and Klein explored rules for the smooth motion of mosaic tiles in animated mosaics. They pursued not only coherence between individual elements, but cohesion in the movement of groups of tiles.

This approach differs radically from the previously mentioned works. The main interest is not to recreate the look of hand painted images or artistic stiles on video sequences but to explore the narrative possibilities of A/S approaches on video signals with temporal coherence. Next two sections will show two different approaches to generate time coherent animations from video data. First, an approach based on the matching of closer objects in consecutive frames is presented. After the matching, the trajectory of the objects can be interpolated or smoothed. This approach possess some similarities with well known problems like the tracking of partials on audio signals with algorithms like the McAulay Quatieri[15] and the general assignment problem in combinatorial optimization [7]. Next we explore a gradient based approach where local rules followed by the synthesis elements recreate a global image. This strategy resembles works on generative computer art. On section 4, results are summarized and some possibilities for future explorations are presented.

2   Correspondences on the Parameters' Domain

Temporal coherence is lost when frames are analyzed independently because the parameters of objects in adjacent frames can change abruptly. Even more, the number of synthesis objects can be totally different in consecutive frames. This rapid appearing and disappearing of objects destroys the effect of motion at the local level and generates a disturbing popping artifact at a global scale. In order to create a coherent animation, the objects on consecutive frames have to be paired. To define this problem as a general linear assignment problem [7] the number of objects have to be the same on every frame. This obstacle is solved by allowing objects of null size (invisible objects) to exist on the less populated frames. This strategy is similar to the one followed in the seminal work of McAulay-Quatieri [15] to handle the death and birth of sinusoidal partials on adjacent audio frames. In their algorithm, they allowed sinusoidal partials of zero amplitude to be matched in previous and subsequent frames. With this consideration the object matching problem can be stated as a linear assignment problem as follows:

Given a cost matrix $C(m, m+1)$ of size $n \times n$ with elements C_{ij} that represents the euclidean distance between the parameters of every object i on frame m to every object j on frame $m + 1$. We want to find the assignment matrix $X(m)$ with elements X_{ij} defined as:

$$X_{ij} = \begin{cases} 1, & \text{if object } i \text{ on frame } m \text{ is matched} \\ & \quad \text{to object } j \text{ on frame } m + 1; \\ 0, & \text{Otherwise} \end{cases}$$

Such that the sum:

$$\sum_{i=1}^{n} \sum_{j=1}^{n} C_{ij} X_{ij} . \tag{1}$$

is minimized.

Subject to:

$$\sum_{j=1}^{n} X_{ij} = 1 \qquad\qquad (i = 1.2...n) .$$

$$\sum_{i=1}^{n} X_{ij} = 1 \qquad\qquad (j = 1.2...n) .$$

$$X_{ij} \in \{0, 1\} \qquad\qquad (i, j = 1.2...n) .$$

This is a standard optimization problem known as the assignment problem, many alternatives for solving this problem efficiently can be found on the literature [7]. After solving this assignment problem a time coherent animation can be produced in different ways:

- Smoothing the trajectories. This creates a trade-off between continuity and accuracy of representation.

– Interpolation. New frames can be generated by interpolating the parameters between the matched objects. A good representation accuracy can be accomplished but the frame rate has to be increased.

Figure 2 shows four frames of a video created with elliptic regions. The ellipse in red color is an example of a matched object.

Fig. 2. Four frames of a synthetic video showing in red an object as it was matched

3   Gradient Based Approach

Another alternative to guarantee temporal coherence is to define a set of rules on the synthesis elements. This set of rules will determine the local behavior of the synthesis objects. Global constraints on the object motion are determined by the input image from video data. This image is used to create a surface. The gradient of this surface is used to generate a vector field of forces that will affect the motion of the synthesis elements. Figure 3 shows a general diagram of this approach.

This approach resembles in some way the practice of generative art [9], where a set of rules is defined over a collection of elements that then behave with some degree of autonomy.

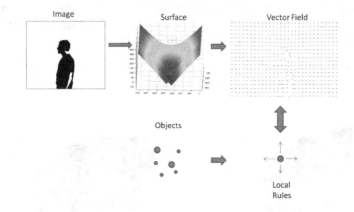

Fig. 3. The generative approach to time coherent animations

3.1   Example 1. A Dynamic Mesh Grid

Figure 4 shows a vector field, in this case generated directly form the gradient of a grayscale image. This vector field is used to attract the nodes of a grid to the dark areas of the input image and repel them from the bright ones. The resulting image is a grid that reassembles the video input. See Figure 5. Internal forces of the mesh such as tension or drag can be modified to produce different visual results.

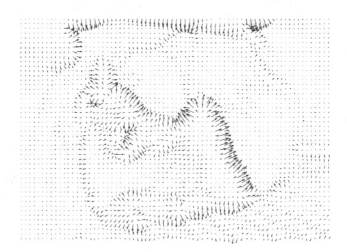

Fig. 4. The vector field obtained with the gradient of a grayscale image), and the mesh grid (Right)

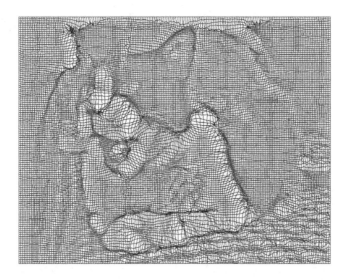

Fig. 5. Mesh grid generated with the vector field

3.2   Example 2. Circle Packing

Figure 6 shows a sequence of frames, where a set of circles of two different sizes are getting attracted by the black areas of a binary video. In order to produce this attraction, the black and white image is used to generate a surface by means of the distance transform. If we define the black pixels of the binary image I, as foreground F and the white ones as background B, then the value of a pixel p on the distance transform image is defined by:

$$Dt\,(p) = \min_{q \in F}\,(d\,(p,q)) \ . \tag{2}$$

A surface is then calculated as:

$$S\,(p) = Dt\,(p) - \bar{D}t\,(p) \ . \tag{3}$$

Where $\bar{D}t\,(p)$ is the distance transform of the logic complement of image I evaluated at pixel p. The gradient of this surface combined with a circle packing algorithm will determine the motion of every circle.

3.3   Example 3. Coherent Straight Lines

Almost the same set of steps used on the previous example can be applied on a different domain. For example to recreate the input image with straight lines moving with time coherency the following strategy can be used:

– Obtain the edge map of the image.

Fig. 6. Some frames of a gradient based animation. The circles started at random position and then they move according to a set of rules and constrained by a surface created with the input image.

- Calculate the Hough transform using the parametrization from [8].

$$r(\theta) = x \cos(\theta) + y \sin(\theta) \ . \tag{4}$$

(x, y) are the coordinates of pixels that belong to an edge.
- Low pass filter the Hough plane image, see left of Figure 7.

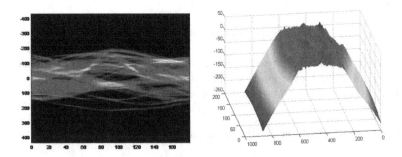

Fig. 7. Left - The low pass filtered version of the Hough transform of an edge image. Right - The surface created applying the distance transform to the Hough plane.

- Get a black and white image by thresholding the resulting image from the previous step.
- Generate a surface using the distance transform as shown in equations 2, 3. See right of Figure 7.
- Generate set of random points on Hough space uniformly distributed. Figure 8 (Left).

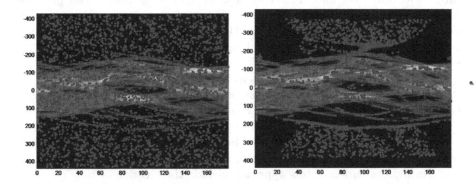

Fig. 8. Left - Random points uniformly distributed on the Hough plane. Right - Dots in the Hough space moving in direction of the peaks.

- Update the position of every point using the gradient of the distance transform and the circle packing algorithm to avoid point collisions. Figure 8 (Right).
- Convert points on Hough space back to lines on the original domain. Figure 9

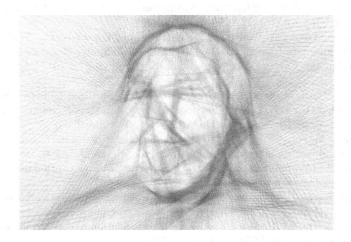

Fig. 9. The image transformed back to the original domain. Every point on Figure 8-Right is now a line.

4   Conclusions

We presented here two separate approaches to generate time coherent animation from video data using analysis and synthesis techniques. The first one uses the matching information of objects in adjacent frames to create smooth transitions or to generate interpolated objects in new in-between frames. This approach still presents a lot of room for exploration, for example: Modifying the cost matrix with direction information to penalize matchings that would produce motion patterns far from the average or fluctuating trajectories. Using optical flow information as preferred direction. Minimizing the maximum error instead of the squared sum (Eq 1) in the matching stage (this variation is known as the bottleneck assignment problem [7]).

The second technique uses a gradient based approach creating a surface in which the synthesis objects can move smoothly. The objects have to be aware of themselves so they do not sink together into a local minimum, that is the reason why this strategy is always combined together with a circle packing algorithm. It was showed that this approach can be extended to parametric curves like straight lines, after a preliminary domain transformation as the Hough transform. Natural extension of this approach include the creation of time coherent animations with different parametric curves like circles, ellipses or parabolas. Future work includes the exploration of synthesis techniques based on the result of well know video tracking techniques as the continuously adaptive mean shift algorithm [6] for region based synthesis and active contours[3] for parametric curve based synthesis.

References

1. Bénard, P., Bousseau, A., Thollot, J.: Dynamic solid textures for real-time coherent stylization. In: ACM SIGGRAPH Symposium on Interactive 3D Graphics and Games (I3D), pp. 121–127. ACM, Boston (2009)
2. Bénard, P., Lagae, A., Vangorp, P., Lefebvre, S., Drettakis, G., Thollot, J.: A dynamic noise primitive for coherent stylization. Computer Graphics Forum (Proceedings of the Eurographics Symposium on Rendering 2010) 29(4), 1497–1506 (2010)
3. Blake, A., Isard, M., et al.: Active contours, vol. 2. Springer, London (1998)
4. Bolter, J.D., Gromala, D.: Windows and Mirrors: Interaction Design, Digital Art, and the Myth of Transparency. The MIT Press (October 2005)
5. Bousseau, A., Neyret, F., Thollot, J., Salesin, D.: Video watercolorization using bidirectional texture advection. ACM Trans. Graph. 26 (July 2007)
6. Bradski, G.: Computer vision face tracking for use in a perceptual user interface. Intel Technology Journal (1998)
7. Burkard, R., Dell'Amico, M., Martello, S.: Assignment problems. Society for Industrial Mathematics (2009)
8. Duda, R.O., Hart, P.E.: Use of the hough transformation to detect lines and curves in pictures. Commun. ACM 15, 11–15 (1972)
9. Galanter, P.: What is generative art? complexity theory as a context for art theory (2003), http://philipgalanter.com/downloads/ga2003_what_is_genart.pdf

10. Hertzmann, A., Perlin, K.: Painterly rendering for video and interaction. In: NPAR 2000, pp. 7–12 (2000)
11. Knowlton. Knowlton mosaics - portraits by computer assisted art pioneer ken knowlton, http://www.knowltonmosaics.com/
12. Levin, G.: Floccular portraits - interactive art by golan levin and collaborators, http://www.flong.com/projects/floccugraph/
13. Levin, G.: Segmentation and symptom - interactive art by golan levin and collaborators, http://www.flong.com/projects/zoo/
14. Litwinowicz, P.: Processing images and video for an impressionist effect. In: Proceedings of the 24th Annual Conference on Computer Graphics and Interactive Techniques, SIGGRAPH 1997, pp. 407–414. ACM Press/Addison-Wesley Publishing Co., New York, USA (1997)
15. McAulay, R., Quatieri, T.: Speech analysis/synthesis based on a sinusoidal representation. IEEE Transactions on Acoustics, Speech and Signal Processing 34(4), 744–754 (1986)
16. Meier, B.J.: Painterly rendering for animation. In: Proceedings of the 23rd Annual Conference on Computer Graphics and Interactive Techniques, SIGGRAPH 1996, pp. 477–484. ACM, New York (1996)
17. Silvers, R.: Robert silvers (2003), http://www.photomosaic.com/
18. Smith, K., Liu, Y., Klein, A.: Animosaics. In: Proceedings of the 2005 ACM SIGGRAPH/Eurographics Symposium on Computer Animation, SCA 2005, pp. 201–208. ACM, New York (2005)
19. Zölzer, U., Amatriain, X., Arfib, D., Bonada, J., Poli, G.D., Dutilleux, P., Evangelista, G., Keiler, F., Loscos, A., Rocchesso, D., Sandler, M., Serra, X., Todoroff, T.: DAFX:Digital Audio Effects, 1st edn. Wiley (May 2002)

Design and Development of an Interactive Virtual Shadow Puppet Play

Abdullah Zawawi Talib[1], Mohd Azam Osman[1], Kian Lam Tan[1], and Sirot Piman[1,2]

[1] School of Computer Sciences
Universiti Sains Malaysia
11800 USM Penang, Malaysia
[2] Department of Business Computing,
Faculty of Business,
Surat Thani Rajabhat University,
Surat Thani, Thailand
{azht,azam}@cs.usm.my, andrewtankianlam@gmail.com,
sirot.cod07@student.usm.my

Abstract. Shadow puppet play has been a popular traditional storytelling method for many centuries in many parts of Asia. This paper describes a method to model a virtual shadow puppet play using sophisticated computer graphics techniques available in Adobe Flash in order to allow interactive play in real-time environment as well as producing realistic animation. Areal-time method is proposed to produce the shadow image that allows interactive play of the virtual shadow puppets by using texture mapping and blending techniques. Special effects such as lighting and blurring effects for virtual shadow puppet play environment are also proposed. Moreover, the use of geometric transformations and hierarchical modeling facilitates interaction among the different parts of the puppet during animation. In essence, our methods and techniques have overcome various limitations of the existing works in virtual shadow puppet play.

Keywords: Animation, Blending, Interactive Play, Real-Time, Shadow Puppet Play, Visual Simulation, Virtual Storytelling.

1   Introduction

Storytelling tradition has been in existence in almost in every culture and society of the world since ancient times. It has been used as a platform for educate the masses and inculcating morals and values to the audience. One of the well-known traditional storytelling traditions in most of Asia is the shadow puppet play theater [1]-[5]. This storytelling tradition as in other well-known traditional storytelling mainly consists of narrations, songs, and accompanied by a musical orchestra and obviously a set of puppets.

Various advances in digital storytelling and virtual storytelling have been reported in the past notably Papous [6], Virtual Storyteller [7]-[8] and CONFUCIUS [9]. Besides, there was an attempt to adapt interactive storytelling in a mixed reality system [10].

A.L. Brooks (Ed.): ArtsIT 2011, LNICST 101, pp. 118–126, 2012.

The art of shadow puppet play is slowly becoming less popular in many countries due to the proliferation of modern digital media entertainment and the lack of interest in the younger generation. Therefore, promoting and providing greater accessibility of this masterpiece using modern technologies such as digital media are needed. Although extensive research works have been carried out in the broader area of virtual or digital storytelling, there was only a handful of research efforts in the area of virtual or digital shadow puppet play such as the development of a framework for the traditional shadow play [11], virtual 'wayang' using 'IRIS Showcase' [12], shadow rendering of Chinese Shadow Play [13], and motion planning algorithm for Chinese Shadow Play [14]. Most of the work involved off-line and non-interactive generation of shadow puppet play. Therefore, in this paper, a method of modeling shadow puppet play is proposed using sophisticated computer graphics techniques available in Adobe Flash that will ensure realistic, fast and interactive play in real-time environment.

2   Related Works

The virtual storyteller Papous [6] can narrate stories in an expressive manner like a real human storyteller. In this system, the scene tags as well as the illumination tags can be changed directly according to the environment. It has some limitations that include flexibility in expressing the emotions and the limited number of available animations for bodily expression. Virtual Storyteller [7]-[8]is an embodied speaking agent that represents the character as semi-autonomous intelligent agent and also incorporates the narrative and the presentation levels as intelligent agents rather than text-based story generation system. However, the knowledge bases are still limited. In CONFUCIUS [9], a story is presented by creating human character animation from natural language using Humanoid Animation (H-Anim) and MPEG 4 SHNC for the animation. Collision detection, autonomy, multiple-character synchronization and coordination are also included. An interactive storytelling that uses a mixed reality system by putting the user as one of the roles in virtual storytelling has also been attempted [10].

In the area of virtual shadow puppet play, a practical framework for mapping the elements of the traditional shadow puppet play as a virtual storyteller was proposed by Chee and Talib [11]. In virtual 'wayang' [12], realistic puppets were created but during animation, the arms and legs of the puppet do not swing. Zhu et al. [13] used photon mapping to render the shadow puppet. Since the rendering has to be done off-line frame-by-frame (key-frames), real-time and interactive play is not possible. However, good shadow effect, blurring effect, animation and illumination are produced. In Hsu et al. [14], motions of the shadow puppet are generated automatically using motion planning technique and RRT-Connect algorithm is used to incorporate motion patterns for the upper body of the puppet. A post-processing procedure is also required to generate the secondary motions in order to ensure that the lower body complies with gravity and obstacles.

The existing works on digital shadow play in the large do not allow interactive play where the user is required to predefine the frames offline and later a commercial software system generates in-between frames for the final play. Therefore, in this paper we propose a virtual shadow puppet play application that allows interaction and real-time play of shadow puppet play by developing new techniques for real-time generation of shadow puppet images and interactive animation of the puppets.

3   System Overview

The overall design of our shadow puppet play system consists of three main elements namely Puppet, Record, and GUI Design as shown in Figure 1. The system enables user to animate the puppet and provides a proper environment and appropriate music that will accompany the play.

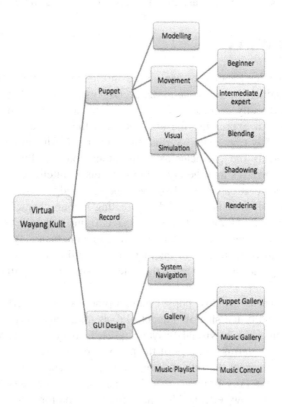

Fig. 1. The Overall Deign

The Puppet module consists of Modeling, Movement and Visual Simulation sub-modules. The Modeling sub-module is the place where all the images are stored. In the module, firstly, images with high resolution are imported to the library. Then, the image of the puppet needs to be broken down into smaller parts as shown in Figure 2. The puppet is broken down into pieces based on specific main body parts. All these parts will be combined in various ways to provide three different types of movement namely Stand, Hand Move and Walk as shown in Figure 2. The Movement sub-module of the Puppet module controls the movement of the puppets and this sub-module provides two different environments for two different categories of users namely Beginner and Intermediate/Expert for novice users and intermediate/expert users respectively. Visual Simulation is the sub-module that touches up the visual simulation after the process of rendering. Blending effect is applied so that the puppet becomes more natural when the brightness of the screen is high. Blurring and shadowing are also required to make the virtual shadow puppets more alive.

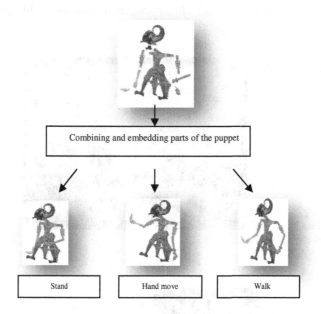

Fig. 2. Puppet Movements

The Record module is the module that allows the shows to be recorded and replay. The recorded file will be saved in the avi format or swf format depending on the user's preference.

The GUI Design module consists of System Navigation, Gallery and Music Playlist sub-modules. The System Navigation sub-module is the main menu of the application where the user can interact with the system. The menu can be added into XML and only three menus can be displayed at a time. The Gallery stores the name of the puppet and music files. XML is used to store the name of the puppets. XML will be loaded and the image of the puppets will be displayed dynamically. Music Playlist plays the music during the show.

4   Implementation

The Virtual Shadow Puppet Play application consists of 8 main scenes. From the first main menu, three choices are provided to the user namely Home, Instruction and User

Level. The Home menu directs the user to the page where all the possible movements of the puppets are displayed. The Instruction menu provides the user manual of this application. Lastly, the User Level menu provides the choice to the user to indicate their level of expertise namely the beginner, intermediate and expert levels.

For the beginner, the user proceeds to play the show without having to choose any music and puppet from the library as shown in Figure 3. The beginner level is suitable for school children or other users who are unfamiliar with the application. This setting provides a virtual joystick to control the puppet movement. The virtual joystick is controlled by an optical mouse. The virtual joystick provides four basic directions namely up, down, left and right. Each direction represents different types of movement.

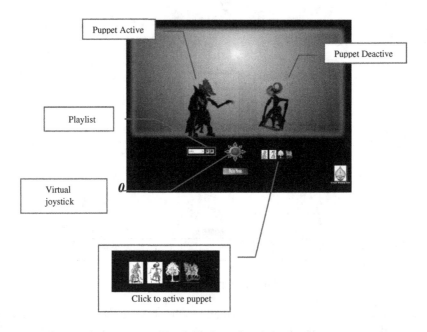

Fig. 3. Beginner Level

The intermediate level provides a slightly different interface. The user needs to choose the puppets from the Puppet Gallery and the music from the Music Gallery. With this level, the show will be accompanied by the traditional music and the user will be able to control the music. Besides, a brightness controller is also provided to allow the adjustment of the brightness. The users can also control the movement of the puppet from the keyboard. All the actions are pre-defined and stored in the short cut key. The expert level provides a better appearance of the stage and the user can choose the puppet immediately as shown in Figure 4. Every puppet is assigned its own unique key for the play. The same goes to the music and brightness of the screen.

Blending effect is added to the puppets based on the brightness of the screen. When the brightness of the screen is high, the blending of the puppet becomes more natural (back to original blending type). Nine types of blending effect can be assigned to the puppet. For example, in the subtract mode, the puppet changes in appearance as shown Figure 5. When the subtract mode of the puppet and the background (screen) has a radial type of the color, the color will be produced according to the brightness of the background (screen).

Fig. 4. Expert Stage

Fig. 5. Puppet with Subtract Mode Blending

Blurring effect to the puppet is also applied during the fading in and out of the puppet. The code for fading in is as follows:

```
if (puppetIn._alpha<100)
    puppetIn._alpha += (100-puppetIn._alpha)*.25;
    myBlure.blurX += (0-myBlure.blurX)/10;
    myBlure.blurY += (0-myBlure.blurY)/10;
    puppetIn.filters = [myBlure];
}
```

The code for fading out is as follows:

```
if (puppetOut._alpha>0) {
    puppetOut._alpha += (0-puppetOut._alpha)*.25;
```

```
puppetOut._x+= ((myWidth/1.5)-puppetOut._width)*.5;
puppetOut._y+=((myHeight/1.5-puppetOut._height)*.5;
myBlure.blurX += (100-myBlure.blurX)/10;
myBlure.blurY += (100-myBlure.blurY)/10;
puppetOut.filters = [myBlure];
}
```

Figure 6 shows the blurring and shadowing effects during fading in (entering the stage). The effects make the show look more real and reflect the traditional shadow puppet play. Figure 7 shows the blurring and shadowing effects during fading out from the stage. After applying the effect, the movie clip will be removed from the stage when the alpha value = 0.

Fig. 6. Blurring and Shadowing Effects on the Puppet During Fading Into the Stage

Fig. 7. Blurring and Shadowing Effects on the Puppet During Fading out from the Stage

5   Discussion

The shadow puppet in [12] can be moved anywhere but the arm of the puppet cannot be moved or animated. In our work, we can generate the same effect like in [12]. However, additionally, we provide realistic, interactive and real time animation that also includes animation of the arms of the puppets. The time taken to render the puppet in [13] does not allow real time and interactive play. The animator (or player) needs to render offline several key frames and use commercial software to generate in-between frames in order to provide a play for a specific storyline. In our work, flexibility and interactive real-time capability are provided without having to preprocess key frames and generating in-betweens. A mechanism that allows the arms of the puppet to swing naturally while the character is walking is provided by [14]. In our work, similar types of movement onto the wrist of the virtual shadow puppet have been successfully implemented. This method is also applicable to other parts of the body of the puppet, thus producing a better effect in expression and body languages. However, in [14] some movements can be made at the same time such as the puppet could swing the hand while running. In traditional shadow puppet play of South-east Asia, the upper part of the body of the puppet always remains static. As such, this functionality is not really necessary and not considered in our work. Furthermore, for the lower part of the puppet, they have to adopt a post processing approach so that the legs can swing like a pendulum and comply with the silhouette of the environments. In our work, there is no such necessity for us to go through the same predetermined step. In [14], an attempt is made to create a shadow play animation with a key-framed based approach. However in our work, realistic and interactive motions can be generated and reusability of different types of motions in real time using just hierarchical modeling is made possible. Since the play can be performed in real-time, user is also able to play interactively and change the storyline at any point during the play.

6   Conclusion and Future Work

In this work, we have provided several solutions for visual simulation and animation of virtual shadow puppet play. Firstly, texture mapping and blending techniques are used instead of rendering technique in order to allow fast and interactive display in real time environment. Besides, several techniques that use various themes (lighting and brightness) and special effects such as blurring to bring the right atmosphere to the virtual shadow play are proposed. Hierarchical modeling method is adopted in order to model a realistic animation for the puppet to include real time elements that allow playing of shadow puppet play naturally in virtual environment. Previous works on shadow puppet play are not interactive and require manual pre-ordering of the play using key-framed approach.

For future work, we will be looking at special devices for the application such as haptic device and developing an intelligent instructional tool for puppeteering that will be used to guide the user in performing the show.

References

1. Matusky, P.: Malaysian Shadow Play and Music: Continuity of an Oral Tradition. Oxford University Press (1993)
2. Edward, V.N.: Javanese WayangKulit: An Introduction. Oxford University Press (1980)
3. Salij, H.J.: Shadow Play and other Stories. Heinemann Singapore (1982)
4. Liu, J.: Chinese Shadow Puppet Plays. Morning Glory Publishers (1998)
5. David, C.: Shadow Puppets & Shadow Play. Crowood Press (2008)

6. Silva, A., Vala, M., Paiva, A.C.R.: Papous: The Virtual Storyteller. In: de Antonio, A., Aylett, R.S., Ballin, D. (eds.) IVA 2001. LNCS (LNAI), vol. 2190, pp. 171–180. Springer, Heidelberg (2001)
7. Theune, M., Faas, S., Nijholt, A., Heylen, D.: The Virtual Storyteller. ACM SIGGROUP Bulletin 23(2), 20–21 (2002)
8. Theune, M., Faas, S., Nijholt, A., Heylen, D.: The Virtual Storyteller: Story Creation by Intelligent Agents. In: Proc. Technologies for Interactive Digital Storytelling and Entertainment, pp. 204–215 (2003)
9. Ma, H., McKevitt, P.: Building Character Animation for Intelligent Storytelling with the H-Anim Standard. In: Proc.of Eurographics Ireland, pp. 9–15 (2003)
10. Cavazza, M., Martin, O., Charles, F., Mead, S.J., Marichal, X.: Users Acting in Mixed Reality Interactive Storytelling. In: Balet, O., Subsol, G., Torguet, P. (eds.) ICVS 2003. LNCS, vol. 2897, pp. 189–197. Springer, Heidelberg (2003)
11. Chee, J., Talib, A.Z.: A Framework for Virtual Storytelling Using Traditional Shadow Play. In: Proc. International Conference on Computing and Informatics (ICOCI 2006) (CD Proc.) (2006)
12. Rahman, K.A.: Wayang "Virtual" Integration of Computer Media in Traditional WayangKulit (Shadow Play) Performance, World Wide Web (1999), http://www.itaucultural.org.br/invencao/papers/Rahman.html (accessed February 9, 2008)
13. Zhu, Y.B., Lee, C.J., Shen, I.F., Ma, K.L., Stompel, A.: A New Form of Traditional Art: Visual Simulation of Chinese Shadow Play. In: International Conference on Computer Graphics and Interactive Techniques Sketches and Applications, p. 1 (2003)
14. Hwu, W.S., Ye, T.: Planning Character Motions for Shadow Play Animations. In: Proc. of International Conference on Computer Animation and Social Agents (CASA 2005), pp. 184–190 (2005)

Interaction Models
for Audience-Artwork Interaction:
Current State and Future Directions

Hanna Schraffenberger[1,2] and Edwin van der Heide[1]

[1] Media Technology Research Group, LIACS, Leiden University
Niels Bohrweg 1, 2333 CA Leiden, The Netherlands
{hkschraf,evdheide}@liacs.nl
[2] AR Lab, Royal Academy of Art, The Hague
Prinsessegracht 4, 2514 AN Den Haag, The Netherlands

Abstract. Interactive art is of great relevance to the arts, sciences and technology alike. A common field of interest among researchers of different disciplines, practising artists and art institutes is the interaction between audience and artwork. This paper reviews existing research concerning interaction in interactive art and discusses its applicability for describing and classifying audience-artwork interaction. In pointing out possible future directions, we identify a need for models describing the relation between the audience's and artwork's actions and reactions as well as the necessity for future research looking at interaction as a continuous bi-directional process between work and audience.

Keywords: Interaction, Interactive Art, Audience-Artwork Interaction, Classification, Taxonomy, Categorization, Model, HCI, Archiving.

1 Introduction

It can be argued that art has always included interaction between artists, audience and performers and that the experience of art is always interactive, considering the interplay of environment, perception and the audience's generation of meaning [13]. However, it is since the 1960s that active audience participation with artworks has created particular interest among artists as well as theorists. A theoretical standpoint in which participation and interaction between audience and artwork are central has for instance been developed by the British artist and theorist Roy Ascott as early as 1966 [1,5]. Even before the personal computer came into existence, Ascott embraced interactivity in computer-based art as an emerging and promising prospect [16].

Developments and accessibility of computer technology have enabled a new kind of interactive art — and with it the possibility for an art-experience in which audience and machine enter into a dialogue that is more than just psychological [13]. Gaining a better understanding of this 'dialogue' – the audience-artwork interaction – has gained growing interest in the arts, technology and science. A

A.L. Brooks (Ed.): ArtsIT 2011, LNICST 101, pp. 127–135, 2012.

structural model for interaction in interactive art will inspire artists to break out of existing habits and facilitate the development of novel forms of interaction, help curators and art experts when comparing artworks as well as support museums and institutes in archiving and categorizing their collections. Modelling the interaction between artwork and audience will furthermore be relevant to research in human-computer interaction (HCI) and elucidate possible differences between interaction in general multimedia applications and interaction in an art context. Most importantly, the development of models describing audience-artwork interaction will go hand in hand with a deeper understanding of interaction in interactive art. Gaining this understanding can be considered one of our main goals.

In this review paper, we survey relevant publications on interaction and interactive art (Section 2), discuss shortcomings of existing research to serve the purpose of describing audience-artwork interaction (Section 3) and conclude necessary directions for future research (Section 4). The paper is written from the perspective of media art research and considers publications by scientists, artists as well as well as contributions by media art institutes. Sociological and psychological studies on interactivity are beyond the scope of this paper. The main selection criterion for the inclusion of publications in the survey has been their applicability for describing audience-artwork interaction.

2   Literature Survey

A prominent figure in interactive art research is the artist and scientist Ernest Edmonds. As early as 1973, Edmonds and Cornock responded to the advent of computer-based interactivity in art and proposed a new concept describing possible relationships between artist, artifact and audience [3,13]. Notwithstanding the age of the publication, the topics addressed and models described are still relevant in interactive art research today. Their categorization which differentiates between *static*, *dynamic-passive*, *dynamic-interactive* and *dynamic-interactive (varying)* art systems has often been used, also in more recent publications. In [5], Edmonds, Turner and Candy outline and extend the originally proposed categories: in *static systems*, the artwork does not change while in *dynamic-passive systems* the art object changes in response to the physical environment or the artist's program. Audience-artwork interaction is reflected in *dynamic-interactive systems*, where the viewer/participant has influence on the art system. The same holds true for *varying dynamic-interactive systems*. Additionally, their behaviour changes, as the systems specifications are modified by a human or software agent. Next to illustrating the categories with artworks by Edmonds, their publication promotes collaborations between technologists and artists and points out that the field of designing interactive art systems can provide a substantial area for future research in user interaction.

The fact that research in user interaction can likewise be relevant to the genre of interactive art has been discussed by Edmonds as well: [6] considers HCI methods and knowledge important to interactive art and suggests that a critical language is needed that can be used to describe, compare and discuss interactive digital art. The text identifies the practice and research known as *experience design* as especially important for interactive art as this field – unlike early HCI – does not focus on interface design but provides a collection of methods that focus on understanding user/audience experience.

A similar strong focus on audience experience is found in [4]. Costello et al. describe a study into the experience of the artwork Iamascope and focus on four categories of what they call 'embodied experience', originally proposed by the creator of the work, Sidney Fels: *response, control, contemplation* and *belonging*. Their publication identifies different classes of movements, vocabulary and behaviour associated with the different categories/stages and adds another stage – *disengagement* – which encompasses patterns that occur around the participant's decision to leave the exhibit.

A rather specific perspective has been taken by two artists, Sommerer and Mignonneau, whose computer installations integrate artificial life and real life [19]. Their text proposes the principle of what they call *non-linear or multi-layered interaction* – interaction which is easy to understand at the very beginning but at the same time rich "so that the visitor is able to continuously discover different levels of interactive experiences." Considering existing interactive artworks, the authors distinguish two types of interaction. Firstly, *pre-designed* or *pre-programmed* paths of interaction, where the viewer can choose a path but where the possibility of discovering unexpected paths of interaction is rather limited. Secondly, interaction in which *evolutionary* processes play an integral role, creating unpredictable and open artworks.

One of the most extended and comprehensive attempts at describing characteristics of interactive artworks yet has been made by Bell [2]. In his dissertation the author identifies 40 characteristics of participatory works of art that use computer technology. Relevant in our context is for example his approach of describing the time based relations between actions. Bell differentiates between two main temporal relationships – *synchronous* and *asynchronous* interaction – and points out how temporal relations relate to the perception of cause and effect. In *synchronous* interaction, events taking place at the same time. *Asynchronous* interaction is characterized by events occurring at different times and is likely to bring about cause-effect reasoning. Regarding interaction between humans and computers in the arts, the author follows a machine-independent approach based on "the input/output (I/O) routes of humans": sound, vision, taste, smell and touch. As those are less likely to change than technology, he proposes different combinations of those inputs and outputs as a defining characteristic of the interaction. Aiming for an easily remembered method to evaluate individual artworks, Bell summarizes the proposed characteristics of participatory works by the degree of control a participant has. An important aspect of this approach concerns the development of a score which describes the change of control over time by plotting the changes in degree of control on a horizontal line like a musical score.

The idea of using a score in order to describe digital artworks has also been explored by Rinehart who presents a formal notation for scoring digital media art [18]. Rinehart builds upon the analogies between digital art and music and considers a score-like mechanism to formally describe media artworks. His proposed Media Art Notation System (MANS) has three levels of implementation that are progressing from simple to more complex. It uses descriptive metadata, XML markup, text, images and other media to document a specific work and ideally could serve as a guide for re-creating the described works.

Important contributions to our field of interest furthermore come from media art institutes with an interest in categorizing and archiving (interactive) media art. One classification of media art relevant to interactive art is provided by the V2_ Institute for the unstable media [22]. Their research on 'capturing unstable media' has resulted in an interaction model which describes several parameters. *Time flexibility or interaction synchronicity* indicates whether the interaction can be experienced at any time or needs to take place at a specific moment and distinguishes between scheduled and not-scheduled. The *interaction location* is classed either as specific or undefined and so indicates whether the interaction has to happen at a specific location or can be experienced at any location. The *user number* takes three possible values: single user, group user and audience. The user number is further classified by defining the *minimum number of users* and *maximum number of users*. The intensity of interaction is described by the *interaction level*; the parameter can take the following values: observational, navigational, participatory, co-authoring and intercommunication. The last parameter, *sensory mode* indicates which senses of the user are involved in the interaction process and distinguishes visual, auditive, olfactory, tactile and gustative. Their study also points out important areas for future research as for example the inclusion of more complex parameters such as *input and output of the interaction*, the *direction of the communication* and a precise description of the user's actions.

A complementary research project has been conducted by the Ludwig Boltzmann Institute Media.Art.Research. [10,11,12] in the context of the Prix Ars Electronica [17]. Working towards detailed differentiations within interactive art, several versions of a taxonomy have been presented. The taxonomy of interactive art builds upon a comprehensive study of existing vocabulary; categories and keywords have been developed and evaluated based on entries in Ars Electronica's archive and competition as well as based on expert feedback. Furthermore, additional keywords used by artists to describe their submitted works have been collected. In the taxonomy presented in 2008, nine keyword categories serve to describe interactive artworks. Interaction is primarily addressed by the categories *interaction partners, the performer (visitor) does* and *the work (project) does*. Keywords for the participant's/performer's actions include: observe, explore, activate, control, select, participate, navigate, leave traces, co-author, collaborate, exchange information and create. The corresponding category *the work (project) does* considers: monitor, serve as an instrument, document, enhance perception, offer a game, enable communication, visualize, sonificate, transform, store, immerse, process, mediate and tell/narrate. It is noteworthy that the keyword category *interaction partners* is not limited to interaction between audience and artwork but allows for several different constellation such as interaction between audience members.

Another notable contribution to taxonomies of interaction in the arts has been presented by Beryl Graham as part of her doctoral thesis [7]. In the chapter *Taxonomies of 'kinds of interactivity' within art* Graham summarizes existing approaches, and consequently develops her own re-interpretation of an unpublished model by Cornock and Edmonds using the metaphor of *conversation*. Her resulting common-language taxonomy uses descriptions of different verbal exchanges and collates audience-artwork interaction with having a real conversation.

In [20], Sparacino et al. discuss authoring techniques for interactive spaces. The authors provide a taxonomy of interactive systems which classifies interactive media applications as *scripted, responsive, behavioural, learning,* and *intentional.* In *scripted systems* the interaction is often restricted to triggering the presentation of new material. In *responsive systems* the system is defined by a series of mappings between user input and system output. In those systems, the same action of the user always results in the same response by the system. In *behavioural systems* the response of the system is dependent on the sensory input as well as on its own internal state. Here, the same sensor measurement does not always result in the same response — the interaction depends on the interaction context which affects the internal state of the system. *Learning systems* are able to learn new behaviours and to modify existing ones. Finally, *intentional systems* are introduced by the authors as a new modelling technique for creating interactive experiences. In intentional systems a perceptual layer is added between the sensory input and the response of the system, which provides the software agent with an interpretation of the audience's actions and intentions. Here, sensor data is first interpreted and then mapped to a response action.

A rather unique taxonomy for media art has been envisioned by Gwilt [8]. The author argues that "a visual taxonomy for New Media Art is an interesting benchmarking device that might be used to establish the parameters of this new genre." Accordingly, he proposes a set of visual icons which can be divided into symbols that describe the composition of the work and those documenting the intended interaction between the viewer and the work.

Taxonomies of interaction in the broader field of multimedia are also of interest, as they can be applied to interaction in the interactive arts. A classification originally proposed in [14] and later applied in [9] distinguishes between different levels of interactivity in multimedia applications: *passive* interaction, in which content is presented linearly and users can only start and stop the presentation of the content; *interactive,* where users can navigate through the content and *adaptive,* in which users can contribute content and control how their content is used. This broader classification has in return influenced the more specific attempts of categorizing interaction in interactive art. Trifonova, Jaccheri and Berguast [21] build upon the latter categorization [9], the differentiation between pre-designed and evolutionary interaction presented in [19] and the varying relationships between artwork, viewer and artist described in [5]. By using the three properties *interac-*

tion rules, *triggering parameters* and *content origin*, they provide a table which covers all of their refereed interaction types. The resulting model considers static and dynamic *interaction rules*; human presence, human actions and the environment as *triggering parameters*, and user input, predefined content by the artist and generated/algorithmic content as possibilities for *content origin*.

A similar approach is followed by Nardelli [15]. The author characterizes and compares interactive digital artworks by approaching "Digital Artworks as Information Technology intensive systems for which spectators are involved in the production of the artistic output." He looks at an artwork as an information system which processes a given input in order to produce a desired output. Nardelli's proposed classification frameworks knows three dimensions: the *content provider*, who produces the raw material which is then processed by the artwork; the *processing dynamics*, describing the variability of the processing itself and the *processing contributors*, the sources which are affecting the processing dynamics.

3   Discussion and Future Directions

The variety and richness of existing approaches suggests the relevance of interaction in interactive art as a broad and interdisciplinary field of research. Although widely discussed, many important aspects of audience-artwork interaction have been left untouched or require further investigation. The following discussion points out those aspects and illustrates the need of a structural method for describing and thereby better understanding interaction in interactive art.[1]

Many of the surveyed publications can be seen as a valuable basis for future models of interaction in interactive art. Research by Edmonds and Cornock [3] has already served this purpose and constitutes a foundation in several succeeding works (see e.g. [5] and [7]). Although remarkable in envisioning and describing interaction in art as early as 1973, their work only provides very generic classifications and does not yet facilitate finer differentiations within the proposed categories. Considering our interest in audience-artwork interaction, differentiations within *dynamic-interactive systems* and *varying dynamic-interactive systems* form a desirable goal of future research.

Another aspect open for future investigations lays in the integration of research focusing on specific aspects, such as audience experience (e.g. [4]), within a comprehensive model of interaction.

More encompassing attempts on the other hand are not necessarily directly applicable either — they quickly result in very complex models which can not easily be used. One example of a comprehensive approach – the study by Bell [2] – solves this by summarizing the complex possible combinations of characteristics by the degree of control a participant has in an interactive artwork. Unfortunate

---

[1] We want to point out, that many of the publications summarized above were not intended to serve the purpose of providing a comprehensive model of interaction in interactive art. Therefore, showing shortcomings in serving this purpose should not be understood as critique of the works per se.

for our purposes, this introduces a strong focus on the human contribution to the interaction and does not include aspects such as the level of control the computer has. Coping with detailed descriptions of interaction while remaining applicable is one of the challenges of future studies on the topic.

Another motivation for future research is the fact that often only few interactive artworks have served as a reference (see e.g. [4]). Consequently, further research is needed in order to evaluate the general applicability and relevance of results gained when studying interaction with a small amount of artworks.

Research done by artists in the context of their art practice (see e.g. [19,20]) raises similar issues. Frequently, such studies are primarily relevant in their specific artistic context. It still has to be shown whether the specific approaches are meaningful and applicable in more general contexts as well. Either way, research realized in the context of artistic practice proposes interesting differentiations and points out possible dimensions to be considered in the future.

An important shortcoming of many classifications lays in the fact that they describe interaction purely by its 'parameters' and thereby disregard the possible relationships between them (see e.g. [22]). A crucial instance is found in [12,10,11], which acknowledges the artwork's and viewer's actions as defining factors, but lacks possibilities to describe the inherent relation between them. Nevertheless, these studies provide a strong basis of keywords and parameters to incorporate in future research and illustrate the remaining challenge of describing their relations and dynamics.

When considering models intended to describe interaction in a multimedia context such as [9], we have to be aware that those – although applicable to interaction between artwork and viewer – do not necessarily provide a level of detail suited for the often rather special aspects of interaction in interactive art. As we are interested in understanding the specific characteristics of audience-artwork interaction as well as in highlighting distinctions between different types of interaction in the arts, those more general approaches can serve as starting points but have to be refined in order to facilitate meaningful classifications in the art context. In line with this, [9,14] call attention to the relationship between interaction and content and can help us identifying pieces belonging to the interactive art genre. Adapting their taxonomy, we can distinguish between art in which interaction serves as a means of accessing the artwork's content on the one hand and works, in which interaction has been used as artistic material and constitutes an integral part of the artwork on the other hand. In our opinion, the latter works form the emerging genre of interactive art relevant to future research on audience-artwork interaction.

A last common shortcoming of existing research for our purposes is the understanding of interaction as a one-way process. One example is found in [21], which considers how the artwork is influenced by the audience and the surroundings but not how the artwork might influence audience reactions in return. Similarly, Nardelli [15] looks at an artwork as an information system which processes a given input in order to produce a desired output and thereby ignores that interaction is a continuous bi-directional process. We consider the feedback loop and continuous process between audience and work important aspects of many interactive pieces and recognize their relevance in future research.

Looking at the presented collection of existing research with respect to its applicability for better understanding and describing audience-artwork interaction, we find – although not conclusive on their own – the presented divergent approaches have the potential to compensate for each other's weaknesses and complement one another in their strengths. As a next step, possibilities of incorporating results from the presented publications in a comprehensive model could be explored.

4   Conclusion

In the course of the presented review, we have highlighted the need for future research into audience-artwork interaction and pointed out possible future directions. In addition to summarizing publications which can serve as a strong foundation for further studies, we have recognized challenges and identified the necessity for future research looking at interaction as a continuous and bi-directional process. The lack of models describing the relationship between defining parameters such as the actions and reactions of audience and artwork has been recognized. By distinguishing between artworks with interaction as integral part of the work and artworks that use interaction to facilitate their contents, we have provided a criterion for identifying pieces belonging to the interactive art genre.

Concluding our review of relevant literature in the knowledge that existing studies as a whole form a good basis for future research, we want to point out that much relevant work in interactive art is actually shared not by means of (scientific) publications but by artworks themselves. Future work should therefore not only build upon existing research but at the same time derive information from examining interactive art pieces and interacting with interactive artworks directly as well as draw from exchange with practising artists and conducting experiments.

We have promoted the term 'audience-artwork interaction' and hope it will serve as a unifying label for future work addressing the discussed topics and thereby foster accessibility as well as exchange among the variety of disciplines contributing to this field of research.

References

1. Ascott, R.: Behaviourist Art and the Cybernetic Vision. Cybernetica: Journal of the International Association for Cybernetics 9(4), 247–264 (1966); 10(1), 25–56 (1967). Excerpted in: Packer, R., Jordan, K. (eds.) Multimedia: From Wagner to Virtual Reality, pp. 95–103. Norton, New York (2001)
2. Bell, S.C.D.: Participatory art and computers: identifying, analysing and composing the characteristics of works of participatory art that use computer technology. Doctoral thesis, Loughborough University of Technology (1991)

3. Cornock, S., Edmonds, E.: The Creative Process Where the Artist Is Amplified or Superseded by the Computer. Leonardo 6(1), 11–16 (1973)
4. Costello, B., Muller, L., Amitani, S., Edmonds, E.: Understanding the Experience of Interactive Art: Iamascope in Beta_space. In: Proceedings of the Second Australasian Conference on Interactive Entertainment, Sydney, Australia, pp. 49–56 (2005)
5. Edmonds, E., Turner, G., Candy, L.: Approaches to Interactive Art Systems. In: Proceedings of the 2nd International Conference on Computer Graphics and Interactive Techniques in Austalasia and South East Asia - GRAPHITE 2004, pp. 113–117. ACM Press (2004)
6. Edmonds, E.: The art of interaction. Digital Creativity 21(4), 257–264 (2010)
7. Graham, C.E.B.: A Study of Audience Relationships with Interactive Computer-Based Visual Artworks in Gallery Settings, through Observation, Art Practice, and Curation. Doctoral thesis, University of Sunderland (1997)
8. Gwilt, I.: Towards a visual taxonomy in New Media Art. In: Proceedings of ENGAGE: Interaction, Art and Audience Experience Symposium, pp. 90–98. Creativity and Cognition Studios Press, Sydney (1997)
9. Hannington, A., Reed, K.: Towards a Taxonomy for Guiding Multimedia Application Development. In: Ninth Asia-Pacific Software Engineering Conference, pp. 97–106. IEEE (2002)
10. Kwastek, K., assisted by Spörl, I., Helfert, H.: Research Project : A Taxonomy of Interactive Art (2007),
    http://media.lbg.ac.at/media/pdf/Taxonomy_IA_200706.pdf
11. Kwastek, K., Spörl, I., with the collaboration of Helfert, H., Sudhoff, N.: Research Report: Taxonomy Interactive Art II. Phase (2009),
    http://media.lbg.ac.at/media/pdf/taxonomy_IA_200911.pdf
12. Ludwig Boltzmann Institute Media.Art.Research. Taxonomies for Media Art,
    http://media.lbg.ac.at/en/content.php?iMenuID=94&iContentID=90
13. Muller, L., Edmonds, E., Connell, M.: Living laboratories for interactive art. CoDesign 2(4), 195–207 (2006)
14. Multimedia Demystified: A Guide to the World of Multimedia from Apple Computer, Inc. Apple-new media series. Random House, New York (1994)
15. Nardelli, E.: A classification framework for interactive digital artworks. Presented at 2nd International ICST Conference on User Centric Media, UCMedia 2010 (2010)
16. Packer, R., Jordan, K. (eds.): Multimedia: From Wagner to Virtual Reality, p. 96. Norton, New York (2001)
17. Prix Ars Electronica, http://www.aec.at/prix/de/
18. Rinehart, R.: The media art notation system: documenting and preserving digital/media art. Leonardo 40(2), 181–187 (2007)
19. Sommerer, C., Mignonneau, L.: Art as a Living System: Interactive Computer Artworks. Leonardo 32(3), 165–173 (1999)
20. Sparacino, F., Davenport, G., Pentland, A.: Media in performance: Interactive spaces for dance, theater, circus, and museum exhibits. IBM Systems Journal 39(3), 479–510 (2000)
21. Trifonova, A., Jaccheri, L., Bergaust, K.: Software Engineering Issues in Interactive Installation Art. International Journal of Arts and Technology 1(1), 43–65 (2008)
22. V2_ Institute for the Unstable Media: Capturing unstable media,
    http://capturing.projects.v2.nl/

Prime Slaughter: Playful Prime Numbers

Andrea Valente and Emanuela Marchetti

Centre for Design, Learning and Innovation
Aalborg University Esbjerg
Niels Bohrs Vej 8, 6700 Esbjerg, Denmark
{av,ema}@create.aau.dk

Abstract. Starting from the difficulty of creating playful representation of domain-specific abstract concepts, this study discusses the design of Prime Slaughter, a computer game aimed at facilitating individual sense-making of abstract mathematical concepts. Specifically the game proposes a transposition of primality and factorization into playful interactions, addressed to primary and early secondary school children. Taking into account individual needs expressed by children regarding play, during a participatory design processes aimed at enhancing learning in museums, Prime Slaughter allows for multiple forms of play and their integration. A simple working prototype has already been developed; it will be tested and re-designed through participatory workshops, involving a group of children in our target group.

Keywords: Non-formal learning, computer games, factorization, play.

1 Introduction

This paper explores the transposition of abstract mathematical concepts into playful visual interaction, by means of computer games. Factorization was chosen as it is representative of algorithmic procedures that are challenging for the learner, yet needed in many fields, being related to fractions (when adding or simplifying them) and to prime numbers. Testing for primality and factorization are also central elements of computer science curricula, where they are considered classical and formative examples of numerical algorithms. Before designing our game, named Prime Slaughter (PS), a survey of math-related games was conducted; the results revealed that these applications are mostly computer-augmented exercises or (virtual) manipulative environments. Genuine math games are rare, especially if one is interested in those related to theory and abstract concepts. PS is therefore an attempt at designing such a game.

The theoretical framework adopted for PS is based on studies about the role of goal-directed activities in learning. Moreover, considering findings from a 1 year participatory design study conducted by one of the authors, about facilitating playful learning in museums, and the lack of playful math-related games, PS has been conceived as an actual computer game, in which the combination of different forms of play are explored and mathematical notions are transposed into goal-directed activities within the gameplay.

A.L. Brooks (Ed.): ArtsIT 2011, LNICST 101, pp. 136–144, 2012.

The following sections of the paper proposes a survey of math-related games in section 2, section 3 instead presents findings from the museum project and the theoretical framework. Section 4 discusses the design of the game, and section 5 presents conclusions and future work.

2   Math-Related Games

The first step toward the creation of PS was to conduct a review of existing games about math learning, specifically focusing on theory coverage and problem solving techniques. Three kinds of games were identified: computer-augmented exercises, exploratory/manipulative environments, and finally very few genuine games.

The category of computer-augmented exercises is the most represented and it includes game such as: *BBC bitesize* and the *Toon University: Prime Factoring*. *BBC bitesize* is a collection of computer-augmented exercises, requiring players to give the right answer. An interesting aspect of *BBC bitesize* is that it provides a concrete context for abstract mathematical operations: for instance in the KS1 section, in the division game, after an answer has been given an animation shows a division as partitioning diamonds among a series of wagons. When a wrong answer is given, some of the wagons are left empty or some diamonds fall on the ground after all wagons have being used. The interface is targeted at primary school children, it has nice and colorful graphics supported by sound effects and voice recordings, which are used to warn about mistakes and about the functions of the buttons. Similarly the *Toon University: Prime Factoring* game requires the players to answer to mathematical questions, by shooting the right answer with a cannon. The goal of the game is to identify the right answer among 3 choices, after having performed mental calculations. This game has a quite low graphic quality and does not offer representations of the steps needed to find the right answer, in this sense is very different from our vision, but represents a typical example of free online math games.

Another approach is to offer a virtual environment, in which the players are supposed to learn by exploring mathematical concepts. An example is provided by *ABCya! Fraction Tiles,* which allows to explore how parts make up a whole, interacting through a desktop-like user interface and a palette of fraction tiles, from 1 to 1/12. The tiles can be taken from the palette and arranged as construction blocks. The width of each tile is proportional to the size of the fraction it represents, so for example two ¼ fractions one aside of the other are as long as a single ½ fraction. The goal here is to let the children explore fractions, freely or under supervision of teachers that could provide challenges or tasks.

An different, and interesting case is provided by the series of *Pixeline* games, which are technically well designed and engaging. These games seem to combine computer-augmented exercises, taken from school curricula, with an exploratory environment. They offer a good context to make exercises more concrete and fun, which are solved by the players through the avatar Pixeline. However, the goal is still solving exercises, theory and problem solving procedures are not directly represented.

The category of genuine games, which better fits our vision, is represented mainly by *number ninjas* (by Armor Games). There the player is a number, who can move around in a side-scrolling world and has the goal to collect shurikens (ninja's throwing stars) and kill other numbers. The player's character is a natural number, initially 1; each shuriken corresponds to an operation, so by killing number 3 with a *plus* shuriken the character becomes number 4 (and 3 dies). In advanced levels there might be multiple ways to finish, by adding, subtracting or multiplying the character's initial value with the available numbers disseminated in the level. The general rule is that if the character becomes more than 9 or less than 0, it will die. This rule contributes to make the solution of the levels more challenging. Decisions involving application of operations to numbers are essential parts of the game, which makes it very interesting and inspiring for us.

In conclusion, the result of our survey suggests that math is typically not effectively transposed into gameplay. And even if some games involve to multiplication and division, we could find not any game that tries to cover more abstract operations, comparable to prime factorization or primality testing.

3   Different Forms of Play

The PS concept is based on findings and reflections from another ongoing research project (conducted by one of the authors [2]) about playful learning and the transposition of abstract notions into playful interactions, specifically regarding museum learning practice and children around 10 years old. A one year Participatory Design (PD) process has been conducted in cooperation with an after-school institution, where a group of 25 children was involved in co-designing a playful learning game about urban development in history [3]. Insights collected through this process, and the related theoretical framework, provided inspiration to try the same approach in factorization and primality. An analogy was identified between the two projects, as in both games the children are supposed to experience theoretical notions and problem solving activities, playing as characters within the provided narrative.

Fig. 1. Different play styles; the mixed group is facing the camera

The theoretical framework adopted for the museum project is based on Rogoff's theory of apprenticeship [4]. According to Rogoff children learn by engaging in goal-directed activities within informal contexts, usually supported by adults when reaching the boundary of their current knowledge [4]. In this study we intend to combine the use of goal-directed activities within play, which is supposed to mediate between the children and the learning content, also in the case they would like to explore the learning domain by themselves. Play is then intended, as in [5], a self-driven activity, which could take different forms according to individual interests.

Observations conducted during the PD sessions have concretely showed that children may express different forms of play, even while playing at the same game and within the same group of players. Some children adopted a form of *military* board games play, usually related to games like chess, Stratego by Milton Bradley Board Games and Monopoly by Hasbro. They placed their tangibles on the board and challenged each other, as they were competing to win control over the other player's land. Other children engaged in a form of *designerly* play, suitable for construction bricks or games like SimCity [1]. They acted as urban planners, arranging their settlement and introducing new buildings or other features (humans, animals, and plants). Some other children combined the two forms of play, they generally started by planning their settlements, in groups or individually, and then engaged in a military play with other children. An interesting case was provided by a group of two girls and two boys: they all started by planning their settlement, but the girls took the designerly phase more seriously and used a lot of time for it. The boys instead placed the tangibles and engaged as soon as possible in the military play form. They had to wait for the girls to be ready, so they started playing by themselves, and after the girls had completed their settlement, they played together in the military way. At the same time other subgroups or individuals played on a parallel basis, as urban planners or fighting landowners, almost as they were in another room (see Fig. 1).

These observations provided a valuable grounding to determine requirements for the museum project and also inspired us to create Prime Slaughter for a different domain. Combining these data and the theoretical framework provided by Rogoff, it was decided to explore a scenario, in which primality and factorization are transposed into playful goal-directed activities embedded in the game. The players are supposed to explore individually theory and problem solving techniques they learned in school, in a tangible and playful way. Then if needed, they may ask support from teachers or parents. In this sense both learning, play, and adults participation are intended as self-driven activities.

4   The Design of Prime Slaughter

Abstractions are commonly used in subjects such as math and computer science, as they allow to effectively represent complex meanings. However, such abstractions are difficult to grasp for novices, therefore, direct manipulation has been introduced for instance in the field of algorithm animation, to allow learners to intuitively experience the semantics of abstract concepts, interacting with their visual representations [7].

In our view PS should follow a similar approach, allowing players to learn abstract notions and procedures related to factorization, through direct manipulation, experiencing the meaning of factorization within a computer game framework.

Moreover, PS should be playable as a real game and not as computer-augmented exercises. By playable we mean also that the children should perceive PS as a game, from their individual perspective of what play is. Therefore, based on the data from the museum project, it was decided to start by supporting both a designerly, generative form of play and a military, dramatic form of play, and possibly emergent combinations of these forms. Furthermore, in our view a playable game should be fun and engaging also for players who do not have solid knowledge of the learning content, in order to motivate them in playing again and learn more.

Starting to design PS we analyzed the typical elements and mechanics of 2D action adventure games, such as *The Legend of Zelda* by *Nintendo,* and *generative games* (or simulation-like games in which the player actively manages or builds part of the simulation), such as *SimCity* by *Maxis,* to gather requirements and support respectively military and designerly forms of play. Then we analyzed the actions involved in prime factorization, such as division, multiplication, and possible visualizations of abstract concepts like the primality or divisibility of a natural number. Finally we defined mappings between math and game dynamics, to create an engaging gameplay. According to our analysis classic 2D action-adventure games have typically a main character, the hero, who is supposed to kill enemies, often represented as monsters, and to explore the world to find tricks or hidden artifacts, which allow to defeat more effectively different monsters. A narrative element, increasing difficulty of levels, and rewards enabling the player to become more effective, provide short terms goals and motivation to continue playing, which may fit well within goal-directed activities. The hero is usually characterize by energy level, experience points, magic or special abilities, and items collected in the game. Long term progress requires strategy in managing experience points or bonuses, and a deeper understanding of the rules of the game, of what is possible to do, including unexpected side-effects of certain actions or artifacts. Similar features are present also in generative games, however, the role of the player is significantly different. The player is often an external agent, who is supposed to act on the world, adding or manipulating some of its features, for instance city infrastructures in SimCity. The goal is to create certain configurations and explore the implications as the simulation unfolds. To keep playing the player simply needs to fulfill some minimal requirements, otherwise she will run out of resources and lose. Finally all these games are enriched by nice colorful graphics and compelling audio effects, providing feedback on the players' performance, and engaging narrative elements disseminated throughout the game.

Factorization requires to see a natural number as a unique collection of its prime factors, in whatever order: for instance 12 is also *2 x 2 x 3*. Regarding actions, a simple algorithm to find the prime factors of an integer number N, is to start from 2 and try to divide N by ever larger primes. And this, in turn, requires to be able to identify prime numbers. Therefore, integer division and multiplication are central concepts in this domain. Divisibility offers yet another way to perceive a number: a number is related to all its factors. For example, the factors of 12 are {1,2,3,4,6,12}. Therefore, a central goal of PS is to allow players to familiarize with the concepts that a natural number has multiple representations, and some properties may become more are clearly visible by manipulating the number to create a different representation.

Hence, initial design phases of PS consisted of an exploration of possible visualizations of the division and multiplication operations, through the creation of simple concept arts, inspired by the games we analyzed. We decided for a representation of division as splitting an object (a cube of jello in the Fig. 2, on the left) into 2 or 3 parts. This representation seems to fit well with the action of slaying of monsters, a typical element of action-adventure games. It was then decided that the monsters would represent numbers to be sliced by the players, also to make fun of the tension often associated to math learning.

Multiplication is instead depicted (in Fig. 2, at the center) as the process of pruning a young tree, to allow it to grow more branches. A tree initially has a value of 1, and a single branch; the top of this tree will have a single leaf of value 1. Cutting the tree in 3 would generate 3 new branches, each with a leaf of value 3. Cutting the tree again in 2, would result in a single trunk, 3 branches and 6 smaller branches. Interestingly, this form of pruning enables players to freely explore the space of the possible tree shapes. Therefore, we decided to map the duality division/multiplication onto the duality killing/growing.

Summarizing in PS the hero is supposed to collect points by fighting monsters with a sword, representing a prime number by which the monsters can be split (as visible in Fig. 2, on the right). The rule for PS is that a monster of value N (or N-monster) can only be sliced by a sword of value M, where M is a factor of N. The sliced monster divides into many smaller monsters; for instance, a sword of value 2 can slice a 12-monster into 2 monsters of value 6. Trying to slice a monster with the wrong sword (e.g. attacking a 9-monster with a 2-sword) results in damage for the hero, who loses energy points, and ultimately dies.

At the beginning of the game, the player's character has a 2-sword (sword of value 2) and monsters are reduced to prime numbers after a few hits; it would be impossible to kill them without acquiring new proper prime-swords. Even further in the slicing process, every number-monster will eventually be reduced to a 1-monster, impossible to kill, since 1 is only divisible by 1. Monsters reduced to value 1 are short lived, and spontaneously disappear. Taking all these points into consideration, it was decided that when a number-monster is prime (for example an 11-monster) it can be frozen by the hero through magic, and transformed into a sword. This double role of the monsters as enemies and material to construct new swords, is intended to enforce the idea that prime numbers are a single fundamental concept throughout the game, and monsters and swords have ultimately the same nature, i.e. they are primes. Finally, number-monsters have different sizes in the game, in relation to their number of prime factors. Hence, a 12-monster has size 3, while a 17-monster has size 1, and 1-monsters have size 0, the minimal possible. In this way the player can use size as a visual indicator of how close the monster is to being prime (and dead).

In alternative to killing monsters, the player can choose to explore the *Natural Bonsais* level, a forest populated by trees representing each a natural number, and like bonsais can be shaped in various forms. Despite many generative games do not have an avatar for the player, in Natural Bonsais the hero is important as it allows to keep the whole game coherent. Moreover, to allow the players to freely choose how to play, it was decided that the killing and the pruning play styles are inherently situated in the levels: some levels only have monsters, others only bonsais, and monsters cannot move across the levels.

In the current prototype, a bonsai starts as a seed with a natural value associated, for example 12; then it can be pruned by the hero's sword, but only if the value of the sword is a factor of the value of the bonsai, in this case 2 or 3. If a newly born 12-bonsai is pruned by a 3-sword, it grows 3 more branches, on top of the existing tree trunk; each of the new branches will have a leaf of value 12/3, i.e. 4. The process of pruning and growth continues until the leaves are primes, then the leaves are replaced by fruits, each with the same value as the leaf that generated it (apples in the current prototype).

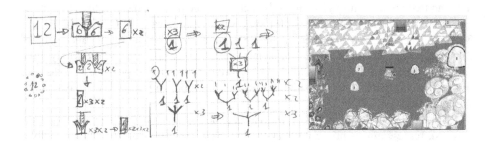

Fig. 2. Splitting numbers could represent division (on the left); pruning a tree can be like multiplication: each new cut creates many new branches (central image). On the right an actual screenshot of the same level in the current prototype.

When the hero collects a number-fruit, his sword is changed accordingly. Points are given during the pruning process, but not when fruits are collected. Old trees can be felled by freezing them, i.e. using the same magic that freezes prime-monsters. When an old tree disappears from the level, a new one is planted at the current position of the hero; this set of rules are meant to suggest players to often fell and re-plant their trees, in order to acquire more points. Moreover, since the bonsai level has no enemies and the player has plenty of time to reflect before acting, making mistakes is punished more severely than in the other levels: for example trying to prune a 12-bonsai with a 5-sword results in reduction of 25% of the hero's current energy. Since the levels of PS contain monsters with values from 1 to 20, the hero needs to collect a number of swords, with all the values of the primes from 1 to 20: 2, 3, 5, 7, 11, 13, 17, 19. The hero in PS can only hold one sword at any given time, so all other swords are kept in an armory. In case the hero dies, he will be re-born in his armory, and all swords collected before dying will still be available. To win the game, the player can collect at least 400 points (by slicing as many monsters as possible) or she can collect all 8 prime-swords in her armory.

The game has goals inspired by the action-adventure genre, i.e. collecting items, increasing the score, or killing monsters. But the actual elements of the game and the actions involved in achieving those goals are related to division, multiplication and factorization. In this sense our game is envisioned as supporting forms of tangential learning, in which learning is not the main focus of players' actions and occurs indirectly [8]. Understanding the built-it mathematical concepts should make you a better player, but you should enjoy playing even with little previous knowledge. Moreover, mathematical concepts should be easily recognizable by player that already studied them in school. Finally, conceptual (mathematical) errors are mapped onto damage points.

5   Conclusion and Future Work

The design of a new game is proposed, aimed at supporting learning of abstract mathematical concepts, specifically factorization. The game is targeted to primary and early secondary school children and is intended to allow them to experience the meaning and dynamics of factorization through direct manipulation. Based on data collected from an ongoing research project about playful learning in museums, and transposition of abstract notions into playful interactions, and from a survey about existing math-related games, it was decided that the game, called Prime Slaughter, should be a fun and playful math game. We map abstract concepts into goal-directed activities within the game framework, and support different forms of play. Taking inspiration from 2D action-adventure games and simulation games, the action of dividing has been transposed into slicing of jello number-monsters with a sword, also representing a natural number, and multiplication has been transposed into pruning and shaping trees in a bonsais forest. The current prototype will be soon tested through a series of participatory workshops, involving children within our target group, to evaluate if the game is really playable as expected and how it actually support learning. Insights collected through the tests will be used to design better version of the game.

References

1. Zeynep, T., Zeynep, C.: Learning from SimCity: An empirical study of Turkish adolescents. Journal of Adolescence 33, 731–739 (2010),
   doi:10.1016/j.adolescence.2009.10.007
2. Marchetti, E.: Myth and Bones: Museum Socio-Epistemic Practice and Children's Values. In: Proceedings of InterSymp 2011, IIAS 2011, 1st Symposium and Panel on the Art of Relational Living in the Communication Age, Baden Baden, Germany, August 1-5 (2011)
3. Rogoff, B.: Apprenticeship in Thinking. Cognitive Development in Social Context. Oxford University Press (1990)
4. Huizinga, J.: Homo Ludens. A study of the play element in culture. Boston Beacon Press (1950)
5. Squire, K., Barab, S.: Replaying history: engaging urban underserved students in learning world history through computer simulation games. In: Proceedings of the 6th International Conference on Learning Sciences (ICLS 2004). International Society of the Learning Sciences, pp. 505–512 (2004)
6. Laakso, M.J., Myller, N., Korhonen, A.: Comparing Learning Performance of Students Using Algorithm Visualizations Collaboratively on Different Engagement Levels. Journal of Educational Technology & Society 12(2), 267–282 (2009)

7. Petersson, E., Brooks, A.: Virtual and Physical Toys: Open-Ended Features for Non-Formal Learning. CyberPsychology & Behavior 9(2), 169–199 (2006)
8. Barendregt, H.P.: The Lambda Calculus its Syntax and Semantics. North-Holland (1984)
9. Valente, A., Marchetti, E.: Programming Turing Machines as a Game for Technology Sense-Making. In: Proc. of IEEE 11th International Conference on Advanced Learning Technologies, pp. 428–430 (2011)
10. Henriksen, P., Kölling, M.: Greenfoot: combining object visualisation with interaction. In: Companion to the 19th Annual ACM SIGPLAN Conference on Object-Oriented Programming Systems, Languages, and Applications (OOPSLA 2004), pp. 73–82. ACM, New York (2004), doi:10.1145/1028664.1028701

Text Invader: A Graphic Interference on Semantic Flow

Onur Yazıcıgil and Elif Ayiter

Sabancı University, Istanbul, Turkey
{Oyazicigil,ayiter}@sabanciuniv.edu

Abstract. In this paper we report on a system of typographic intervention which aims to bring about a typesetting environment which automates the aesthetic as well as contextual concerns previously manifested in the output of deconstructivist typographers throughout the 20th century. While in the current state of the undertaking a commercial font design software named FontLab has been used to bring about a virus which substitutes vectors for semantic patterns found in bodies of text, future work will evolve towards the creation of a standalone application which may aid in a convergence of the fields of textual authorship and graphic design.

Keywords: Typography, Automated, Controlled, Generated, Font, Virus, Graffiti.

1 Background

The motivation for creating Text Invader lies in a strong interest in the work and appended philosophical concerns of a number of deconstructivist graphic designers of the late 20th century who investigated breaking type and semantic flow on typeset pages through techniques which can best be described as painting with type, which involved experimental broken type setting. Particularly noteworthy amongst these designers are Neville Brody and David Carson, who initiated the Grunge Type movement which has been vastly influential onto this day [1].

Beyond designers such as Brody and Carson, the origins of typographic deconstruction can be traced to much early times, especially to Futuristic typography in the early decades of the 20th century. Thus, Marinetti writes in 1913 that his revolution is aimed at the so-called typographical harmony of the page, which is contrary to the flux and reflux, the leaps and bursts of style that run through the page adding that *"with this typographical revolution and this multicolored variety in the letters I mean to redouble the expressive force of words."* [2]

One of Marinetti's basic Futuristic tenets, the relegation of human experience to a continuum of sensations, underlay the techniques he proposed to use in achieving a Futurist literary expression. Marinetti described these procedures by declaring that *"nouns will be scattered at random, infinitives with their greater elasticity will replace the pedantic indicative"* [3].

Although separated in time though a period of 80 years, Ellen Lupton seems to pick up on certain aspects of Marinetti's outcry when she sees deconstruction in graphic design as a process - an act of questioning typographic practice. In Derrida's

A.L. Brooks (Ed.): ArtsIT 2011, LNICST 101, pp. 145–151, 2012.

original theory deconstruction asks several questions which are crucial to typographic design as well: How does representation inhabit reality? How does the external appearance of a thing get inside its internal essence? How does the surface get under the skin?

A crucial opposition in Derrida's theory of deconstruction, and one which is also highly pertinent in terms of typographic design, is speech versus writing. The Western philosophical tradition has denigrated writing as an inferior, dead copy of the living, spoken word. When we speak, we draw on our inner consciousness, but when we write, our words are inert and abstract. The written word loses its connection to our inner selves. Language is set adrift.

Parallel questions for graphic design which preoccupy Lupton are how visual form may get inside the content of writing and through what means has typography refused to be a passive, transparent vessel for written texts, instead developing as a system with its own structures and devices throughout the ages? A typographic work can be called a deconstruction when it exposes and transforms the established rules of writing, interrupting the sacred inside of content with the profane outside of form [4] whereby *"communication for the deconstructivist is no longer linear, but involves instead the provision of many entry and exit points for the increasingly over-stimulated reader"* [5]. Thus the page is no longer to be just read but also to be perceived, beyond the pure textual content, into all of its associative conjunctions: In other words, we are also meant to feel rather than just to read a page, which brings up back to the considerations of graphic designers such as Brody and Carson who brought about such mind states by individually crafted works of typography in which the requisite interventions had been painted in by hand.

Can this process of breaking typesetting or painting with type happen generatively? Instead of typographically painting each individual composition, could there be a generative system comprised of fonts which would recycle and paint differently each time due to the nature of different word combinations? Bill Hill, who is renowned for his work on Microsoft's ClearType system proclaims that *"reading is like trail tracking which is a series of pattern recognition movements"*, a stance which is further elaborated upon by Gerard Unger [6]. Can such semantic patterns be visualized by substituting some of the letters, words or even paragraphs with graphic elements? If so, can this repetitive semantic pattern result in an aesthetic investigation?

Yet another query to which this project is related concerns the notion of 'the designer as author' whereby according to Poyner [7] certain examples of experimental typography could be considered as a post-structuralist revaluing of the co-production of meaning by both author and reader. Poyner elaborated this view in 1996 and commented that experiments in typography *"reflect a deep skepticism about received wisdom and a questioning of established authorities, traditional practices and fixed cultural identities"* [8]. While Poyner's concerns for a redefinition of the agency of the designer as author, whose job definitions should go well beyond those of a merely efficient *"service-provider whose job is to convey a given message to an audience as efficiently as possible"* are duly noted, nonetheless of equal importance would appear to be the unleashing of a novel means of transdisciplinary expression in its own right - one which stands between the traditionally well demarcated fields of design and literature.

2 Text Invader

In 1996, Adobe collaborated with Microsoft on developing a format for scalable computer fonts. This new format, named OpenType, was intended to expand the use of typographic behaviors as well as to provide a platform where all the world's writing systems could be managed in a single font file. It is a cross-platform format which is recognized both in MAC OSX and Windows operating systems. OpenType fonts allow around a hundred specifications for typographic behavior. This provides the typesetter with the choice to apply various glyph substitutions in order to enrich the content like, small caps, ligatures, text figures, scientific numerals, and alternative glyphs, which are just five specification features out of the many available variables. These OpenType features are programmed in FontLab where much of the type-design work takes place.

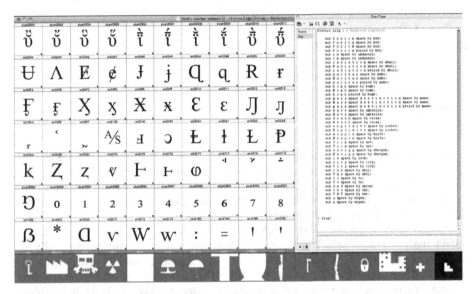

Fig. 1. Screenshot showing the process whereby glyphs become substituted by vector drawings through codified intervention

OpenType programming has a very basic substitution principle which is activated when certain combinations are juxtaposed. The common use of these typographic substitution behaviors are used to enrich the coherency level of the flowing text. For instance the f and i combinations in serif typefaces appear often times as the fi ligature and is activated in order to compensate the awkward negative space, to smoothen the reading direction, and to enrich legibility. In order to activate the fi ligature the typesetter has to enable this behavior via the OpenType panel in Adobe InDesign. This could as well be used for aesthetic reasons such as ct, st and sp ligatures. These are called discretionary ligatures, which still need to be enabled by the typesetter. This is a simple OpenType feature which is coded as "liga" for standard fi and ffi fl ligatures or "dlig" for discretionary ligatures in the OpenType coding panel.

The Text Invader method aims to use FontLab's OpenType panel as a creative medium in which to generate typefaces that modify the intended use of common typographic behaviors. It aims to experiment with the possibilities that are provided by the OpenType format in order to create the unexpected rather than the established conventions of typesetting. In other words, to interfere with the conventions that serves for linguistic flow. Unlike the liga feature where the typesetter can enable or disable this feature, the rlig (Required Ligature) feature is added in order to enforce this substitution without having the typesetter's will:

```
feature rlig { # Required Ligatures
   # Latin

      sub f u s i o n space by key;
      sub i n space by industry;
      sub R a d i a t i o n space by skull;
      sub n u c l e a r space by nuke;
      sub b o m b space by bomb;
      sub e x p l o s i v e space by rocket;
      sub h a v e space by umbrella;

   script DFLT;
   } rlig;
```

In the code above 'sub' stands for substitution whereas 'by' literally means by and 'space' denotes a hit on the space bar button. Anything after 'by' is a specific name that is given for each graphic to be called from the glyph library. Thus, sub f u s i o n space by key = substitute whenever the letter combination fusion comes together and forms the word fusion with the graphic that is called key.

As the name suggests, Text Invader aims to generate fonts that can attack and infect the content in search for a pattern that may alter the context ironically or metaphorically. The Text-Invader virus may be implanted as various visuals: graphic images, letters, and abstract forms, which will be generated as an OpenType font format. Virus images are not used arbitrarily to alter the look of the content, rather they substitute the images with certain repetitive letters, words and even lines of text in search for creating a meta-text: Text in which the author's intentions have been intermediated by the Text Invader. This methodology in generating a virus font initiates a discourse and discussion about the author's and designer's roles in typesetting.

2.1 The Workflow of Text Invader

The system was tried out during a 2 day long workshop held at the graphic design department of Bilkent University, Ankara in April 2011, with 10 participating students who utilized Text Invader to create a series of typographic interventions on text harvested from various sources. The following table shows the workflow through which the outcome was generated during the workshop.

As is evident from the table above, the two creative tasks which fell upon the workshop participants were the selection of the font and font sizes which would bring about the body text and more importantly the creation of the vector files which would substitute the keywords.

Table 1. Workflow of Text Invader

Phase	Tasks
Language	English, Turkish, French, etc.
Topic	Art & Design, Law, Ethics, Sports, etc.
Textual Research	Keyword selection
Visual Research	Creating visual elements (vector drawings)
Font	Choosing continuous text fonts
Virus	Importing vector drawings into FontLab
OpenType	Programming OpenType features (rlig)
Generation	Generating it as a usable font (.otf)
Invasion	Output

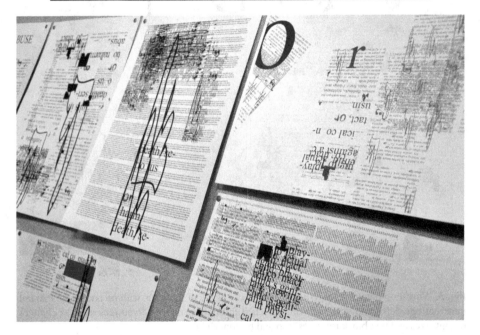

Fig. 2. Workshop output. Bilkent University, April 2011.

The system is based upon a dichotomy in that it is both controlled as well as generative at different levels of the output: While the substitution of vector files for specific keywords all of which are determined by the user brings forth a level of control as far as single words are concerned, the combination of these words into semantic patterns brings forth a novel layer/level of unpredictability in which the vector drawings conglomerate into a combined visual output which is ever changing based upon the variance with which the keywords converge throughout the text.

3   Future Work

While the virus was used with great enthusiasm and provided the mainstay of textual transformations affecting semantic flow, nonetheless further manual interventions were also embarked upon by the participants. These involved changes in font sizes, rotations of text blocks and even analog additions such as the crossing out of words and sentences on printouts. Observing the design behaviors which the young designers who participated in the workshop exhibited has inevitably led to further thoughts as to whether such enhanced strategies which involve layout and composition can also be incorporated into the design environment as a novel layer of viral intervention wrought upon the semantic flow which, again, works through keywords and their juxtapositions and proximity within a given body of text.

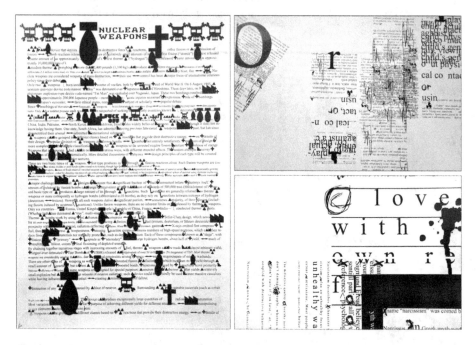

Fig. 3. Workshop output. Typesetting through sole usage of the virus with no additional manual interventions (left), and viral behavior enriched through manual interventions such as changes in font sizes and text block rotations (top and bottom right).

While in its current state Text Invader works primarily as a typesetting environment, further viral infections which are programmed to evoke changes that go beyond the text and affect layout will inevitably entail a transition from pure typesetting to a fully fledged design application, in which design principles such as Gestalt and visual hierarchies will have to become sets of rules to be programmed as viral invasions which affect semantic flow not only as discrete vector elements but as the instigators of overriding compositional systems.

Amongst graphic design software which works under generative principles Adrian Ward's AutoIllustrator from 2002, and Samul Lising/Peter Spreenberg's n-Gen Design Machine from the late 1990's stand out. While a close scrutiny as to how aesthetic principles were adapted with remarkable mastery into both of these applications is in order; nonetheless it is prudent to also bear in mind that Text Invader operates under an entirely different premise in that the primary concern does not revolve around pure visuality but rather around semantic flow, i.e., the transformation of textual content.

Utilizing the principles of generative systems as the founding strategies for design applications has been under discussion within the community of design theorists for quite some time [9]. The matrices for these discussions are often derived from self-organizational systems such as biological swarms and colonies, evolutionary systems and shape grammars, the last of which which have been deliberated upon for the better part of 4 decades as a means for novel forms of artistic production [10]. It is generally held that generative design strategies may prove to be potent platforms for bringing about novel structures, behaviors and relationships as well as in providing stages upon which the complex and interconnected relationships between the design organism and its environment can be acted out.

For Text Invader the desired outcome is seen to be a creation of such novel structures, behaviors and relationships that will manifest not solely in the graphic design field but at the intersection of two fields, namely typography and semantics. Thus the aim is to bring about a transdisciplinary creative system in which designers and writers can find fertile ground for collaboration, as well as undertake personal artistic investigations which may bear novel forms of semantic as well as aesthetic expressions.

References

1. Meggs, P.B., Purvis, A.W.: Meggs' history of graphic design, 4th edn., pp. 494–495. Wiley, N.Y. (2006)
2. Marinetti, F.T.: Destruction of Syntax—Imagination without strings—Words-in-Freedom (1913), http://www.unknown.nu/futurism/destruction.html (accessed on June 01, 2011)
3. Cundy, D.: Marinetti and Italian Futurist Typography. Art Journal 41(4), Futurism, 349–352 (1981)
4. Lupton, E.: A Post-Mortem on Deconstruction? AIGA Journal of Graphic Design 12(2), 45–47 (1994)
5. Cahalan, J.M.: The guilty forgiving the innocent: Stanislaus, Shaun, and Shem in Finnegans Wake. Notes on Modern Irish Literature 6, 5–11 (1994)
6. Unger, G.: While you're reading, pp. 82–85. Mark Batty, New York (2007)
7. Poyner, R.: Typography Now: The Next Wave, p. 7, 15. Internos Books, London (1991)
8. Poyner, R.: Typography Now Two: Implosion, p. 15. Booth Clibborn Editions, London (1996)
9. McCormack, J., Dorin, A., Innocent, T.: Generative Design: a paradigm for design research. In: Redmond, J., et al. (eds.) Proceedings of Futureground, Design Research Society, Melbourne (2004)
10. Stiny, G., Gips, J.: Shape Grammars and the Generative Specification of Painting and Sculpture. Republished in Petrocelli, O.R. (ed.) The Best Computer Papers of 1971, Auerbach, Philadelphia, pp. 125–135 (1972)

Using the Voice to Design Ceramics

Flemming Tvede Hansen[1] and Kristoffer Jensen[2]

[1] The Royal Danish Academy of Fine Arts - The School of Design
fth@dkds.dk
[2] Department of Architecture, Design and Media Technology (ad:mt), Aalborg University
{Esbjerg,krist}@create.aau.dk

Abstract. Digital technology makes new possibilities in ceramic craft. This project is about how experiential knowledge that the craftsmen gains in a direct physical and tactile interaction with a responding material can be transformed and utilized in the use of digital technologies. The project presents SoundShaping, a system to create ceramics from the human voice. Based on a generic audio feature extraction system, and the principal component analysis to ensure that the pertinent information in the voice is used, a 3D shape is created using simple geometric rules. This shape is output to a 3D printer to make ceramic results. The system demonstrates the close connection between digital technology and craft practice.

Keywords: Experiential knowledge, design method, CAD, generative 3d software, interaction audio features.

1 Introduction

This project builds on McCullough's [1] idea about a close connection between digital work and a craft practice, and that the hand and brain activities related to computer technology may be analogous to practical activities where tacit knowledge, according to Polanyi [2], is involved. McCullough's research is based on studies of crafts; design processes and tools related to fundamental human activities. The results of these studies are related to the artist Bernard Leach's [3] idea about crafting and execution as a unity that is intuitive and humanistic - *One Hand, One Brain*. Thus McCullough suggests that computer systems should be developed much more from the user's perspective (here, the designer) to utilize tacit knowledge.

The overall field of this research is about integration of digital technology in the field of 3D design, especially in fields rooted in arts and craft such as ceramics. In this case it is about how experiential knowledge of craftsmen is transformed and utilized in the use of digital technologies. Specifically, the project focuses on the development and exploration of a digital interactive design tool that uses voice as input and 3D physical form as output by rapid prototyping. As the voice is among the main communicative and expressive parts of the human, this project, which we call SoundShaping, is made to investigate what the voice is capable of creating in 3D ceramics.

Firstly, this concept implies the study of the interaction between the designer using voice as input and a real time dynamic and responding 3D graphics. Secondly, it

A.L. Brooks (Ed.): ArtsIT 2011, LNICST 101, pp. 152–159, 2012.

focuses on the output in 3D physical form, i.e. actual and real, a form that can be viewed, touched, and thus examined from different angles. This part is done with digital-based 3D printing in order to obtain ceramic items from the digital tool. The project distinguishes itself exactly by the combination of interaction and 3D tangible form.

The approach is driven by a desire to *humanize* the use of digital technology in the field of design. By humanizing we mean that the involvement of the body is being exploited in the use of digital technology—and that it is reflected in the product. It can be hand gestures, body movement, or as in this project the voice, that forms the basis for an interaction through digital technology.

This approach is seen as a contrast to the predominantly use of mouse click and typing in numbers, which does not utilize the body as a tool to accentuate the design with digital technology.

The article reports from the first stage of the technically, artistically and experimentally development of this design tool, which is done in collaboration with students from ad:mt at Aalborg University in Esbjerg.

2   Field of Research

The overall research field is characterized by a creative use of equipment within digital technologies, e.g. the work from the research cluster Autonomatic [4] that explores the use of digital manufacturing technologies in the creative process of designing and making three dimensional objects. One example is Drummond Masterton's [5] intense process of testing CNC milling, adjusting large segments of machine code and changing or making tools for the machine to use. This work is seen as a transformation of how a silversmith might use a range of hammers and stakes to create a certain form or texture (according to Bunnell [6]). Another example is Tavs Jørgensen [7] use of CAD programs that enable production of flat patterns from which prototype models are constructed. The methods is similar to that used for traditional origami models, but the complexity of the shapes means that they could never have been realized without the use of IT tools. The complexity of the shapes is contrasted by the simplicity of the plaster moulds used to cast the ceramics pieces [7]. These are examples that integrate manufacturing with digital technologies in a way that builds on a craft tradition.

An overlooked area within the field of ceramics is the experiential knowledge that the ceramicist gains in a direct physical and tactile interaction with a responding material. Manuel de Landa [8] describes it as ...*a form that we tease out of those materials as we allow them to have their say in the structures we create*, and Leach [3] as ....*a living embodiment of the intention*... Hansen [9] argues that this experiential knowledge of craftsmen can be transformed and utilized by the use of digital technologies. It is knowledge based on tacit knowledge experienced from an experimental, explorative and tactile interplay with a physical material. This approach, that Hansen calls the *interactive material-driven designing,* is characterized by two layers. Firstly the craftsman developing his own material and technique, and secondly by examining the potential of the material by interacting with it and being attentive to its response. This is about an intimate relationship between the designer and the material, which is reflected as a unique artistic fingerprint in the final artefact.

Hansen's conclusion is that such an approach to designing is utilized with digital technology, when the designer develops his own digital *material* [9]. If the designer is not able to develop his own digital *material*, he should collaborate with relevant specialists to make this possible. This project constitutes such collaboration.

A parallel to the idea of a responding material is to be found in the generative potential within digital technologies. It means that the computer is able to produce results based on input. An important development in this field of design can be referred to the animation techniques introduced by Greg Lynn and the experimental use of diagrams introduced by Peter Eisenman during the nineties (according to Sevaldson [10]). This is also about a focus on how interrelated forces in a complex dynamic system works as a kind of *abstract machine* [11], which is utilized as part of the design process.

The aspect of interaction within digital technologies is well known in the field of interaction design and event based productions such as computer games, interactive art installations, performance etc. Such a use employs the digital technology as part of its own medium and makes up a clear distinction from a tool [12] that is the purpose of this project.

An example is the interactive dance-architecture Sea Unsea [14], which takes place on an interactive stage informed by a camera interface (by motion capture). The performers' movements affect a sonorous field of sound and explore, attracting, repulsing and entwining their bodies and voices within an evolving patterns of a swirling hypnotic synthetic sea (CITA 2011) [13]. Another example is World Ripple by Ståle Stenslie [15]. World Ripple builds sculptures out of emotions rendered real. It is an invisible, immaterial sculpture made sensually *senseable* by a tactile, wireless, mobile bodysuit with a binaural sound system. The sculptures are triggered by GPS coordinates.

Thus the digital tool is about connecting the aspect of interaction with a generative responding potential material through digital media. This integrates digital technology in design practice in a way that utilizes the experiential knowledge about the design process of craftsmen, and thus the intimate relationship between the designer and the material. This is what we call humanizing the digital technology as a tool for 3D design.

Such a research firstly is about an experimental development of a generative digital responding material in a close relation with a programmer or suchlike. Secondly it is about examining the potential by interacting with the body (in this case by the voice) and being attentive to the response. These are two coherent and interrelated issues; it is in the light of this interaction that the generative digital responding material is developed and programmed.

3   Experiment

In this research we employ the *research through design* methodology (Frayling [16]), which for our purpose is defined as an experimental design practice that is part of the design research and contributes empirical data. The method is explorative and experimental, which in this study means that the research questions and empirical series of experiments are produced and developed in the process of research. This approach is seen as a *reflection on action* similar to Schön's ideas [18]. The method begins with a definition of a frame for carrying out experiments, which is defined by the overall research question. This approach is inspired by Binder and Redström's [19] notion of *exemplary design research*:

> It is 'exemplary' in the sense that it enables critical dissemination
> primarily by creating examples of what could be done and how, i.e.
> examples that both express the possibilities of the design program as well
> as more general suggestions about a (change to) design practice.

The intention with this paper is to give an insight into one of these experiments in this frame and the potential it may exhibit.

Sound is invisible, but when it hits the ear membrane, it is *translated* into intelligible sound by the brain using neuronal signals. We are interested in the idea of a translation of the audio, but a subjective translation to a three-dimensional form, which can be seen and touched as a kind of physical memory and that reflects the audio experience.

The subjective translation is viewed as an artistic fingerprint, which motivates the interactive process and the artistic intention. The translation is seen as a responding generative 3D graphic that transforms the designer's audio input. Interaction is an unpredictable and surprising process that motivates an exploratory and experimental process for the designers and researchers.

3.1   Overview

The SoundShaping system overview can be seen in figure 1. It consists of an *Audio Feature* estimation module, a *PCA* module to extract the most important information from the audio features, a *Shape Creation* module, and the *3D print* module.

In this work, we consider the voice as an expression of information through the use of vowels and consonants [21], and as an expression of emotions [22] through the prosody, i.e. the use of mainly pitch and loudness contours. The *Audio Feature* module extracts intuitive features with a clear relationship to humans, such as pitch and loudness, but also less intuitive features, such as spectrum. In the case of a craftsman using this system, two situations may arise, 1) the craftsman uses intuitive features, such as pitch/loudness, e.g. by singing, or 2) the craftsman does not use these features, but expresses the voice differently, e.g. whispering. If 1) then the craftsman has potential for conscious control of the shape that is created, but in the case of 2), the craftsman has lost the conscious control of the system, because the system does not respond to that category of features and/or other non-intuitive features are used. In order to increase the potential for utilizing any expression of the voice as well as retaining the possibility of a conscious control of the system, the PCA [23] module is introduced. This module extracts pertinent information from the voice, which may be expressed differently from time to time, but the output of the PCA is supposed to reflect the intent of the craftsman, no matter how he or she expresses the voice.

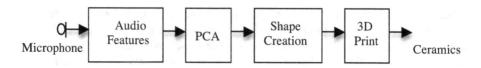

Fig. 1. Overview of SoundShaping system

To decide what the resulting shape has to fulfil, it is needed to look at the purpose. In this research we want to investigate the use of 3d digital designing in ceramics. The 3D print technique is based on the use of a Z Corp 3d powder printer [17], which is changed to use ceramic powder. This technique allows us to print the 3D geometry directly in ceramics. Thus the 3d print has to fulfil the general requirement for firing a ceramic artifact. A ceramic artifact needs to have strong walls, which can resist the heat since the ceramics softens during firing. At the same time the walls should not be too thick since this produces cracks during firing. Thus it is a matter of the construction. The artifact should not be too curved and have a certain strength to support itself, a hollow inside with walls is useful. These requirements had to be fulfilled.

3.2   Audio Features

It is necessary to know what kind of parameters to be used to describe the audio. It is on the basis of the audio parameters an idiom and a dynamic interactive graphics is developed and programmed. Audio can be described using temporal and spectral envelopes that give an overview of the quality of the sound. Furthermore, dependent if the sound is voiced or unvoiced, more parameters can be used to describe the sound in more detail. In this work, the MIR toolbox [20] is used as the basis for audio feature extraction. The *Brightness*, *Roughness*, and *RMS* (loudness) features are used to capture the specific features, and the *Chromagram* is used to capture pitch information. These features capture mainly the prosody - emotional expressions [22] of the voice. The *Spectrum* captures detailed spectral information, and the *MFCC* captures the spectral overview, the spectral envelope. These features capture mainly the information expressed by the consonants and vowels [21]. A frame length of *50 ms* seems to work well in this context.

All in all, the audio features consist of a few hundred values for each frame (time step). In order to lower this number, and to ensure that the most pertinent information from the audio is used, the Principal Component Analysis (PCA) [23] transformation is used on the audio features. This ensures that the output variables are uncorrelated and account for as much of the variability of the voice as possible.

3.3   3D Graphic

The experiment is based on 6 variables (N), and time as a feature. The 3D digital geometry is seen as one object, which evolves in the length over time. The position of the centre is determined by N=1, N=2 and time (figure 2 left). The cross section is determined by N=3, N=4, N=5 and N=6 (figure 2 right), which are connected with a parameterized curve. To make sure there is variation in all shape dimensions, the variables (output of the PCA) are normalized in order to have equal standard deviations.

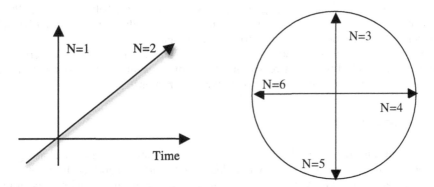

Fig. 2. The position of the evolving 3d geometry is determined by N=1, N=2 and time (left), and the cross section of the 3d geometry is determined by N=3, N=4, N=5 and N=6

Sometimes, the results showed a much-curved and very thin shape, which did not fulfil our requirements. As the voice is a very expressive organ, the resulting shape can be very different. Therefore, many possibilities of parameterization are included, that adjust the resulting rendering. This is utilized to explore and specify the idiom in different categories of sound based on the introductory proposal, e.g. screaming, babbling, talking, singing, etc. and at the same time fulfil the realizable requirements. The options include *Frame size*, choice of *Audio Features*, order of *PCA variables*, *smoothing* length and *curve* parameters. Figure 3 (left) shows a 3D object with smoothing, and the order of *PCA variables* and *curve* parameters options. In figure 3 (right) the same shape is shown as created in ceramics.

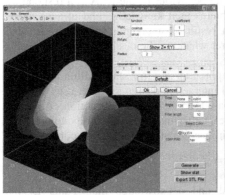

Fig. 3. The SoundShaping interface (left), including curve parameterization and PCA variable order options. The same object created in ceramics is shown right.

This development with parameters makes up an excellent basis to investigate the responding aspect. The exploration of the introductory responding generative system allows adjusting the shape with the voice. At this stage the SoundShaping system creates one object at a time. Each time the PCA is recalculated it creates a shape based on a responding generative system inherent in a complexity within audio features. Thus, with time, the designer explores and obtains the behaviour of the PCA as tacit knowledge. This enables the designer to explore the voice in an individual way and reflects the designers fingerprint in the design.

Such an approach is based on the designer's and the researcher's experiential knowledge, which this project relies on, and permits examining the potential of the material by interacting with it and be attentive to its response.

4   Conclusion

We have in this article introduced an approach to integration of digital technology in the field of 3D designing, especially in fields rooted in arts and craft such as ceramics. The approach is driven by a desire to *humanize* the use of digital technology in the field of design and is characterized by an interaction and a responding 3D graphic that has proven useful to explore and to experiment by interacting with the voice. We have exemplified and discussed this issue based on an experiment.

The experiment was based on the use of a generative system that converts audio into features, and variables (based on PCA) that accounts for the main part of the voice expression. The use of PCA ensures that the craftsman expresses the voice in any manner while still being sure that the output – the 3D object – reflects his/her intent.

A comprehensive and flexible generative system with a parametric user interface was developed. This was utilized to identify different categories of audio, which at the same time was utilized to fulfil our requirements for a ceramic design. The use of PCA showed a potential to generate and reflect a complexity within audio features, which is utilized and transferred to the idiom in the generative system and thus a ceramic design. With further use, the designer gains an intimate relationship to the digital material based on this complexity. The behaviour of the PCA is a responding generative system of which the designer obtains tacit knowledge and utilizes in his own right. This is reflected in the design result as a complexity and a personal fingerprint, as the system using PCA interpret whatever the designer expresses in his voice.

All in all the experiment showed a useful potential at a first stage within the idea of the development and exploration of a digital interactive design tool that uses voice as input, but requires further investigation based on real time interaction. Also our experiment was only based on one 3D model. Other models have to be explored e.g. one which only reflects a frozen moment in a constantly change without time as a feature.

Acknowledgement. We are very grateful and acknowledge that Yanis Lisima participated in the discussions and in the elaboration of the SoundShaping software prototype.

References

1. McCullough, M.: Abstracting Craft. The Practiced Digital Hand. MIT Press (1998)
2. Polanyi, M.: The Tacit Dimension. The University of Chicago Press, USA (1966)
3. Leach, B.: A Potter's Book. Faber and Faber, London (1940)
4. Autonomatic, http://www.autonomatic.org.uk/ (visited October 3, 2011)
5. Masterton, D.: The Hunt for Complexity. Paper presented at the Autonomatic 1 Symposium, University College Falmouth (2005)
6. Bunnell, K.: Craft and digital technology. Paper presented at the World Crafts Council 40th Anniversary Conference in Metsovo, Greece (2004)
7. Jørgensen, T.: Helix - ceramic origami (2009),
   http://www.oktavius.co.uk/ceramic_origami.html
   (retrieved March 1, 2009)
8. Landa, M.d.: Material Complexity. Paper presented at the Digital Tectonics, University of Bath Department of Architecture and Civil Engineering (2002)
9. Hansen, F.T.: Materialedreven 3D digital formgivning: Eksperimenterende brug og integration af det digitale medie i det keramiske fagområde, PhD-report, Danmarks Designskole (2010)
10. Sevaldson, B.: Developing Digital Design Techniques. Investigations on Creative Design Computing. Oslo School of Architecture and Design (2005)
11. Deleuze, G., Guattari, F.: A Thousand Plateaus: Capitalism and Schizophrenia. Athlone Press, London (1988)
12. Paul, C.: Digital Art. Thames & Hudson (2003)
13. CITA. Sea Unsea (2010), http://cita.karch.dk/Menu/Projects/
    Interface+Ecologies/Sea+Unsea+(2006) (retrieved March 5, 2010)
14. Ramsgaard Thomsen, M.: Sea Unsea..I: Arkitekten (6), p. 47 (2007)
15. Stenslie, S.: Haptic Hedonism - Designing Pleasure for the Flesh. Paper presented at the Nordes, Engaging Artifacts, Oslo (2009)
16. Frayling, C.: Research in Art and Design. Royal College of Art Research Papers 1(1), 1–5 (1993)
17. Z Corporation, 3D Printers,
    http://www.zcorp.com/en/Products/3D-Printers/spage.aspx,
    (visited October 3, 2011)
18. Schön, D.: The Reflective Practitioner. How Professionals Think in Action. Basic Books, New York (1983)
19. Binder, T., Redström, J.: Exemplary Design Resarch. Paper presented at the Design Research Society, Lissabon, Portugal (2006)
20. Lartillot, O., Toiviainen, P.: A Matlab Toolbox for Musical Feature Extraction From Audio. In: International Conference on Digital Audio Effects, Bordeaux (2007)
21. Fant, G.: Acoustic Theory of Speech Production. Mouton De Gruyter (1970)
22. Pittam, J., Scherer, K.R.: Vocal Expression and Communication of Emotion. In: Lewis, M., Haviland, J.M. (eds.) Handbook of Emotions. The Guilford Press, New York (1993)
23. Pearson, K.: On Lines and Planes of Closest Fit to Systems of Points in Space. Philosophical Magazine 2(6), 559–572 (1901)

Numerical Investigation of the Primety of Real Numbers

Kristoffer Jensen

ad:mt, Aalborg University Esbjerg
Niels Bohrsvej 8, 6700 Esbjerg, Denmark
krist@create.aau.dk

Abstract. The Farey sequences can be used [1] to create the Eulers totient function $\phi(n)$, by identifying the fractions for number n that did not occur in all Farey sequences up to $n\text{-}1$. This function creates, when divided by n-1, what is here called the Primety measure, which is a measure of how close to being a prime number n is. $P(n)=\phi(n)/(n\text{-}1)$ has maximum 1 for all prime numbers and minimum that decreases non-uniformly with n. Thus $P(n)$ is the Primety function, which permits to designate a value of Primety of a number n. If $P(n)==1$, then n is a prime. If $P(n)<1$, n is not a prime, and the further $P(n)$ is from n, the less n is a prime. $\phi(n)$ and $P(n)$ is generalized to real numbers through the use of real numbered Farey sequences. The corresponding numerical sequences are shown to have interesting mathematical and artistic properties.

Keywords: Farey sequences, Totient function, Primety, Selfsimilarity, Fractals.

1   Introduction

The quest for (large) prime numbers is one of the important problems in mathematics, with repercussions into fundamental mathematics as well as contemporary society, with the use of prime numbers in coding and security systems. With the unpredictability of prime numbers, only brute force methods are guaranteed to render a result as to if a number is prime or not. Many mathematicians will find the mathematics involved in prime numbers beautiful, or even artistic in its own right. [2] states it *Mathematics, as I have been describing it, is an art form. The words ambiguity and metaphor are much more acceptable in the arts than they are in the sciences. But ambiguity and metaphor are the mechanisms through which that ultimate ambiguity, the one that divides the objective from the subjective, the natural world from the mind, is bridged.*

In addition to art in mathematical problem solving, the numbers can represent art in itself. Certainly, the Golden Ratio, and the accompanying Fibonacci numbers are found in many art works [3]. Another mathematic area of interest with artistic outcomes is fractals. Fractals are objects that are self-similar (i.e. details looks like the whole). Fractals are divided into exact or statistic self-similar objects, full or partial fractals, natural and mathematic fractals, etc. A common natural fractal is the coastline that was used as an example by the 'father' of fractal geometry, Benoit

A.L. Brooks (Ed.): ArtsIT 2011, LNICST 101, pp. 160–167, 2012.

Mandelbrot [5]. Common examples of mathematic fractals are the Cantor set, the Koch curve, and the Mandelbrot set. Fractals have two possible definitions [6], both proposed by Mandelbrot, the first saying that the Hausdorff dimension strictly exceeds the topological dimensions, and the second saying that the fractal is a shape made of parts similar to the whole in some way. Often, fractals are created using some kind of feedback mechanism, in which the input of the next step is a function including the output of the current step.

Larry Austin composed several music pieces based on natural fractal shapes [7], including Maroon Bells (1976), based in part on a mountain range, and Canadian Coastlines (1981), based on actual coastlines.

This work proposes to investigate the Farey sequence, in particular in the case of real numbers, and show some interesting and aesthetic outcomes of these sequences.

2   Mathematical Development

The Farey sequence [1] for a number n consists of [*0/n, 1/1, 1/2, 1/3, 2/3, ..., 1/n, ..., n-1/n*]. For $n=0$, it is the empty set [], for $n=1$, it is [*0,1*], for n=2, it is [*0,1/2,1*], for $n=3$ it is [*0,1/3,1/2,2/3,1*], etc. If all unique elements up to $n-1$ are retained, then for $n=1$, 2 there is one new element and for $n=3$ there are two new elements. For $n=4$, there are 2 new elements [*1/4, 3/4*], etc. The number of new element is [*1,1,2,2,4,2,6,4,6,4,...*] and it corresponds [1] to the Euler totient function $\varphi(n)$. $\varphi(n)$ has the property [2] that $\varphi(p)=(p-1)$ for p primes, and that $\varphi(n)\leq(n-1)$, equal only in the case of n prime.

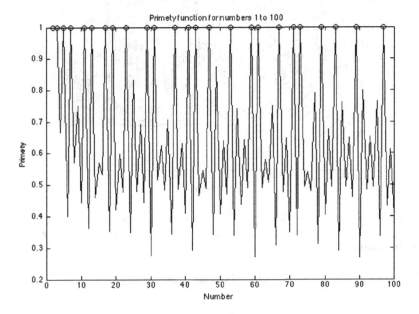

Fig. 1. The Primety for numbers 1 to 100

Therefore,

$$P(n) = \phi(n)\big/_{n-1} \qquad (1)$$

is here set as the Primety function, i.e. a numerical indication of how close to being prime a number is. The Primety values are shown in figure 1 for the numbers 1 to 100. The Prime numbers, for which $P(n)=1$, are denoted with a ring.

Now, if we use real numbers in the construction of the Farey sequence, $[0/r, 1/r, ..., r/r, ..., 1/(r+\delta), ..., (r)/(r+\delta),...]$, and then find all new unique rations for each incremental δ, it is possible to show that the Primety function for real numbers,

$$P(r) = \phi(r)\big/_{r-1} \qquad (2)$$

where $\phi(r)$ is calculated as the new unique element in the Farey sequence for increasing real numbers (r). $P(r)$ follows a simple rule, as is shown in figure 2.

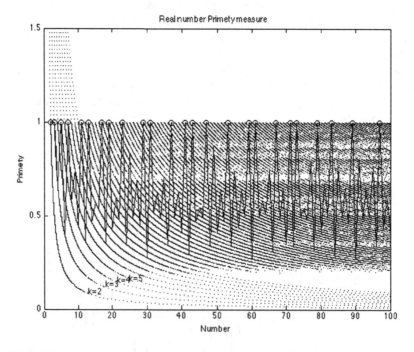

Fig. 2. The Primety values for real numbers between 1 and 100. The integer numbers are shown in the figure, and the primes are denoted with 'o'. The eq. (2) is shown, for low numbers $(2 \leq k \leq 10)$, in dashed.

The Primety values are always found on one of the curves;

$$c_k = k\big/_x, \qquad (3)$$

where k is an integer, and $x>0$ is an arbitrary value. $P(r)$ jumps between the different c_k, as r is increasing, so it is not possible to predict $P(r)$ from it. Nonetheless, this seems like a promising area of further research. For instance, the eq. (3) gives an absolute minimum for the value of $P(r)$. The maximum value seems to be equal to one for all values of x, with the exceptions of $r=1$. For $r<1$, $O(r)=0$. All integer values approaches full Prime number Primety value; $P(r) \to 1$ as $r \to n$. It is not clear how this relates to the fact that many of these integer numbers has Primety values less than 1.

This is investigated further by transforming $P(r)$, so that the shape of it, according to eq. (3) is visible. By identifying the values of $P(r)$ that correspond to each c_k, and then multiply the found values by x a constant function is obtained. The result is shown in figure 3. It is clear that $P(r')\cdot r'$, where r' corresponds to the values where $P(r)==c_k$, is a constant function equal to k. The min and max index values shown in the right of figure 3 indicates that the minimum index is equal to k, and the maximum index is fluctuating slowly.

The first index corresponds to $P(r) \to 1$ as $r \to n$. The last index fluctuates slowly, in a non-predictable way, it seems. The Primety function for real numbers has the appearance to bring new findings in the quest for the understanding of prime numbers, but more work is necessary in order to assert this further. Hopefully this will allow more inspiring and artistically ambiguous mathematic development and further the art of mathematics and the mathematic art. Some initial investigations of the latter are made in the next section.

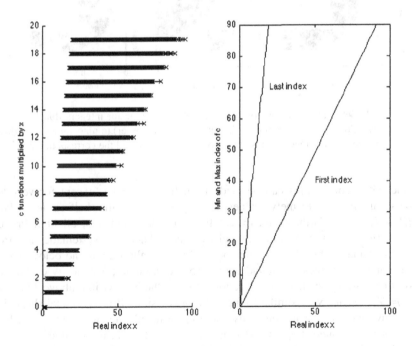

Fig. 3. Transformed real value Primety function (left) with corresponding min and max index values (right)

3   Fractal Behaviour

This section will show some of the fractal behaviours of the Primety function, and the related Farey sequence. First, we calculate the Primety for all numbers up to a large number, and show the scatterplot, i.e. the following Primety value as a function of the current value, as seen in figure 4.

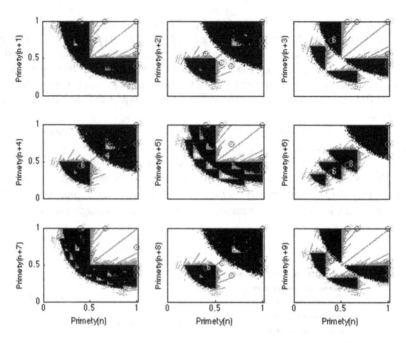

Fig. 4. Next Primety values as function of current Primety value for integers (black) and real numbers (grey). Context going from next Primety (upper left corner) to nine values after (lower right corner). The first 8 integer values are denoted with a ring, and the corresponding value of n.

Some initial conclusions can be made from figure 4. First, except for very low numbers, all integer Primety values are found above the half-circle - $P(n)-1)^2+(P(n+1)-1)^2=z$. Furthermore, except for a few low numbers, all high Primety values – $P(n)>0.5$ gives $P(n+1)<0.5$ and vice-versa. There is a systematic shift from high to low values. Thus, all even numbered Primety values are found below 0.5 and all odd numbered values are found above 0.5. Furthermore, a majority of $P(n)$ are found at or close to small integer fractions. Inside, the hole visible above $P(n)=1/3$, $P(n+1)=2/3$, a shape very similar to the full plot is visible. If it is a fractal shape, it is a very slow one, i.e. the fractals only show up in detail after many numbers. Each scatterplot reveals interesting and informative aspects of the Primety values.

For the real numbered Primety values, $P(r)$, even though the scatterplots place the real Primety values in the vicinity of the integer values, the situation is different, as it seems the scatterplot reveals lines; $P(n+k)=(l/m)*P(n)$, where l and m are low integers. For instance, (for the next value scatterplot), for the line leading to the '2', $l=m=1$, for '3' $l=2$, $m=3$, for '4', $l=3$, $m=2$, etc.

More fractal behaviour is coming from the Farey sequences. The difference signal of the integer Farey sequence has a characteristic shape, which is independent on the size of the Farey sequence. Furthermore, this same shape is exactly replicated inside the larger shape (assuming n is large). These findings are shown in figure 5 for three different sizes, $n=100$ (left), $n=1000$, and $n=10000$ (right). All three sizes have the same shape, albeit the small sequence (left) is coarser. The peaks of the differences are found on small integer ratios, ($1/2$, $1/3$, $3/8$, $2/5$, $5/12$, etc)

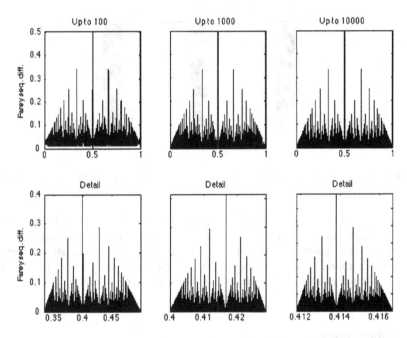

Fig. 5. Difference of Farey sequence for three sizes (top), and three different details of the large size (bottom). The different sizes show how the Farey difference signal always retains the same shape, and the different details show how the outer shape is copied in the details.

Figure 5 show the fractal behaviour of the Farey difference signal, both for different sizes (top), and for different details (bottom), and for different details (bottom).

In addition to this, the real signal Primety function $P(r)$ exposes an interesting behaviour. In figure 6, the real values Primety function is show for $0<r<10$, along with the first to third difference signals (top) and spectrograms (bottom). It is interesting to observe how the difference signals look similar to the Primety signal itself, although with larger values for each difference, and also clearly changing shape at each integer value for higher difference signals. Treated as an audio signal, this function exposes a characteristic toned and rhythmic sound that eventually blends into a noisy signal. The sound is very similar across the Primety difference signals.

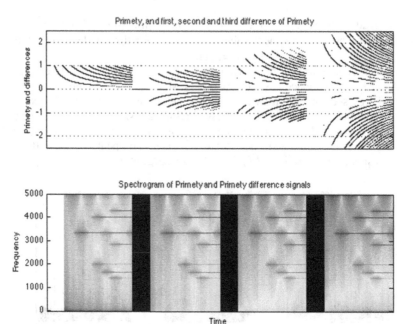

Fig. 6. Real value Primety function and first three difference signals (top), and spectrograms (bottom)

It is certain that the nature contains vast amount of at least statistic self-similarities fractals [5]. Many artists have, consciously or not, integrated fractal shapes in their art. Among audio signals to potentially be used in music, as shown above, fractals have a long tradition for quasi-artistic qualities. While the figures shown here are not necessary polished enough, or do not contain the aesthetic or otherwise qualities to be used in artwork, it is still possibly to envision such a use.

4   Conclusions

The Farey sequence of real numbers, along with the introduction of the Primety value permits to expose a certain number of laws that governs prime numbers. Among these are that the Primety values are always found on functions of the shape $c_k = k/x$, which enables to assert a (low) lowest possible value of the Primety function. Furthermore, all even Primety values are less than one half, and all odd are more than one half.

Three interesting visual results from this research are; 1) the k/x shape of the Primety function, 2) the almost fractal scatterplot of the Primety function, and the complete fractal shape of the Farey difference signal. Some interesting visual and sonic results are obtained from these signals.

Fractals and related mathematic results, as presented here, are placed in a double art context, first, because the quest for the mathematic results leads to ambiguity, *one of art's most potent aesthetic functions* [2], secondly, because the end result, graphics, plots, music, represents art in itself.

References

1. Sylvester, J.J.: On the number of fractions contained in any 'Farey series' of which the limiting number is given. The London, Edinburgh and Dublin Philosophical Magazine and Journal of Science 15(5), 251–257 (1883)
2. Byers, W.: How mathematicians think: using ambiguity, contradiction, and paradox to create mathematics. Princeton University Press (2007)
3. Posamentier, A.S., Lehmann, I.: The fabulous Fibonacci numbers. Prometheus Books (2007)
4. Graham, R.L., Knuth, D.E., Patashnik, O.: Concrete Mathematics, p. 147. Addison-Wesley (1989)
5. Mandelbrot, B.B.: How long is the coast of Britain? Statistical self-similarity and fractional dimension. Science 156, 636–638 (1967)
6. Addison, P.S.: Fractals and chaos: an illustrated course. The Institute of Physics, London (1997)
7. Dodge, C., Jerse, T.A.: Computer Music: Synthesis, Composition and Performance, 2nd edn. Macmillan Library Reference (1997)

Mobile Game for Virtual Heritage Exploration – MHEX

Kian Lam Tan, Chen Kim Lim, and Abdullah Zawawi Talib

School of Computer Sciences, Universiti Sains Malaysia,
11800 USM Pulau Pinang, Malaysia
andrewtankianlam@gmail.com, kim86_lavender@hotmail.com,
azht@cs.usm.my

Abstract. In this paper, we present a virtual heritage application called MHEX (Mobile Heritage Exploration for George Town) that provides a technology-integrated environment that allows users to gain knowledge of various heritage sitesthrough gaming on mobile platform. With this application, everybody can learn about the significance of various heritage sites through a game that combines the games of monopoly and treasure hunt. The game is implemented and tested within the urban environment of George Town, Malaysia, running on iPhone from Apple.

Keywords: Game,mobile platform, panoramic view.

1   Introduction

Interactive entertainment systems traditionally offer a limited choice of user interface technologies and interaction styles that make little use of the human body and require low physical exertion. The first-ever mobile phone game was the black-and-white Snake that was embedded in Nokia 6110 model in 1997. Recently, a new generation of mobile phone games that encourages new styles in interactive recreation began to emerge in the market. An application with rich interactive entertainment is very much needed to transform the heritage sites into an interactive entertainment application.In this paper, we preset a virtual heritage exploration system that allows the user to explore the heritage sites through gaming on a mobile platform.

2   Overview of the MHEX

The MHEX architecture is based on multi-tier that consists of the Monopoly and Treasure Hunt modules as shown in Fig. 1. MHEX is implemented using the Objective C programming language and Apple X-Code as the Integrated Development Environment (IDE) to develop the game's platform.The main purpose of MHEX is to facilitate digital preservation of the heritage site using leading edge technologies. The application enables user to learn about the heritage sites while playing the games.

The MHEX application is designed based on the classical board game called Monopoly together with the game of Treasure Hunt. The player can control the virtual

A.L. Brooks (Ed.): ArtsIT 2011, LNICST 101, pp. 168–170, 2012.

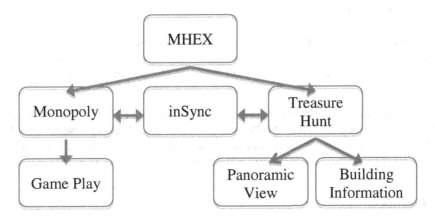

Fig. 1. Architecture of the MHEX Application

character (an icon) by rolling a dice to move around. The Monopoly component consists of Game Play module where it stores all the icons, board, and properties. inSync is the component where it serves as the intermediate cell or bridge between Monopoly and Treasure Hunt to allow the user to play Monopoly and Treasure Hunt concurrently without any delay. The Treasure Hunt component consists of Panoramic View and Building Information. Panoramic View module stores all the heritage sites' view while Building Information module stores all the information of the heritage sites. All the Panoramic View and Building Information are presented in a table format through inSync component. The layout of MHEX for the heritage zone of George Town is as shown in Fig. 2. The main window is based on the monopoly platform. The monopoly map takes a huge portion of the screen in order to ensure that the players have a proper view of the route. MHEX provides a game background that is customized for the core of heritage zone of George Town, Penang in Malaysia.

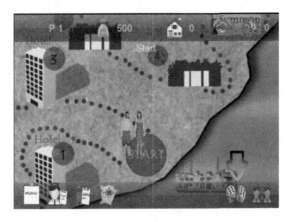

Fig. 2. The Interface for MHEX

3   Conclusion

The application is created as close as possible to the heritage sites in George Town, Penang. It allows the users to explore and learn about the heritages sites of the core heritage zone of the citythrough the mobile game anywhere and anytime.

Acknowledgement. This work presented is supported by Research Univerisiti Grant U0829 and scholarship from MyPhD, MyBrain15 for Malaysia researchers. The authors would also like to thank Tan Kian Guan, Poon Pui Yee, Kong Yng Jye and Chin Kew Yee for their contributions in the development of MHEX.

References

1. Lam Tan, K., Kim Lim, C., Zawawi Talib, A.: A Mobile Gaming Approach to Virtual Heritage Exploration. In: Ariwa, E., El-Qawasmeh, E. (eds.) DEIS 2011. CCIS, vol. 194, pp. 493–500. Springer, Heidelberg (2011)
2. Kim Lim, C., Lam Tan, K., Zawawi Talib, A.: A Low-Cost Method for Generating Panoramic Views for a Mobile Virtual Heritage Application. In: Ariwa, E., El-Qawasmeh, E. (eds.) DEIS 2011. CCIS, vol. 194, pp. 501–512. Springer, Heidelberg (2011)

Art Evolves through Technology:
Haptic after the Hegemony of Visual Art

Sandra Coelho

Faculdade de Engenharia, Universidade do Porto
Rua Dr. Roberto Frias, 4200-465 Porto, Portugal
sandra.coelho@fe.up.pt

Abstract. Recently and from now on, we'll be hearing the word haptic regularly in consumer multimodal devices. In an era of transition from sight hegemony, the sense of touch is getting a place of visibility. Still, most of us don't think of the sense of touch as being a primary sense. Possibly it is because we don't know this sense well enough. This paper introduces a haptic art concept for a touch reactive dynamic surface as an awareness project. It is intended to construct the knowledge of the self through the sense of touch, following the latest technological advances in smart materials that provide physical interactivity for art explorations.

Keywords: art, technology, sense of touch, haptic, organic user interfaces, smart materials, shape shifting materials, dynamic surfaces.

1   Introduction

Art is highly dependent on the technology available. In this sense, art characterizes the development state of its tools and means.

Art is in constant renewal following advances in technology. The definition of art changes and its manifestations vary through time and geography. Throughout history, the tools have been characterizing the art making. Cultural changes have named art periods. Some were ephemeral, and others perdure, a few as classic while others persist resistively. What was mostly an artifact is now produced and maintained by computers. The authorship is dislocated from authors to participants, and in an era of easy access to creative software, creators emerge increasingly. New technological tools democratized the art creation and interconnected computers expanded means of exhibition.

As technology evolves, new metaphors provide answers to previous inquiries while other challenges arise. Art used to be static, as a frame capturing a moment, now is moving and changing its form in semi-living and self-sufficient compositions. Digital art works are aware of the surroundings, capable of choosing in what to transform after collecting data information. Emergent technological materials are giving to tangible art works, the ability of transformation from one state to another. It is mainly the capacity of replicating living abilities that raise much curiosity in their creation. New digital art works are earning attitude and a life-like statement. They are organic and ever changing, challenging our behaviors towards them.

A.L. Brooks (Ed.): ArtsIT 2011, LNICST 101, pp. 171–176, 2012.
© Institute for Computer Sciences, Social Informatics and Telecommunications Engineering 2012

Driven by inherent curiosity, artists explore and extend to new technological materials to provide better the intended concepts and meanings. Artists appropriate of new dynamic materials that weren't initially developed for a creative use. As artists have always challenged imagination through the use of new tools, new media art works fuse transversal disciplines. They move without frontiers between science and technology, involving critically in their creation with a purpose of transformation of thought and action.

2   Fundamental Reasons for Art Existence

Art disrupts established norms, and structures comprehension. The purpose of art is to make us think differently from what we are used to, is to provide us with a new understanding of ourselves and what surround us. Art is concerned with questioning and to bring awareness to what might seem understated can make it explicit and reachable for better understanding. Art actively aims to be thought-provoking, stimulating and inspiring. Art creation comes from a restless mind as a representation of inquietude or something that needs to be answered or better explained. Sometimes turning difficult issues accessible to public critical understanding.

3   Advances in Technology Predict Art Evolution

Art works used to be perceived at distance, untouchable, but now to be fully experienced they have to be maneuvered requiring physical interaction. Stated by Pallasmaa the "tactile sensibility replaces distancing visual imagery by enhanced materiality, nearness and intimacy." [4]

To stress the need for physicality, one envisions that computers of the future will have any organic form or shape demanding new ways of interaction and new body approaches to shape shifting devices. The device itself will change its physical interface, sensing and responding accordingly to real time physical input. Organic user interfaces will transform the way we use computers. Adding the dynamic response to our physical inputs will certainly change our interactions with computational devices radically. The objects will adapt physically to our biological nature. The dynamic surfaces will change their physical appearance and texturing when we touch or hold them. Prompting new experiential dimensions and renewed haptic relationships between the human body and its surroundings. Technology will be at our use effortlessly, changeable and controllable at our moods and desires along the digital everyday devices become increasingly complex, smaller, less obtrusive, and with minor technological appearance. The technological devices of the future will have distinct physical appearance from today, as they will be everywhere, in any material or surface, flexible or rigid, liquid or solid. Electronic components will be assembled combined with the most disparate materials (paper, fabric, plastic, ceramic, glass, concrete, fluids), providing a variety of different and endless textural possibilities for tactility. Our lifeless everyday objects will soon become lively interfaces for interactions, demanding new physical relations and changing body behaviors. As touch suggests variations between activity and passivity, renewed perceptual means will give rise to the interplay between subject and object.

Since ever, artists explore, appropriate, and recreate the means. Attentive to what is happening in technological developments to adopt the ultimate technologies as their creative tools.

Examples of explorations on sensory experiences, which in different ways relate to the haptic interfaces or explore the tactile qualities of surfaces, artists have integrated new materials by way of technology transfer potential in technology-based art works:

The Water Logo '09,by Kenya Hara, et al. [3], is a surface that mimics the lotus leaf. Drops of water create a sign on top of a water-repellent fabric giving the audience a multisensory experience. When water droplets fall on lotus leaves, they bead up into balls. This effect happens because the infinitesimal hairs coating the surface of the leaves repel water. The Water Logo uses the Monert material, which is processed by a Nano-tex technique for an ultra water-repellent fabric.

The surface slopes slightly down to the front, so that whenever a drop reaches a certain size, it begins to roll down the sloping surface under the influence of gravity. A drop of water grows up to take the place of each drop that rolls away, to the water logo being constantly renewed. Driven by a hidden mechanism, the water seeps through the fabric in groups of drops that spell out "Senseware" coupling a visual experience with a tactile appearance.

Another example is Six-Forty by Four-Eighty, by Marcelo Coelho, et al. [2], that is an interactive lighting installation, composed of an array of magnetic physical pixels. Reacting to touch each pixel-tile change the color and communicate its state to other tiles by using the human body as the conduit for color information. Touching a pixel-tile makes it cycle through a color palette. When touched for a short time, the pixel-tile starts pulsing to indicate its transmission state. By keeping the first hand in the tile and touching other pixel-tiles with the other hand, the color is copied and pasted from one pixel-tile to another. When is detected a touch, the brightness of the light changes according to an exponential decay based on the behavior of incandescent light bulbs also simulates a soft object elastically deforming with applied pressure. The pixel-tiles can create patterns and animations when grouped together, serving playfully for customizing physical spaces with ferrous surfaces.

Conventional materials incorporate new technologies disrupting traditional uses. The new technological materials are active and participative. The smart materials sense, react and change reversibly in appearance, shape and texture, in response to the environment, adding functionality and meaning to interactive art means.

Currently, sustainability issues require materials to have increased functionality and adaptive capabilities. Mimicking processes and structures of nature through biomimetics and nanotechnology, the smart materials do more and better with fewer resources. These materials identify an era to which art is not indifferent. Technology-based art is representative of its time concerning economic, social, political, cultural, and ecological dispositions. The smart materials adapt well to a fast evolving society, as "their properties are changeable and thus responsive to *transient* needs" as Schodek and Addington asserted. [6]

The option for smart materials for creative applications is seductive due to their behavioral characteristics. Succinctly explained by Schodek and Addington [6], they are suitable because of the "immediacy" as these materials respond promptly.

Because of the "transiency" as they respond to several environmental state. Because of the "self-actuation" as they possess a molecular structure that responds to external influences. Because of the "selectivity" as they respond in a distinct and controlled way. Because of the "directness" as they respond *in loco* to a stimulus, and the most salient, because of the reversibility as they change back to their initial state.

Activated through chemical, electrical, magnetic, optical, thermal, or mechanical stimulus depending on their properties, these responsive materials interact with the environment in which we intervene disobeying the conviction of the "hegemonic material as visual artifact" that Schodek and Addington correspondingly claimed [6], defying our sensory perceptions to transformative material surfaces.

4   The Exaltation of a Sense in the Reactant Surface

Senses act interrelated, but notice can be given to senses individually, it depends on the emphatic attention to a particular sense. As Merleau-Ponty explained "the experience of the separate 'senses' is gained only when one assumes a highly particularized attitude." [5]

Touch is indispensable for our existence, but its capabilities haven't been exhaustively studied as those of sight and hearing. The sense of touch is ontological and phenomenologically of utmost importance for our normal functioning and well-being. Still there is a lack of haptic knowledge, on what we are able to obtain through tactile sensations, because much is performed unnoticed below the conscious threshold. The difficulty is in the interpretation of haptic sensations experienced by the body.

Knowing that the physical response to an event is determined by subjective sensitivity, previous experiences, and state of awareness, this research intents to infer the importance of the level of expectancy. Inquiring how does the tactile interaction intensify the subjective experience, and how does the change of the tactile stimulus enhance the sensation, for a consciously inner augmented tactile feeling.

Outwardly, it is through touch that we act upon the environment. Touch is the only sense capable of changing its surroundings. Equivalent to what Wallace claims when relates action and its consequent reaction "it is the ability of one substance to act on another that explains why it is possible to identify agents and reagents in the order of nature." [7]

Mimicking forms of nature, The Reactant is a surface concept that goes through a physical change during a reaction. Through a tactile reaction, this sensitive surface change sits physical nature as it may grow or shrink when we press a finger on it altering our tactile sensations. As texture keeps active the stimulus of this sense, the tactile qualities of the means influence the quality of the experience.

Using for this purpose a shape memory alloy (SMA) actuator wire. The Nitinol, which is a deformable temperature-responsive metal compound, made of nickel and titanium, that assembled with electronic components and combined with non-woven fabrics, allowing flexibility of movement and easing the cooling of the SMA actuator, produce a life-like movement when activated by an intentional stimulus. While in tactile feedback screens, the physical changes happen under the glass, unreachable for the eye and are developed to deceive our cutaneous system; The Reactant is a tactile sensitive surface that shifts its appearance from one physical state to another. Making use of the recent developments in smart materials, that interact with the environment it is able of responding to changes through emergent sensitive technologies. As sensors and actuators become more sensible, accessible, sustainable, and affordable, permit the artists to explore innovative technologies. This project benefits from the technological evolution of smart materials that reversibly change shape in response to electrical stimuli, mixing the organic with the electromechanical components and systems, to ally the aesthetic to functional adding an inquiring purpose. The Reactant is a haptic art project conceived with the purpose of awareness to a sense that is often neglected.

The concept focuses on how we perceive and retain our surroundings through our sense of touch that provide us a conscious existence of physicality. The way we behave depends directly on the way we perceive our environment. It is the perception of the self in relation to reality. According to Ackerman, the sense of one's self "has to do with touch, with how we feel" [1]. In relating the haptic perception of the self to the surfaces and spaces around, Pallasmaa states that "touch is the sensory mode that integrates our experience of the world with that of ourselves." [4]

The dynamic surface, The Reactant, is a visual and tactile metaphor created to show how our actions influence the behaviors of others. How our immediate reactive instinct predicts our consequent behaviors. Concerning the instinctive action to an unexpected touch, or the first reaction to the embodied experience of feeling something in our skin. The first moment we experience something new is the alluring of an instant that will determine our future behaviors to similar experiences. A lasting involvement depends on the quality of the first impression. We are moved by sensations, constantly looking for unforgettable ones. Commonly, beyond our survival instincts, it is our desire to enhance our experiences when dealing with the most disparate things, from the everyday simplest actions to interactions that challenge our knowledge. Those improvements are related to how we use our senses when experiencing those things. When forming first impressions, it is what we see, hear, smell, taste, and touch that influence our assessments and future behaviors.

5   Contributions

The main purpose of this research is to deliver a comprehensive understanding of the phenomenology of the haptic being the expected results of subjective analysis prompted by individual descriptive meanings. To deliver an insightful interpretation on how we've been relating to touch, and why the sense of touch is essential to us, attempting to unravel its hidden characteristics and abilities through art survey. Encompassing a multidisciplinary overview, relating philosophy, psychology, cognitive and natural sciences, social and cultural history, and engineering, aimed to be a useful theoretical framework about the haptic, with convergences between perception, aesthetics, creativity, behavior, and technology. Aims to develop collaborative relationships between research in art and design, as a way to explore future technological implications for public involvement and awareness. Aims to improve our awareness to tactile sensations when interacting with tangible media and intensify the physical experience between users and digital systems.

6   Conclusions

Hitherto, consumer haptic devices are devoted to the feedback feeling, but lack the tactual sensation of the material that is usually slick and cold and not truly tactile stimulating.

Besides, people know very little about the sense of touch. Often restrict it to the sensations felt on the skin. They only know the surface of this sense. The sense of touch is critically vital, from controlling the body to perceiving, learning from, and interacting with the environment.

Art can make it explicit and reachable for better understanding, reordering the knowledge of it. The proposed texture shape-changing surface crossing differentiated practices from the inquisitive art to the resolvable design, from the explainable natural sciences to the conceivable engineering, is intended to be an open-ended, critical, and thought-provoking project to raise individual awareness. Meant to be an analytical project through investigation, it is open to questioning one's subjective perceptions challenging each one to know oneself through their touch behavioral reactions.

In collaboration, artists and technologists have an interdependent relationship. They act interrelated pushing each other further. Art stretches technical developments and technology listens to art technical requirements albeit constrained by technical skills, scientific knowledge, and technical limitations. Artists develop, modify and use technical means and tools to stir social awareness and renew aesthetic experiences.

Acknowledgments. To The Fundação para a Ciência e a Tecnologia (FCT) for funding this research (SFRH/BD/33952/2009) through the UT Austin | Portugal program for the Doctoral Program in Digital Media by Universidade do Porto (U.Porto).

References

1. Ackerman, D.: A Natural History of the Senses. Random House USA Inc., Vintage Books, NY, USA (1992)
2. Coelho, M., Zigelbaum, J., Kopin, J.: Six-Forty by Four-Eighty. MIT Media Lab and Zigelbaum+Coelho (2010),
   http://zigelbaumcoelho.com/six-forty-by-four-eighty
3. Hara, K., et al.: Water Logo 2009. Nippon Design Center Hara Design Institute + Atelier OMOYA. Tokyo Fiber 2009 Senseware (2009), http://tokyofiber.com/en
4. Pallasmaa, J.: Hapticity and time. Notes on fragile architecture. Architectural Review 207(1239), 78–84 (2000)
5. Ponty, M.: Phenomenology of Perception. Translated by Smith C. Routledge Classics, Taylor & Francis Ltd., London, UK and NY, USA (2002 (1945))
6. Schodek, D., Addington, M.: Smart Materials in Architecture and Design. Architectural Press, London (2004)
7. Wallace, W.A.: The Modeling of Nature: Philosophy of Science and the Philosophy of Nature in Synthesis. The Catholic University of America Press, Washington (1996)

Author Index